Secured Computing

A CISSP STUDY GUIDE

Endorf Technical Research

Author: Carl F. Endorf, *CISSP, MCSE, CCNA, GCIA, CIW*
Editor: Chad Johnson
Trafford Publishing - Copyright, 2001

Acknowledgements

To my beautiful wife, two children and my family for letting me spend my time on this book and not with them, I appreciate it.

To Chad Johnson for helping to edit the book, you are a gentleman and scholar.

Disclaimer

CISSP™ is a registered Trademark of ISC2, Inc. This publication is not endorsed nor sponsored by ISC2, Inc. The information here within is that of the author and his intent to consolidate this information. The test and quiz questions arenot official test questions set forth by ISC2, but intended only for the purpose of learning the knowledge needed to prepare for this test.

*Pass or Money back Guarantee

We Guarantee, you will pass the CISSP certification exam! We offer you a 120-Day 100% Money Back Guarantee. If you do not pass the CISSP test on two attempts within 120 days of the purchase we will refund 100% of your money back, less shipping and handling. Send both of the original letters of failure notification and original receipt of book purchase to:

Endorf Technical Research
1716 Taft Dr.
Normal, IL 61761

We will refund your money and send the letters of failure back to you.

National Library of Canada Cataloguing in Publication Data

```
Endorf, Carl F., 1969-
  Secured computing


  ISBN 1-55212-889-X


  1. Electronic data processing personnel--Certification. 2. Computer networks-
-Examinations--Study guides.  I. Johnson, Chad, 1973-  II. Title.
QA76.3.E52 2001          005.8           C2001-911250-5
```

TRAFFORD

This book was published *on-demand* in cooperation with Trafford Publishing.
On-demand publishing is a unique process and service of making a book available for retail sale to the public taking advantage of on-demand manufacturing and Internet marketing.
On-demand publishing includes promotions, retail sales, manufacturing, order fulfilment, accounting and collecting royalties on behalf of the author.

Suite 6E, 2333 Government St., Victoria, B.C. V8T 4P4, CANADA

Phone	250-383-6864	Toll-free	1-888-232-4444 (Canada & US)
Fax	250-383-6804	E-mail	sales@trafford.com
Web site	www.trafford.com	TRAFFORD PUBLISHING IS A DIVISION OF TRAFFORD HOLDINGS LTD.
Trafford Catalogue #01-0291		www.trafford.com/robots/01-0291.html

10   9   8   7   6   5

Contents

Preface **viii**
Overview of CISSP and the Exam **viii**
How to Use This Book **ix**
The Study Plan **ix**
Test Day Tips **x**

Chapter One
Domain 1 — Access Control Systems and Methodology
    Definitions 2
    Access Control Techniques **3**
    Access Control Layers **5**
    Types of Access Control **6**
    Account, Log and journal Monitoring **7**
    Access Control Models **9**
    The three Basic Principles of I&A **12**
    Passwords **13**
    Centralized Remote Authentication Access Controls **15**
    Decentralized Remote Authentication Access Controls **16**
    Methods of Attacks **17**
    Monitoring **18**
    Test Your Knowledge **23**

Chapter Two
Domain 2 — Telecommunications & Network Security
    Definitions **31**
    ISO/OSI Model **31**
    Network Topologies **35**
    Protocol Vulnerabilities **37**
    WAN Protocols **44**
    Identification and Authentication **46**
    Data Communications **48**
    Web Security Protocols **51**
    Network Components **53**
    Network Availability **54**
    Test Your Knowledge **58**

Chapter Three
Domain 3 — Security Management Practices
    Definitions **66**
    Security Management Concepts and Principles **66**

Protection Mechanisms *67*
Change/Control Management *67*
Data Classification Schemes *68*
Employment Policies and Practices *71*
Policies, Standards, Guidelines, and Procedures *73*
Risk Management *75*
Countermeasures *79*
Roles and Responsibilities *82*
Security Awareness *83*
Security Management Planning *84*
Test Your Knowledge *86*

Chapter Four

Domain 4 — Applications & Systems Development
Definitions *92*
Application Issues *92*
Local/Non Distributed Environment *96*
Data Information Storage *100*
Knowledge Based Systems *101*
Security Control Architecture *102*
System Development Controls *105*
Test Your Knowledge *111*

Chapter Five

Domain 5 — Cryptography
Definitions *116*
Uses of Cryptography *117*
Cryptographic Concepts, Methodologies, and Practices *118*
Key Management *122*
Ciphers *123*
Cryptographic Algorithms *125*
Public Key Infrastructure *133*
Application and Network Based Protocols *136*
Methods of Attack *139*
Test Your Knowledge *141*

Chapter Six

Domain 6 — Security Architecture and Models
Definitions *147*
Principles of Common Computer and Network Architecture and Design *147*
Principles of Common Security Models, Architectures, and Evaluation Criteria *150*
NSA/NCSC Rainbow Series *154*
Objects and Subjects *165*
Common Flaws in Security Architecture *161*
Test Your Knowledge *164*

Chapter Seven
Domain 7 — Operations Security

Definitions **169**
Administrative Management **170**
Computer Operations Concepts **171**
Test Your Knowledge **174**

Chapter Eight
Domain 8 — Business Continuity Planning and Disaster Recovery

Definitions **180**
Business Continuity Planning **181**
Disaster Recovery Planning **183**
Recovery Planning Development **184**
Test Your Knowledge **188**

Chapter Nine
Domain 9 — Laws, Investigations, and Ethics

Definitions **196**
Types of Laws **196**
U.S. Laws **198**
International Computer Crime Related Laws **200**
BS17799 **201**
Investigations **201**
Types of Computer Crime **205**
Incident Handling/Response **206**
Ethics **207**
ISC2 Code of Ethics **207**
Test Your Knowledge **211**

Chapter Ten
Domain 10 — Physical Security

Definitions **216**
Administrative and Physical Controls **216**
Personal Identification systems **217**
Elements of Physical Security **221**
Facility Requirements **221**
Noise **223**
Fire Access and Controls **223**
Physical Access Controls **224**
Technical Controls **225**
Environment/Life Safety **225**
Test Your Knowledge **226**

Chapter Eleven
Methods of Attacks

Definitions **233**

Virus Types **234**
Other Attacks **235**
Secret key algorithm attacks **236**

Whatis.com Definitions 239
References **254**
Recommended Study Aids **255**
Glossary 256
CISSP Practice Exam **289**

Acknowledgements

To my beautiful wife, two children and my family for letting me spend time on this book and not with them, I appreciate it.

To Chad Johnson for helping to edit the book, you are a gentleman and scholar.

To Ken Newton for just being Ken.

Disclaimer

CISSP™ is a registered Trademark of ISC2, Inc. This publication is not endorsed nor sponsored by ISC2, Inc. The information here within is that of the author and his intent to consolidate this information. The test and quiz questions are not official test questions set forth by ISC2, but intended only for the purpose of learning the knowledge needed to prepare for this test.

*Pass or Money back Guarantee

We Guarantee you will pass the CISSP certification exam! We offer you a 180-Day 100% Money Back Guarantee. If you do not pass the CISSP test on two attempts within 180 days of the purchase we will refund 100% of your money back for the book only, less shipping and handling. Send both of the original letters of failure notification and the original receipt of book purchase to:

**Endorf Technical Research
1716 Taft Dr.
Normal, IL 61761**

We will refund your money for the book and send the receipt and letters of failure back to you.

Secured Computing, A CISSP Study Guide, Copyright 2001

Preface

The Common Body of Knowledge is a large group of commonly accepted security practices covering ten domains: *Access Control Systems and Methodology, Telecommunications and Network Security, Security Management Practices, Applications and Systems Development Security, Cryptography, Security Architecture and Models, Operations Security, Business Continuity Planning and Disaster Recovery, Laws, Investigation and Ethics* and *Physical Security.*

The purpose of this book is to put all this information into one succinct place that can be easily read and understood. I have tried to make the information easy to read and study without a lot of dry jargon and by getting to the point of the information. This book is geared toward the security professional that already has a base knowledge in security, _not the beginner wanting to pass an exam_. This book should not be the "end all be all" source for your studies, but hopefully will enhance your pursuit for the Certified Information Systems Security Professional (CISSP) certification. What I have attempted to do is take all the information available from my personal experience, books (see bibliography), lectures, and exams while preparing for the CISSP and put it into one volume for others to successfully study the material.

Overview of CISSP and the Exam

ISC2, Inc. is a non-profit organization that has put together security professionals to help identify and help qualify a "common body of knowledge" (CBK) that every security professional should work towards understanding. The CISSP designation is the most well respected certification in the security industry at this time. It covers a broad scope of security related subjects.

Only those who have three years or more of security experience in one or more of the domains can take the exam. The exams are given at various locations around the world. See the ISC2 website for more information at, www.isc2.org. The test contains 250 questions, of which 25 are used for research purposes for future exams. The test covers all ten domains in no particular order. You have six hours to complete the exam.

How to Use This Book

This book is designed to make your study towards passing this exam as easy as possible. Each chapter covers one of the ten domains. Throughout each chapter I have included questions to help you better remember the information. Much of this book consists of simple definitions of terms and knowledge areas needed for the test.

The Study Plan

Instead of giving time lines on how long to study for the test I will give an idea of what is the best way to study the material. This is not an easy test! Some things you will be very familiar with and others will be new to you. First, read through the book and decide what you understand and what is difficult. Once you have identified your trouble areas, set forth a study plan. Below is an example study plan that could be beneficial to follow:

- Read over all chapters and take the chapter tests after each one.
- Read through all the glossary terms (This is very important!!).
- Decide, based on the chapter tests and reading, what areas you need to focus on the most.
- Read the chapters that need more focus again and take chapter tests.
- Read, or at least skim, the recommended study aids in the back of the book.
- Read through all glossary terms and make sure you could explain each of these in your head just by seeing the word.
- Scan the Internet for related topics on security, keeping up to date on current attacks and events.
- Take the CISSP practice exam in the back of this book
- Take the real exam and PASS!

Again, it is hard to say how much time you will need to study. It will depend largely on your study habits and comprehension. I would suggest <u>at least</u> an hour a day for 60 days. Be diligent and you will do fine!

<u>Test Day Tips</u>

- Eat something before and during the exam (you will need to bring it yourself).
- Do not study the day of the exam.
- Dress comfortably – you will be sitting for a long time.
- Arrive early.
- Take frequent breaks (about one an hour) and stretch.
- Caffeine will help – it is a long test.
- Eliminate the obviously wrong answers in the questions and then make your choice.
- RELAX!

Domain 1

Access Control Systems and Methodology

ACCESS CONTROL SYSTEMS & METHODOLOGY

Access controls are mechanisms that permit system administrators, managers, and analysts of a network or particular system to allow or deny access, direct influence, or help secure the content of a computer system. The whole idea of access controls can be summed up by one word – *accountability*.

Definitions

Accountability — The means of linking individuals to their interactions with an IT product, thereby supporting identification of and recovery from unexpected or unavoidable failures of the control objectives. These actions include violations and attempted violations of the security policy, as well as allowed actions on a system to be traced to individuals who may then be held responsible for their actions.

Access control mechanism — Security safeguards designed to detect and prevent unauthorized access, and to permit authorized access in an IT product. Hardware or software features, operating procedures, management procedures, and various combinations of these designed to detect and prevent unauthorized access and to permit authorized access in an automated system.

Authentication — To validate a claimed identity. To provide protection against fraudulent transactions by establishing the validity of a message, station, individual, or originator. The process of verifying an identity claimed by or for a system entity.

Identification — Process that enables recognition of an entity by an IT product. This can be done by machine-readable names, such as the MAC address or IP address or the hostname for the machine.

CIA Triad

Access controls are designed to meet three main objectives:

Confidentiality: Preventing the disclosure of sensitive information.

Secured Computing: A CISSP Study Guide, Copyright 2001

Integrity: Preventing unauthorized modifications to information and maintaining internal and external consistency.

Availability: To assure that the system and its data are accessible when they are needed.

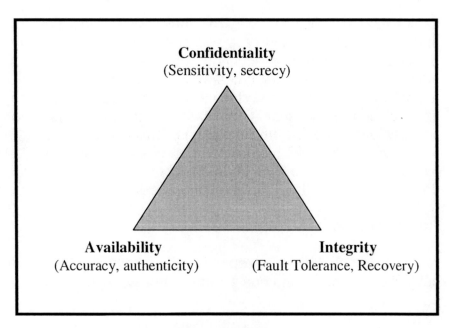

Confidentiality
(Sensitivity, secrecy)

Availability
(Accuracy, authenticity)

Integrity
(Fault Tolerance, Recovery)

Figure 1.1- CIA Triad

Access Control Techniques

Mandatory Access Controls

Mandatory access controls cannot be made more permissive by subjects and are dictated by the system. They are based on information sensitivity such as security labels (classification levels). For example, you write a document that is labeled top secret, but you yourself may not be able to go back and read it as you only have clearance for confidential materials that are less restrictive.

Discretionary Access Controls

Discretionary access controls allow subjects (users) to specify the access controls, with certain limitations, without the intercession of a system administrator. Most commonly done through an Access Control

List (ACL). For example, you may be able to create a document with write access for yourself and read for everyone else. You set these permissions.

Lattice Based Access Control

Lattice based access controls are a lattice model where every resource and every user of a resource is associated with one of an ordered set of classes. The subject associated with that class is as high as or higher than that of the resources may only use the resources associated with a particular class. For example, a dominate security level (a security level that is dominate over another if it is a higher security level), like security level Z1, is dominate over security level Z2 if the classification of Z1 is greater than or equal to that of Z2. Another example would be the level of an object of high integrity may be defined to be "less than" the level of an object of low integrity.

Rule Based Access Control

An access control based on specific rules relating to the nature of the subject or object beyond one's identity. For example, security labels or classifications.

Role Based Access Control

Role based access control (RBAC) is an alternative to discretionary access models (DAC) and mandatory access control (MAC) policies. RBAC security is managed at a level that corresponds with the organization's structure. Roles can be hierarchical in nature. Each user may be assigned one or more roles and each role is assigned one or more privileges that are permitted to users in that role. For example, someone may be assigned a role as a security analyst, advisor to a project, and job tasker for the unit. The analyst role may include all privileges available to the project role, which in turn includes all the privileges available to the job tasker role.

Access Control Lists

An access control list (ACL) is a table that tells a computer operating system which access rights each user has to a particular system object, such as a file directory or individual file. Each object has a

4

security attribute that identifies its access control list. The list has an entry for each system user with access privileges. The most common privileges include the ability to read a file, to write to the file or files, or to execute the file. Most of the popular operating systems today make use of ACLs.

Constrained User Interfaces

These restrict users' access to specific functions by not allowing them to request that information.

Capability Tables

Tables of protected identifiers that allow a subject specific rights based on the capability or ticket they possess.

Content Dependent Access Controls

Content dependent access controls utilize information in an object being accessed. These are usually applicable to database systems as the data is structured.

<u>Access Control Layers</u>

Access controls can be separated into three main layers — administrative, physical, and technical (logical). See figure 1.2.

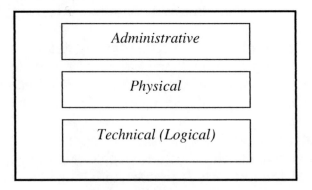

Figure 1.2 — Access control layers.

Administrative access controls include:
- Security awareness training
- Policies and procedures
- Testing
- Personnel controls

Physical access controls include:

- Data backup
- Building security such as alarms and sensors
- Closed work areas

Technical (logical) access controls include:

- File access
- Encryption
- System access

Types of Access Controls

There are many types of access controls and in this section we will examine these types in more detail.

Preventative Controls

Preventative access controls are put in place to avoid the occurrence of an unwanted event. This could include fences, security guards, biometrics, locks, or keys put in place to avoid unauthorized access to facilities.

Sensitive system protection is a type of preventative control that is made up of a control zone. Control zones are usually regarded in feet or in radius and are the area that surrounds sensitive information and the equipment that handles that information.

Environmental controls are a preventative control that is put into place to save the environment, which include people and their operations. Types of environmental controls include temperature, humidity, access, and policies.

Secured Computing: A CISSP Study Guide, Copyright 2001

Storage areas are also used as preventative controls. They help protect media by using logs, physical across controls, and environmental controls. They require monitoring at all times.

Detective Controls

Detective controls are put in place to alert you or identify when an access is violated. These controls include closed circuit TV, intrusion detection systems, sensors, and alarms.

Corrective Controls

Corrective controls are designed to remedy any unauthorized access or restore the original controls. For example, an account lock out after three incorrect log in attempts is a corrective control.

Deterrent Controls

These include controls that try to discourage violations. For example, a warning banner or something that warns what the consequences are for doing certain things would be a deterrent control.

Recovery Controls

These controls restore resources, capabilities, or losses back to a normal working state. This would include any procedures or automated responses that would return a machine back into working order.

Compensating Controls

Compensating controls are an alternative control, such as supervision of an area. The person supervising can help to compensate for others' lack of knowledge.

Account, Log, and Journal Monitoring

Logging is the activity that consists of collecting information that will be used for monitoring and auditing. Detailed logs combined with active monitoring allow detection of security issues before they negatively affect your systems.

Secured Computing: A CISSP Study Guide, Copyright 2001

Logging Schedule

Logging of systems is an ongoing task. They should be logged 24 hours a day 7 days a week. Logging can be storage and CPU intensive, but should be done as much as resources allow. At the least, the following should be logged:

- Login and failed login attempts
- Servers
- Routers
- Processes
- Critical file modification and access

There are several things that should be considered when logging:

- All clocks should be synchronized to a central timeserver.

- Logs should be centralized for ease of use and access.

- All critical logs should be encrypted.

- All security relevant events must be logged.

- Logs should be kept for a specific period of time and then discarded properly when not needed.

- Keep logs in a secure place and make sure only authorized personnel have access to them.

Establishment

Establishment, also referred to as authorization, should determine who has trusted authorization for a specific purpose.

File and Data Owners, Custodians, and Users

Data Owners are responsible for information assets. Responsibilities include determining the sensitivity and criticality of the information, reviewing classification to ensure that it still meets the business needs, ensuring that security controls are in place commensurate with the

Secured Computing: A CISSP Study Guide, Copyright 2001

classification, and reviewing and ensuring currency of the previously granted access rights.

Custodians are often an information systems person. The custodian operates as the owner's delegate with primary responsibility for backup and recovery of the information. Responsibilities include performing backups according to requirements established by the information owner and, when necessary, restoring lost or damaged files.

The U*sers* are any employees, contractors, or other users who access the information from time to time. Their responsibilities include maintaining confidentiality of usernames and passwords.

Principle of Least Privilege

The *principle of least privilege* refers to granting users only those accesses required to perform their job duties. *Segregation of duties and responsibilities* refers to dividing roles and responsibilities so that a single individual cannot sabotage a significant process. The *rotation of duties* is important to deter against fraud and provides cross training for individuals.

Access Control Models

Bell-LaPadula Confidentiality Model

The Bell-LaPadula (BLP) model is an *information flow* model that prevents users and processes from reading above their security level. In addition it prevents processes within a given classification from writing data associated with a lower classification. The model describes a set of access control rules. In this formal model, the entities in a computer system are divided into abstract sets of subjects and objects. The notion of a secure state is defined, and it is proven that each state transition preserves security by moving from secure state to secure state; therefore showing that the system is secure. A system state is secure if only the permitted access modes of subjects (users) to objects (computers) are in accordance with the security policy set forth. In order to determine whether or not a specific access mode is allowed, the clearance of a subject is compared to the classification of the object and a determination is made as to whether the subject is authorized for the specific access mode.

BLP rules are for *discretionary access control* (DAC), a specific subject is authorized for a particular mode of access. Abstract formal treatment of DoD security policy, lattice-based model (dominance relationships) to determine whether a subject can access an object based on:

- The classification or sensitivity of the object
- The clearance or privilege of the subject
- The security policy that is in effect.

The BLP model sets forth certain relationships or rules between security levels known as the *dominance relation*. These relationships are as follows:

> **Star Property (* Property):** A rule that allows a subject write access to an object only if the security level of the object dominates the security level of the subject. It helps to prevent a process with a given classification from writing data associated with a lower classification. Simply stated — **can't write down, but can write up**. You can read and write, but only at the same level. **The same level is okay.**
>
> **Simple Security Property:** A rule (part of the lattice model) that allows a subject read access to an object only if the security level of the subject dominates the security level of the object. The processes with a given classification will not be able to read data associated with a higher classification. Simply stated — **can't read up, but can read down. The same level is okay.**
>
> **Strong Star Property:** A rule that only allows the subject to stay at the same level. **No write up and no read down.**

More on the BLP in Domain Six

Biba Integrity Model

The Biba model is an integrity model in which a subject cannot depend on a less trusted object, including another subject. Biba discovered a plausible notion of integrity, which he defined as prevention of unauthorized modification. For example, if a process could write above its security level, trustworthy data can be contaminated by the addition of that less trustworthy data.

Biba's model is based on a hierarchical lattice of integrity levels. He defined elements in integrity terms, set of subjects and set of objects. Sets of subjects are active and process information. Sets of objects are passive, receiving and are a place for information to be stored.

More on the Biba in Domain Six

Clark and Wilson Integrity Model

The Clark and Wilson model's approach is to provide data integrity for common commercial activities like software engineering, allocations of least privilege and separation of privilege. What the model is trying to do is preventing unauthorized users, from making modifications, maintaining internal and external consistency and preventing authorized users from making improper modifications. It is based on Well-formed transactions that control the applications used to make the modifications and Preserve/ensure internal consistency so that the user can manipulate data only in ways that ensure internal consistency. Well-formed transactions must be:

> *Logged* — all access and changes to the data must be logged.
> *Untampered* — data cannot be tampered with, even as it undergoes changes.
> *Consistent* — the data must be consistent, whether or not there is a change.

Separation of duties attempts to ensure external consistency and prevent authorized users from making improper modifications. The operation is divided in sub parts where a different person executes each part and ensures external consistency as well as prevents authorized users from unauthorized modifications

More on the Clark and Wilson model in Domain Six

State Machine Model

A state machine model captures the state of a system. The state of a machine can change only at discrete points in time that are initiated by a specific event. Both the Bell LaPadula and Biba models are state machine models. The state should capture the essential features of the system under investigation

Access Matrix Model

The access matrix model is used to describe which users have access to what objects. This is usually done through ACL's or capability tables.

There are four parts to an access matrix model:

- A list of the subjects
- A list of the objects
- A "T" function that will return an objects type
- The matrix itself

Information Flow Model

The *Information Flow model* is a variation of the access control model, in that it is based upon information flow and not access controls. This model makes it easier to look for cover channels and is often implemented in a lattice format.

The Three Basic Principles of I&A

- **Something you know** — A password, pass phrase, or a personal identification number (PIN). If you know the password you must be the owner. Problem is if it is easily guessable or it is given to someone it is not secure at all.

- **Something you have** — Keys, tokens, badges and smart cards that you must have to "unlock" your terminal or account. Problem is that you may lose the key or it may get stolen.

- **Something you are** — Physiological or behavior traits, such as fingerprints, handprint, retina, iris, voice, signature. Biometric systems compare your trait against the one stored for you and determine if you are who you claim to be. The iris scan is the most accurate of the biometric choices.

Passwords

Passwords should be selected carefully so they cannot be easily guessed, but are not too difficult to remember. Keys to password management are:

Secured Computing: A CISSP Study Guide, Copyright 2001

- Login user ID should be unique to each user

- Minimum of 6 alphanumeric characters

- Kept private

- User accounts lock out after 3 unsuccessful attempts

- Successful logins will display date and time of last logon

- ID and password suspended after long periods of non-use

Password factors

- Length range — length of characters in a password

- Composition — types of characters used in a password, upper case, lower case, alphanumeric, special characters

- Lifetime — the amount of time between password changes. Many times users are asked to change their password every 30, 60, or 90 days.

- Source — how is the password generated? Secure token? User generated?

- Distribution — the methods of distributing passwords

- Storage — how the password is stored, encrypted, plaintext

- Transmission — how passwords are transmitted. Do they use SSL or plaintext?

Pass Phrase

A pass phrase is a sequence of characters or words that are used instead of a password. Usually they are longer and more difficult to break, but they take longer to enter and are permanently stored.

Secured Computing: A CISSP Study Guide, Copyright 2001

One-Time Passwords

One-time passwords change after every use. Smart tokens that dynamically generate passwords can create one-time passwords.

There are two types of token devices:

- Asynchronous token devices use a challenge response scheme based on a one-time pad.

- Synchronous token devices that are based on time or events. For example, a time based device would provide a password every 60 seconds where an event based token would produce a password every time you pushed a button.

Tokens

Tokens consist of memory cards and smart cards:

- Memory cards store but do not process information (ex. Magnetic striped card). Usually used with a combination of what the user possesses and what they know, as in a personal identification number (PIN).

- Smart cards have processing capabilities. Each card contains unique information such as their identity or privileges. The card's processor performs a one-way transformation of the user's PIN.

Biometrics

Biometrics are based on something that you are and therefore are not easily forgeable. Biometrics are not yet widespread as there is much trepidation of others to use measuring devices. In practice, it is generally necessary to adjust the equipment used in biometrics for a compromise between rejection of correct individuals (type I error, false negative) and false acceptance of imposters (type II, false positive).

Single Sign-On (SSO)

One of the frustrations of passwords is that users may accumulate many and start writing them down or using easily guessable ones. This is where

Secured Computing: A CISSP Study Guide, Copyright 2001

single sign-on comes into play. SSO attempts to make the use of multiple passwords transparent to the user. Writing a script that contains the various passwords and user ID for that user or authenticating to a security server can do this and this removes the burden from the user, but transfers it to the administrator. SSO grants access to workstations, servers and applications. Since there is only one password this helps to encourage the use of one stronger password by users. The disadvantage is that once you are in you have access to everything without constraint.

Secure-single sign on (SSSO) is the ability for a user to use a single user ID and a single password to logon once and gain access to all resources that one is allowed to access while that information is encrypted.

Kerberos

Kerberos is a third party authentication service that is based on the MIT project named Athena and depends on passwords and symmetric cryptography (DES) to implement ticket-based, peer entity authentication services and access control services distributed in a client-server network environment. The Kerberos authentication server is a central system that knows about every principal and its passwords. It issues tickets to principals who successfully authenticate themselves. These tickets can be used to authenticate one principal (a user) to another (a server application). Kerberos sets up a session key for the principals that can be used to protect the privacy and the integrity of the communication. For this reason, the Kerberos system is also called a Key Distribution Center (KDC).

SESAME

Secure European System and Applications in Multi-vendor Environment (SESAME) is a project of the European Computer Manufacturer's Association (ECMA). It is a distributed access control for SSO using symmetric and asymmetric cryptography techniques. It helps to provide a global access identity.

Centralized Remote Authentication Access Controls

With the growth of Virtual private networks (VPN), mobile computing and multi-platforms centralized authentication services such as RADIUS,

TACACS, and DIAMETER fill the need. They are less expensive, easy to implement, and more flexible than remote access servers (RAS).

RADIUS, TACACS, and DIAMETER are all considered to be authentication, authorization, and accounting (AAA) servers. A more detailed description follows:

RADIUS

RADIUS is the most widely used AAA service used because it uses open source code. It is a handshaking protocol in which an authentication server provides authorization and authentication information to a network server to which the user is attempting to link. It provides a centralized server for a single point of authentication.

TACACS

TACACS is an UDP-based authentication and access control protocol in which a server receives an identifier and password from a remote terminal and passes them to a separate authentication server for verification. After the user is authenticated it forwards the login info to the data server requested by the user. In 1990 it was extended to include additional functionality and is referred to as XTACACS. Cisco also adopted TACACS and added some new features and extensibility and calls it TACACS+.

DIAMETER

DIAMETER was designed to support roaming applications and to overcome the extension limits of both RADIUS and TACACS. It will support any number of AAA connections using a base of protocols. It is built on the RADIUS protocol, but is more enhanced.

Decentralized Administration

Decentralized administration is controlled directly by the owners or creators of the files, often the function manager. This keeps control in the hands of those most accountable for the info, but leads to inconsistency in the procedures and criteria for granting user access and capabilities. Examples of decentralized access control are:

Domains — a domain is a unique context in which a program is operating: in affect, the set of objects that a subject has the ability to access.

Trusted computer system — a trusted computer system is a system that employs sufficient hardware and software integrity measures to allow its use for processing a range of sensitive or classified information.

File and data ownership

- System owners must identify, describe, and designate the sensitivity of their present and proposed application systems.

- System owners must ensure proper security control requirements.

- Prior to implementation system owners must assess security requirements by identifying threats and vulnerabilities.

- They must create and implement a solid security plan.

- Test systems and software for security specifications before put into production.

- Create a contingency plan for users to perform essential functions in the event that normal operations are interrupted.

- Maintain written policy stating who specifically is authorized to use their systems and the users understand that.

Methods of Attack

Buffer Overflow Attack	This is the most common kind of Denial of Service (DoS) attack. You are sending more traffic to a buffer than the buffer can handle and cause the system to crash.
Man in the middle	A man in the middle attack is one in which the attacker intercepts messages in a public key exchange and then retransmits them, substituting their own public key for the requested one, so that the two original parties still appear to be communicating with each other directly. The attacker uses a program that appears to be the server to the client and appears to be the client to the server. The attack may be used simply to gain access to the messages, or enable the attacker to modify them before retransmitting them.

17

Illicit Server	When you have an unauthorized daemon or service running on your system that can cause harm. An Illicit server can secretly open a port and provide service that is not authorized.
Ping Of Death	A Hacker will crash a system when sending an ICMP-based packet that is more than 65,536 bytes, which causes a buffer overflow.
Land Attack	A Hacker can send an IP packet (Spoofed) to another computer and have the identical Source / Destination address.
Smurf Attack	The attacker sends an IP PING request to another site. The ping packet can specify that it be broadcast to a number of hosts within the receiving site's local network. The packet can also indicate that the request is from another site, the target site that is to receive the DoS. (This is called spoofing.) The result will be MANY ping replies flooding back to the spoofed host. If the flood is big enough, the spoofed host will no longer be able to receive real traffic. They will be DoS and non-functional. To protect, filter ICMP packets at the firewall.
Teardrop Attack	This attack exploits vulnerabilities in the IP protocol. The attacker sends a large packet that must be divided up and then sets a confusing offset value in the second frame causing the system to crash.
Physical Attacks	This would be a maliciously cut cable or any physical damage that is done purposely.
Brute Force	Brute force is exhausting all possible combinations of codes and words using computer software. This can be done using password crackers
Dictionary attacks	This is a brute force attack using a dictionary as the source of the guesses.
Root Kits	They are very hard to detect but may be found with checksum analysis and port scanning. They are comprised of many programs that replace legitimate ones.
Social Engineering (Non-Direct attacks)	A way for hackers to trick users into giving up their credentials or accidentally giving hackers access to resources through trickery or mistake. Hackers might imitate others and trick a Help Desk agent into changing a password. (As an example)
Hijacking	This is similar to the man-in-the-middle attack, except the hacker intercepts the data and ACTS as or IMPERSINATES the other person you think you are in contact with.

Monitoring

Monitoring is an ongoing activity that checks on the system, its users, or the environment. In general, the more real-time the activity is, the more it falls into the category of monitoring. Monitoring is not risk mitigation; just an alarm that alerts you to what may be an anomaly of some sort.

Secured Computing: A CISSP Study Guide, Copyright 2001

Intrusion Detection

Intrusion detection is a technique that attempts to detect network attacks by observing network traffic. The two ways that it examines this traffic is through signatures and anomalies:

- Attack signatures are specific patterns in the IP packet data that allow an analyst or intrusion detection system (IDS) to identify that information as a highly probable attack. This is done by comparing past intrusions and developing models and then comparing these "signatures" to current traffic. This type of analysis is weak against new types of attacks.

- Anomaly identification is an anomaly-based approach that focuses on building a statistical model of users' normal behavior (sequential patterns) and generating an alarm when the activity falls outside the modeled norm. This is referred to as time based inductive learning and is a detection of deviations from these sequential rules. This is also called *time-based induction machine* (TIM), which observes the process, identifies the patterns, sets a hypothesis, inputs episodes, and gives a user profile.

There are four main types of intrusion detection systems: statistical, rule based, signature based, and adaptive real-time anomaly based.

Statistical Intrusion Detection

Statistical intrusion detection compares audit files and logs and then develops and maintains profiles for what is considered normal behavior.

Rule Based Intrusion Detection

Rule based intrusion detection compares audit records to specific rule set forth by the system. Many use expert system technology and attempt to repeat human experts reasoning.

Signature Based Intrusion Detection

Signature based intrusion detection develops models of attacks based on past intrusions. Then the system tries to recognize the signature or patterns of these attacks. One problem is that it is weak against any new attacks.

Adaptive Real-time Anomaly Detection

Adaptive real-time anomaly detection inductively generates sequential patterns that describe behavior. Any deviations from these patterns are considered an alert because they are out of the norm. They detect these deviations using a time based inductive learning approach, which detects the deviations from the sequential rules.

Alarms

Alarms are used to detect and signal unauthorized entry or attempted entry. Holds up alarms are manual as with tilt switches, vibration detectors or mechanical contacts for doors and windows. Testing must be done periodically and the power supply should always be monitored.

Corrective Procedures

Corrective procedures can be manual or automated. These are procedures that put a system or device back into normal working condition.

Audit Trails

Audit trails are a one time or periodic event to evaluate security is the definition of auditing. A periodic review of system-generated logs can detect security problems, including attempts to exceed access authority or gain system access during unusual hours. They help to recreate an event, help in problem analysis, intrusion detection and individual accountability. There are three audit record types:

- **System events** are used for special access to alter configuration files and to monitor and fine-tune performance. Examples would be log on ID, types of devices used and dates and times of log on/off attempts.

- **Application** events are used for error messages and any violations found in an application. Examples include data files that are opened and closed, modification of any records and the actions taken within the application (read, write, delete etc.)

- **User events** are used to hold individuals accountable, expose any security violations and to do key stroke monitoring. Examples include any user-initiated command, files accessed and authentication attempts.

Penetration Testing

Penetration testing is attempting to break into ones own system, also referred to as a tiger team approach. Use of automated tools and manual attempts are used. It should always be done under management consent. Typically, the team doing the penetration test starts out with the same type of information that a hacker would, and initiates similar attacks to simulate breaking into your system. If they cannot break in, then the attack has demonstrated that the level of security implemented is good. If they are successful, then it demonstrates what vulnerabilities exist, how they can be used, and what areas of improvement should be taken.

There are many methods of Penetration Testing but the most common methods of gathering information during the penetration test are:

- Social engineering
- Dumpster diving
- Eavesdropping
- Sniffing the network
- War dialing

Once the information has been gathered, it is used to try and gain unauthorized access to the organizations systems. The result is a report to management identifying what information was collected, what methods were used, what vulnerabilities were found and how they were exploited.

The methods of planning a penetration test are as follows:

1. Create a test plan — outlines goals and objectives of the test as well as expectations. This is also were we would want to get managements approval and buy in.

2. Perform the test — Once the test plan is completed it is time to perform the test. This can be broken into three main areas; Reconnaissance, Attack and Occupation (optional).

   - Reconnaissance is the "discovery" portion, when you try to survey the scene and gather information about what you are going to attack.

- Attack is when you exploit the weaknesses you found in the reconnaissance stage.

- Occupation is when the attacker gains entry into the system and uses it as a base of operations. This may be done if the attacker wants to gather more information, monitor activities, or launch attacks on other systems from that base.

3. Report results — this is the final step and should answer the expectations set forth in the test plan.

Test Your Knowledge

1. What are the three principles of A & I?

   A. Something you know, something you are, something you would like to be
   B. Something you know, something you are, something you have
   C. Something you are, something you would like to be, something you know
   D. Something you are, something you have, something you control

2. What type of attack is it when you try all possible combinations to break a code or password?

   A. Dictionary attack
   B. Black Ops
   C. Brute Force
   D. Penetration testing

3. What are specific patterns in the packet data that allow an Intrusion detection system (IDS) to identify that information as a highly probable attack?

   A. Packet analysis
   B. Pattern based idioscopy
   C. Packet anomaly
   D. Signature analysis

4. What network access technique is it when users log into a single centralized server that contains a database of authorized accounts?

   A. TACACS
   B. RADIUS
   C. DOMAINS
   D. DoS

5. What are used to allow management to allow or deny access to objects in a computer system?

   A. Permissions
   B. Access Controls
   C. Controlling attributes

D. ACL's

6. What refers to dividing up roles so that one single individual cannot have sole responsibility of critical processes?

   A. Principle of least privilege
   B. Discretionary access control (DAC)
   C. Segregation of duties
   D. ACL's

7. _____ access controls cannot be made more permissive and are based on security labels?

   A. Lattice based access controls
   B. Mandatory access controls
   C. Discretionary based access controls
   D. The principle of controlling attributes

8. _____ is the ability to assure individual accountability of classified and sensitive information whenever a discretionary security policy is used?

   A. Accountability
   B. Invincibility
   C. RBAC
   D. DAC

9. What access control is based on specific rules relating to the nature of the subject or object, beyond ones identity?

   A. Role based
   B. Rule based
   C. Authentication based
   D. Discretionary based

10. What model is an information flow model?

    A. Biba
    B. Clark & Wilson
    C. Bell - LaPadula
    D. Cheech & Chong

11. What relationship or rule in the Bell – LaPadula model states <u>CAN'T WRITE DOWN, CAN WRITE UP</u>.

    A. *- Property
    B. Simple secure property
    C. Complex/Simplex Property
    D. Information flow

12. The area that surrounds sensitive information and the equipment that handle that information is called?

    A. Lock down area
    B. Control zone
    C. Secured site
    D. Confidential library

13. What are the three layers of access controls?

    A. Confidentiality, authentication and Identification
    B. Confidentiality, Integrity and availability
    C. Administrative, physical and logical
    D. Administrative, Authentication and logical

14. File access, encryption, and system access are examples of what kind of access control?

    A. Physical
    B. Logical
    C. Administrative
    D. Authentic

15. What type of access control is in place when they try to alert you or identify when an access is violated?

    A. Detective
    B. Preventative
    C. Isolated
    D. Deterrent

Secured Computing: A CISSP Study Guide, Copyright 2001

16. What type of intrusion detection approach focuses on building a statistical model of users' normal behavior and generating an alarm when the activity falls outside the modeled norm?

   A. Gnomonical event
   B. Anomaly detection
   C. Signature detection
   D. Statistical comparatives

17. What type of access control is based on specific rules relating to the nature of the subject or object, beyond ones identity, like security labels or classifications?

   A. Role based
   B. Lattice based
   C. Action based
   D. Rule based

18. Length range, composition, lifetime, source, ownership, distribution, storage, entry, transmission, authentication period are what?

   A. Password factors
   B. Anomaly factors
   C. Pass phrase parameters
   D. Password matrices

19. What type of audit events are user-initiated commands, files accessed and authentication attempts?

   A. System events
   B. User events
   C. Application events
   D. Control events

20. _____ is a third party authentication service that depends on passwords and symmetric cryptography to implement ticket-based, peer entity authentication service and access control service distributed in a client-server network environment?

   A. KDE
   B. Kerberos
   C. TGS

Secured Computing: A CISSP Study Guide, Copyright 2001

D. Ticket

Answers

1.B, 2.C, 3.D, 4.A, 5.B,

6.C, 7.B, 8.A, 9.B, 10.C,

11.A, 12.B, 13.C, 14.B, 15.A,

16.B, 17.D, 18.A, 19.B, 20.B

References

Information in this chapter was referenced from the following sources:

1. Computer Security Handbook, Third edition, Arthur E, Hutt et al. 1995 John Wiley & Sons Inc.

2. *Information Security Management Handbook, 4th edition, Harold F. Tipton, et al. 2000, Auerbach Publications.*

3. *RFC 2828*

4. *RFC 2196 Site Security Handbook, RFC 2196, author B. Fraser, 1997*

5. *Security in Computing, Second edition, Charles P. Pfleeger, 1997 Prentice Hall*

<u>Notes</u>

2

Domain 2

Telecommunications & Network Security

Telecommunications and Network Security

The telecommunications and network security domain encompasses the transmission methods, structures, transport formats, availability, authentication and confidentiality of information over public and private communications networks.

Definitions

Datagram — A self-contained, independent entity of data carrying sufficient information to be routed from the source to the destination.

End-to-end encryption — Continuous protection of data that flows between two points in a network, this is provided by encrypting the data at the source and decrypting only when the data arrives at the intended destination.

Link encryption — Stepwise protection of data that flows between two points in a network, provided by encrypting data separately on each network link, i.e., by encrypting data when it leaves a host or subnetwork relay and decrypting it when it arrives at the next host or relay. Each link may use a different key or even a different algorithm.

Network security — The protection of networks and their services from unauthorized modification, destruction, or disclosure. Providing an assurance that the network performs its critical functions correctly and there are no harmful side effects. Includes providing for information accuracy.

Protocol suite — A complementary collection of communication protocols used in a computer network.

ISO/OSI Model

Short for *Open System Interconnection*, an ISO standard for worldwide communications that defines a networking framework for implementing protocols in seven layers. Control is passed from one layer to the next,

Secured Computing: A CISSP Study Guide, Copyright 2001

starting at the application layer down the chain to the physical layer and back up again. Many vendors support the model loosely, but OSI mainly serves as the teaching model for all other protocols. See figure 2.1.

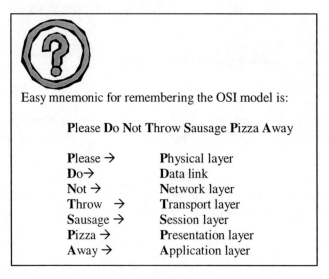

Easy mnemonic for remembering the OSI model is:

Please Do Not Throw Sausage Pizza Away

Please →	**P**hysical layer
Do →	**D**ata link
Not →	**N**etwork layer
Throw →	**T**ransport layer
Sausage →	**S**ession layer
Pizza →	**P**resentation layer
Away →	**A**pplication layer

Figure 2.1 – OSI Model

Communications and Network Security

Physical Media

Twisted-pair cable consists of copper wires surrounded by an insulator. Two wires are twisted together to form a pair, and the pair forms a circuit that transmits the data. Unshielded twisted-pair (UTP) is the most commonly used type of twisted-pair cable.

Shielded twisted-pair (STP) provides protection against crosstalk. Twisted-pair cable is the most commonly used cabling and is used in Ethernet, Fast Ethernet, token ring, and other network topologies.

The EIA/TIA has defined the five categories of twisted-pair cable:

- Category 1- this is traditional telephone cable.
- Category 2- can send data transmissions up to 4 Mbps.
- Category 3- transmission characteristics are specified up to 16 MHz. This is used by 10BASE-T and 100BASE-T4 installations.

- Category 4- transmission characteristics are specified up to 20 MHz. It is used by 10BASE-T and 100BASE-T4 installations.

Layer	Name	Function	Protocol
7	Application Layer	Program-to-program communication.	TFTP, BOOTP, SMTP, MIME
6	Presentation Layer	Manages data representation conversions. For example, the Presentation Layer would be responsible for converting from EBCDIC to ASCII.	
5	Session Layer	Responsible for establishing and maintaining communications channels. In practice, this layer is often combined with the Transport Layer.	
4	Transport Layer	Responsible for end-to-end integrity of data transmission.	TCP UDP
3	Network Layer	Routes data from one node to another.	IP, OSPF RIP, IGMP
2	Data Link Layer	Responsible for physical passing data from one node to another.	ARP, RARP PPP, SLIP
1	Physical Layer	Manages putting data onto the network media and taking the data off.	Ethernet, ISDN

Secured Computing: A CISSP Study Guide, Copyright 2001

- Category 5- transmission characteristics are specified up to 100 MHz. It is used by 10BASE-T, 100BASE-T4, and 100BASE-TX installations. The cable normally has four pairs of copper wire. Category 5 is the most popular cable used in installations today.

10BASE-T Standard

10BASE-T is the IEEE 802.3 standard for Ethernet signaling over unshielded twisted-pair wire at 10 Mbps. *Base* stands for base band, which is a technology that transmits direct-current pulses rather than as modulated signals on separate carrier frequencies.

100BASE-T Standard

The 100BASE-T Fast Ethernet standard is based on the 10BASE-T standard and retains nearly all elements of the original IEEE 802.3 Ethernet specification, while greatly increasing the network's overall throughput.

100BASE-TX Specification

100BASE-TX designates the IEEE 802.3 specification for 100 Mbps Ethernet signaling with CSMA/CD over two pairs of Category 5 UTP or STP wire. The pairs of wires used for transmitting and receiving signals are the same as those used for 10BASE-T.

100BASE-FX Specification

100BASE-FX is the IEEE 802.3 specification for 100 Mbps Ethernet signaling over two strands of multimode fiber-optic cable. This is used for transmissions over long distances, downlinks, and backbones, and is very useful in an environment subject to electrical interference.

Secured Computing: A CISSP Study Guide, Copyright 2001

Installation

When installing cabling it is important to install it where it is unexposed and protected. It should be laid in pairs and in separate tubing. Use a pressurized conduit so that if you see the pressure drop it may indicate an intrusion.

Two other terms that you will want to be aware of is cross talk and attenuation:

- *Cross talk* is the electromagnetic interference that occurs when the electrical signal on one wire changes the electrical properties on an adjacent wire. Using shielded cables can prevent this.
- *Attenuation* is the degradation of a signal because energy is lost as it moves down the wire. Repeaters are used to re-amplify signals that experience attenuation.

Network topologies

Theses are the three principal topologies (See figure 2.2) used in LANs today:

- Bus topology: devices are connected from a central cable, called the bus or backbone. Bus networks are the least expensive and easiest to install for small networks. Ethernet systems use a bus topology.

- Star topology: The devices are connected to a central hub and extend out from there. Hence the name star as they look like a star. Star networks are easy to install and manage, but they can bottleneck because all data must pass through the hub.

- Ring topology: devices are connected to each other in the shape of a closed loop. This way the device is connected directly to two other devices, one on either side of it. Ring topologies are more expensive and difficult to install than a Bus topology, but they offer high bandwidth and can span large distances.

Secured Computing: A CISSP Study Guide, Copyright 2001

These topologies can be mixed. For example, a bus-star network consists of a high-bandwidth bus, called the backbone, which connects a collection of slower-bandwidth star segments.

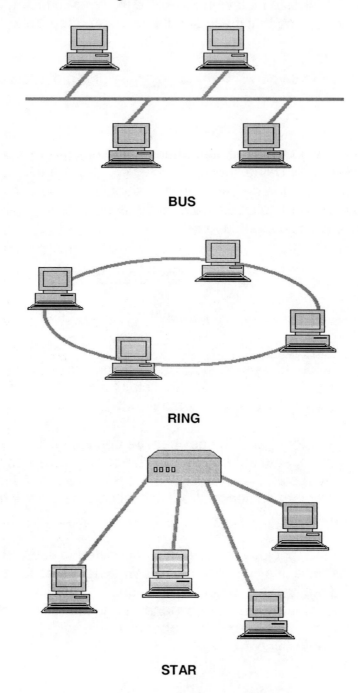

BUS

RING

STAR

Figure 2.2 —Network Topologies.

36
Secured Computing: A CISSP Study Guide, Copyright 2001

Protocol Vulnerabilities

A protocol is a set of rules that determine how computers communicate across a network.

FTP

FTP (File Transfer Protocol) is exploited frequently. It is best to keep your FTP server in a DMZ and only allow anonymous access, as FTP sends passwords in clear text.

FTP has many vulnerabilities such as sending passwords in clear text and hackers will look for a directory with WRITE access to either upload Trojans, viruses, or fill the server with so much space that it takes up all hard disk space. To help mitigate this it is important to have your operating system on a different hard disk on the server.

SMTP

Attacks against email servers are common. SMTP was not designed with security in mind so there are many attacks that can be spread by users. The best ways to protect an email server is to either have it scan each message, or set up a filtering firewall or proxy to scan all messages.

HTTP

HTTP is traffic is usually the most common of network traffic. It is what most web traffic is made up of. HTTP alone is not nearly as unsecured as when CGI, Java applets and Active X are used. Port 80 is the default port for HTTP. It is best to have all web servers located in a DMZ.

TELNET

Telnet is the part of the TCP/IP stack and used to establish terminal emulation between a client and a server. The main security issues are that passwords are sent in clear text. It is best to use SSH instead of telnet as SSH uses public key encryption.

Secured Computing: A CISSP Study Guide, Copyright 2001

SNMP

SNMP is considered an unsafe protocol as it allows clear text passwords. Everything is done via community name and if that name is compromised, then all SNMP-enabled devices with that string could also be compromised. This best filtered at the firewall.

DNS

DNS can be easily attacked if not properly secured. Intruders can try to attack the DNS server zone files using either NSLOOKUP or when the secondary name server queries the primary zone files. "Name Poisoning" is when a Hacker is able to insert wrong or false DNS information into a Zone Transfer – usually between a Master and a Slave.

ARP and RARP

ARP (Address Resolution Protocol) is a protocol for mapping an IP address to a physical machine address that is recognized in the local network. A table, usually called the ARP cache, is used to maintain a correlation between each MAC address and its corresponding IP address. ARP provides the protocol rules for making this correlation and providing address conversion in both directions.

RARP (Reverse Address Resolution Protocol) is a protocol by which a physical machine in a local area network can request to learn its IP address from a gateway server's Address Resolution Protocol table or cache.

TCP/IP Characteristics and Vulnerabilities

Transmission Control Protocol/Internet Protocol (TCP/IP) is a suite of protocols that are the de facto standard of internetworking. The entire Internet is based on the TCP/IP protocol. The major protocols include:

IP

IP is an Internet standard protocol (IPv4 and IPv6) that moves datagrams from one computer to another across an internetwork. IP does *not* provide reliable delivery, flow control, sequencing, or other end-to-end services that TCP provides.

Secured Computing: A CISSP Study Guide, Copyright 2001

The datagram (See figure 2.3) is a unit of data with the associated header that is sent from the source host to the destination host. Each datagram is sent out in sequence and can be routed individually. Due to this capability there is no guarantee that datagrams will arrive in the proper sequence, or for that matter, arrive at all. As each data packet is sent out a header is attached.

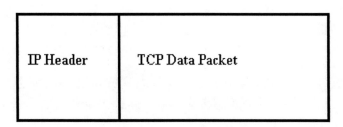

Figure 2.3. - Datagram Composition

The header that is attached to the datagram contains a wealth of information in order to allow the datagram to reach its destination (see figure 2.4). The information contained in the header consists of:

1. Version - The version of IP that is being used
2. Header Length - The length of the header in 32 bit words
3. Type of Service - Describes the priority, delay, throughput and reliability of service for the datagram
4. Length of Datagram - This is the total length of the datagram as measured in octets (eight-bit bytes). This limits the type of networks that the datagram can travel along, unless fragmentation is allowed
5. Identifier - This contains a number identifying which message the datagram belongs to
6. Flags - The first flag is used to show if the datagram can be broken down if necessary in order to cross a network that cannot handle a datagram of this size. The second flag indicates if this is the last fragment or if there are more fragments to follow
7. Fragment Offset - This gives the offset of the data fragment from the beginning of the message in eight octet blocks
8. Time to Live - Contains the number of seconds remaining before this datagram is discarded (maximum value of 255 seconds)
9. Protocol - This defines the protocol that the packet is intended for (TCP - 6, UDP - 17)

10.Checksum - A calculated checksum for the header. This value changes as the time to live value is decreased or if changes are made to the header due to options that were set

11.Source Address - The IP address of the source computer

12.Destination Address - The IP address of the destination computer

13.Options

14.End of Option List - Padding

15.Padding

16.Data

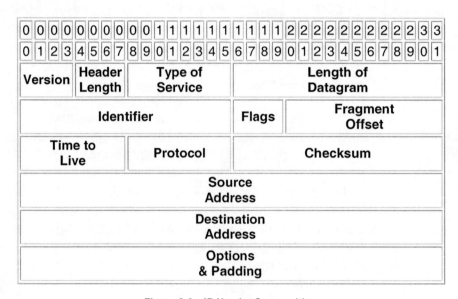

Figure 2.4 – IP Header Composition

Ipv4

Internet Protocol version 4 (IPv4) has been in use since the late 1970s. IP currently runs on top of a large number of media. The IP delivery system is connectionless and unreliable. IP packets are treated independent of each other, therefore, they can be lost, duplicated or delivered out of order. A more detailed overview of IPv4 can be found in RFC 791.

There are few security mechanisms for IPv4; access software can use the source and destination addresses and ports in order to authorize access. IP has user-defined field that could be used for security labeling, but it usually isn't found in the commercial world. In addition, there are privileged ports, those under 1024, but that is not specified in the protocol.

Secured Computing: A CISSP Study Guide, Copyright 2001

Currently, IP based protocols, such as Telnet, FTP, and Mail, use clear text messages. With the current 4 byte (32 bits) addresses used in IPv4, the Internet was expected to run out of new addresses as early as 2002, but with the high use with subnetting and private addressing schemes they are lasting longer. With the mass installation of Ipv4 it will need to be a very gradual migration to Ipv6, which offers more security features and many more addresses.

IPv6

IPv6 expands addresses to 16 bytes (128 bits) to allow for the continued growth of the Internet while making changes to improve efficiency for hosts and routers connected to a large-scale network. In addition, IPv6 also incorporates new functionality to provide security, multimedia support, and plug and play capability, features necessary to push the Internet into the future.

IPv6 mandates specific routines for packet-level encryption and authentication. Future applications can depend on having these functions available. Encryption scrambles the data packet to prevent unauthorized people from reading the message. Authentication verifies that the source address was not forged and that the packet was not tampered with while in route to its destination. IPv6 can be configured to encrypt or authenticate particular streams of data, or can automatically apply security to all communications between specified hosts. IPv6 also includes the MD5 algorithm for message integrity and authentication.

TCP

Transmission Control Protocol enables two hosts to establish a connection and exchange streams of data. TCP guarantees delivery of data and also guarantees that packets will be delivered in the same order in which they were sent.

A connection using TCP is achieved after the following steps have taken place. The host computer opens the port telling the port to listen for requests. The client computer sends a handshaking signal to the host requesting a connection. The host computer upon receiving this signal sends out an acknowledgement and its own handshaking signal. Once the host signal is received by the client, it sends out an acknowledge message and notifies the application program that a connection has been

41

established. When the clients acknowledge the host receives a message, it informs the application connected to that port that a connection has been established.

TCP attaches a header to each data packet that it sends. This header and data packet make up the information passed to IP as a package of data to be delivered. The contents of the TCP header segment (see Figure 2.5) are:

1.Source Port - This is the port that the message was sent from
2.Destination Port - This is the port that the message is destined for
3.Sequence Number - Used to keep track of the data being sent
4.Acknowledgement Number - Used to acknowledge the last data sequence number received
5.Header Length - The length of the header in 32 bit words
6.Reserved Section
7.Code Bits - Used to send control codes between the computers

- Urgent
- Acknowledge
- Push - data sent by user
- Reset - used to terminate a connection
- Synchronize - used to establish a connection
- Finish - used to terminate a connection

8.Window - Used to control the size of data packets that can be sent and for flow control
9.Checksum - This is a checksum for the combined header and data packet
10.Urgent Pointer - Indicates where in the data packet urgent data is located
11.Options - Settings that allow further description of the data packet size and flow control
12.Padding

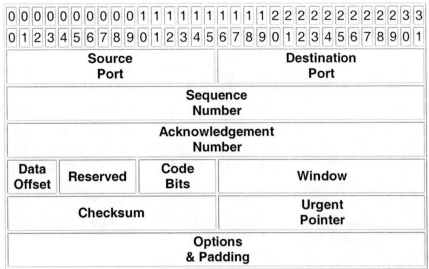

Figure 2.5 – TCP Header Composition

UDP

User Datagram *Protocol (UCP),* a connectionless protocol that, like TCP, runs on top of IP networks. UDP/IP has little error recovery services, offering instead a direct way to send and receive datagrams over an IP network. UDP is much faster than TCP and therefore is primarily for broadcasting messages over a network.

ICMP

The *Internet Control Message Protocol (ICMP)* is an extension to the Internet Protocol (IP). ICMP supports packets containing error, control, and informational messages. The PING command, for example, uses ICMP to test an Internet connection.

The main vulnerabilities associated with TCP/IP are:

- TCP/IP is a bandwidth hog
- It is easy to tap into
- Vulnerable to hacking/spoofing

WAN Protocols

HDLC

High-level Data Link Control is a transmission protocol used at the data link layer (layer 2) of the OSI model for data communications. HDLC embeds information in a data frame that allows devices to control data flow and correct errors. One station is primary and the other secondary to establish any HDLC communications. A session will use one of the following connection modes, which determine how the primary and secondary stations interact:

- Asynchronous: The secondary station can initiate the message.

- Normal unbalanced: This is where the secondary station responds only to the primary station.

- Asynchronous balanced: Both stations send and receive over its part of a duplex line. This mode is used for X.25 packet-switching networks.

VOIP

Voice over IP is a voice delivered using the Internet Protocol. It is a term used in IP telephony for a set of facilities for managing the delivery of voice information using the Internet Protocol. Rather than send information in the traditional circuit-committed protocols of the public switched telephone network (PSTN) it sends voice information in digital form called packets. The major advantage of VoIP is that it avoids the charges by the ordinary telephone service.

HSSI

High Speed Serial Interface is a short-distance communications interface that is commonly used to interconnect routing and switching devices on local area networks with the higher-speed lines of a WAN. HSSI is used between devices that are within fifty feet of each other and achieves data rates up to 52 Mbps. HSSI can be used to interconnect devices on token ring and Ethernet LANs with devices that operate at Synchronous Optical Network (Synchronous Optical Network) Optical Carrier levels (OCx)

(Optical Carrier 1) speeds or on T-carrier system lines. HSSI is also used for host-to-host linking, image processing, and disaster recovery applications.

ISDN

Integrated Services Digital Network is an international communications standard for sending video, voice, and data over a digital telephone line or normal telephone wires. ISDN supports data transfer rates of 64 Kbps. ISDN lines offered by telephone companies give you two lines at once, called *B channels.*

PPP

Point-to-Point Protocol is a protocol that helps communication between two computers using a serial interface. PPP uses the Internet protocol (IP) and is designed to handle others. Essentially, it packages your computer's TCP/IP packets and forwards them to the server where they can actually be put on the Internet.

DSL

Digital Subscriber Line is a technology for bringing high-bandwidth information to homes and small businesses over ordinary telephone lines. *X*DSL refers to different variations of DSL, such as, HDSL, ADSL and RADSL. It may be possible to receive data at rates up to 6.1 megabits per second of a theoretical 8.448 megabits per second, enabling continuous transmission of motion video, and audio, as well as 3-D effects. More typically, individual connections will provide from 1.544 Mbps to 512 Kbps downstream and about 128 Kbps upstream. A DSL line can carry both data and voice signals and the data part of the line is continuously connected.

SMDS

Switched Multimegabit Data Service is a public, packet-switched service intended for enterprises that need to exchange large amounts of data with other enterprises over the wide-area network on a nonconstant basis. SMDS extends the performance and efficiencies of a company's LAN over a wide area on a switched, as-needed basis. It is connectionless so there is no need to set up a connection through the network before sending data. This provides bandwidth on demand for the "bursty" data transmission typically found on LANs.

Identification and Authentication

User identification and authorization is used to identify who is attempting to establish a connection. They are used to identify the source that is attempting establish a connection. This can be done through audit logs and the network access used. Two popular authentication protocols are CHAP and PAP:

Challenge Handshake Authentication Protocol (CHAP) is a type of authentication in which an authentication agent, usually a network server, sends the client program a key to be used to encrypt the username and password. This allows the username and password to be transmitted encrypted to protect them against eavesdroppers.

Password Authentication Protocol (PAP) is the most basic form of authentication, in which a user's name and password are transmitted over a network and compared to a table of name-password pairs. Typically, the passwords stored in the table are encrypted. The Basic Authentication feature built into the HTTP protocol uses PAP. The main weakness of PAP is that both the username and password are transmitted in the clear.

Firewalls

Many firewalls use many techniques (see figure 2.6). A firewall is considered a first line of defense in protecting private information. For greater security, data can be encrypted. A firewall is a system designed to keep out unauthorized access to or from a private network. Firewalls can be used to prevent unauthorized Internet users from accessing private networks connected to the Internet; this is especially true in intranets. Firewalls can come in the form of both hardware and software, or a combination of both. All messages entering or leaving the intranet pass through the firewall, which examines each message and blocks those that do not meet the specified security criteria.

There are four main purposes to a firewall:
- Implement Company's Security Policy
- Create a Choke point
- Log Internet Activity

- Limit Network Exposure

Stateful Inspection

Stateful inspection is when all data is captured and analyzed at all communication layers for a more detailed analysis. The state and the context of the data are stored and updated dynamically. This helps to track data from connectionless protocols such as UDP and RPC. This is firewall type has the best protection and analysis.

Packet-filtering Firewall This firewall works at the network layer and can be performed by routers	Looks at each packet entering or leaving the network and accepts or rejects it based on user-defined rules, ACL's. Packet filtering is effective and transparent to users, but it can be difficult to configure. It can be susceptible to IP spoofing.
Circuit-level Gateway Works at the session layer	Applies Access controls when a TCP or UDP connection is established. Once the connection has been made, packets can flow freely between the hosts without further checking. It helps to provide security for a wide variety of protocols and is easier to maintain than an application firewall.
Application-level Gateway Works at all seven layers of the OSI	Applies security mechanisms to specific applications, such as FTP and Telnet servers. It can mask the origin of the initiating connection. This is very effective, but can impose performance degradation because it analyzes each packet and must make a decision about access control.
DMZ Demilitarized Zone	A DMZ is a separate network that sits between the Internet and your internal network. This zone may contain FTP servers, e-commerce systems, and web servers. One firewall protects the zone from the Internet the other firewall protects the internal network.
Proxy Server	Stands in between and intercepts all messages entering and leaving a network. The proxy server can effectively hide the true network addresses from outsiders. Proxy servers have two main purposes: to filter requests and to help improve performance.
Screened Hosts	Offers added security by using Internet access to deny or permit certain traffic from the Bastion Host. This is the first stop for traffic, which can continue only if the Screening Router lets it through.
Screening Routers	Basic type of firewall that uses only the packet-filtering capability to control and monitor network traffic passing through the border. Can block traffic between networks or to and from specific hosts on an IP-port level. A CHOKE router is the only point in.

Figure 2.6 – Firewall Techniques

Secured Computing: A CISSP Study Guide, Copyright 2001

Data Communications

Extranets and Intranets

An intranet is a private network that is separated from the general Internet through an access-limiting device, like a firewall. An extranet, is a private network that is outside the intranet. The purpose of the extranet is to extend services from the intranet to the extranet. An extranet may be part of the Internet, or protected through an access-limiting device.

LAN's and WAN's

A LAN is a local area network, which is generally a small network to connect computers together. It lies with in a limited spatial area and has a specific topology. It is most often connected with a form of Ethernet technology. LANs can come in several different topologies. These include Star, bus, ring, mesh and several hybrids.

A WAN is a wide area network that is used to connect LANs that are separated by large geographical areas. They are privately operated for a specific group and usually support many protocols and network services. Wan technologies that are able to carry data over large areas include:

Frame Relay

Frame relay is a packet-switching protocol for connecting devices on a Wide Area Network (WAN). Frame Relay networks in the U.S. support data transfer rates at T-1 (1.544 Mbps) and T-3 (45 Mbps) speeds, In Europe, speeds vary from 64 Kbps to 2 Mbps.

X.25

X.25 is a standard for packet switching networks that was approved by the ITU in 1976. It is defined at the 1, 2, and 3 layers in the OSI Reference Model.

Network Switching

A circuit switched network is a physical and permanent connection. It is a transparent path to the terminal equipment that experiences no or little data manipulation. A Packet switch network has all the data traveling in

Secured Computing: A CISSP Study Guide, Copyright 2001

packets and relies on switches to route the data to the next destination. At the destination the packets may or may not arrive in order but are reassembled according to their sequence number. See figure 2.7

Circuit Switching	Packet Switching
Fixed delays	Variable delays
Connection orientated	Connectionless
Constant traffic	Bursty Traffic
Voice Orientated	Data Orientated

Figure 2.7-- Circuit/Packet Switching

WAN's use logical or virtual circuits to ensure the communications are reliable. There are two types of virtual circuits:

- Switched Virtual Circuits (SVR)- these circuits are established on demand and terminated when the transmission is complete. They are more often used when there is not a constant flow of data.

- Permanent Virtual Circuits (PVC)- are circuits that are in one mode only, transfer mode. They are used when there is constant data flow.

WAN Devices

There are many devices that are specific to a WAN environment. It is important to have a basic understanding of each of these:

- WAN Switch- is a multi-port device that is used in carrier networks that delivers multi-service access and switching across private and public networks

- Access server- is a connection point for dial in and dial out connections.

- Modems- this is a device that modulates and demodulates analog and digital signals. For example the digital data from your computer is converted to analog signals to travel across an analog communication line and then is demodulated back to digital when it arrives at the receiving computer.

- CSU/DSU- these are Channel Service Units (CSU) and Data Service Units (DSU). They are the digital interface that adapts the physical interface on data terminal equipment (DTE) to the interface of a data circuit-terminating device (DCE) in a switched carrier environment.

- ISDN terminal adapter- these are devices that connect a basic rate interface (BRI) to other interfaces. It can be looked at as an ISDN modem.

- ATM Switch- this device provides high speed switching. It is scalable and is great for video, voice and data applications. The data travels in fixed sizes called cells.

Virtual Private Network

A Virtual Private Network (VPN) is a type of connection in which the transmission from one computer to another is done through a private channel in the network. This is generally setup by creating an encrypted session between the two computers that no one else can access. A VPN can be run through a small network, through a large intranet, or through the Internet.

Tunneling, also called encapsulation, works by encapsulating a network protocol within packets carried by the second network. It does this by embedding its own network protocol within the TCP/IP packets carried by the Internet. An example is Microsoft's PPTP technology, which enables organizations to use the Internet to transmit data across a virtual private network.

VAN

A Value Added Network (VAN) is a concept from the electronic data interchange (EDI) services realm. It is a dedicated circuit that a VAN provider supplies that provides a secure connection. The VAN allows users to connect and transfer documents, while the VAN makes guarantees about delivery, quality of service, and security.

Web Based Environment

A web based environment makes it easier for users to access information, has platform independence, is faster, has common protocols and is rich with information. The drawbacks are that there are thousands of users, limited bandwidth, security problems and scalability issues.

Web Security and Protocols

SKIP

Skip was originally developed by the NSA and formerly classified. Skipjack is a Type II block cipher with a block size of 64 bits and key size of 80 bits. The algorithm uses 80-bit keys, compared with 56 for DES, and has 32 computational rounds or iterations. Skipjack provides high-speed encryption when implemented in a key-escrow chip.

SSL

SSL is a protocol developed by Netscape for transmitting documents securely via the Internet. SSL works by using a private key (symmetric) to encrypt data that's transferred over the SSL connection. This is secure connection that can send any amount of data once established. Many Web sites use the protocol to obtain confidential user information, such as credit card numbers. Web pages that require an SSL connection start with *https*: instead of *http*.

IPSEC

IPsec short for IP Security, it is a set of protocols being developed by the IETF that helps to support secure exchange of packets at the IP layer. IPsec used to implement Virtual Private Networks (VPNs).

IPsec has two encryption modes: Tunnel and Transport. The Tunnel mode encrypts both the header and the payload of the packet. The transport mode encrypts only the payload of each packet, but leaves the header untouched. Both the sender and the receiver must use the same IPsec-compliant device to encrypt/decrypt each packet. Both the sending and receiving devices must share a public key. This is accomplished through a protocol known as Internet Security Association and Key Management

Secured Computing: A CISSP Study Guide, Copyright 2001

Protocol/Oakley (ISAKMP/Oakley), which allow the receiver to obtain a public key and authenticate the sender using digital certificates.

S-RPC

Secure Remote Procedure Call (S-RPC) should be transparent to the end user. The user supplies their password once and it is used to authenticate to the server based on that original password. The client acts on behalf of the user for the protocol exchanges. Servers provide the requested services and require that users be authenticated before providing the services. The authentication server provides the public and private keys to servers and clients. Secure RPC uses Diffie Hellman.

S-HTTP

Secure HTTP is Unlike SSL; S-HTTP is designed to transmit *individual* messages securely. SSL and S-HTTP are complementary rather than competing technologies.

Hash Totals

A hash total is a number generated from a string of text. The hash is substantially smaller than the text itself, and is generated by a mathematical formula in such a way that it is quite unlikely that some other text will produce the same hash value.

Hashes are used to ensure that transmitted messages have not been tampered with. The sender generates a hash of the message, encrypts it, and sends it with the message itself. The receiver then decrypts both the message and the hash, produces another hash from the received message, and compares the two hashes. If they're the same, there is an exceedingly high probability that the message was transmitted unharmed.

S/MIME

Short for *Secure/MIME,* a new version of the MIME a specification for formatting non-ASCII messages so that they can be sent over the Internet. Many e-mail clients now support MIME, which enables them to send and receive graphics, audio, and video files via the Internet mail system. In addition, MIME supports messages in character sets other than ASCII.

Secured Computing: A CISSP Study Guide, Copyright 2001

Protocol that supports encryption of messages. S/MIME is based on RSA public-key encryption technology.

SET

Secure Electronic Transaction, a standard that will enable secure credit card transactions on the Internet. SET will enable merchants to verify that buyers are who they claim to be, by employing digital signatures. And it will protect buyers by providing a mechanism for their credit card number to be transferred directly to the credit card issuer for verification and billing without the merchant being able to see the number. Virtually all the major players in the electronic commerce arena, including Microsoft, Netscape, Visa, and MasterCard, have endorsed SET.

Network Components

Bridges

A bridge is a network device that connects two physical networks together. A bridge receives traffic and only forwards that which is not local to the subnet. Bridges are capable of storing and forwarding a complete packet, while a repeater forwards electrical signals only. Bridges are protocol independent, as they work as the physical or MAC layer.

"Smart" and "Dumb" Hubs, Concentrators, & Repeaters

A "dumb" hub is a device that allows multiple 10baseT/100baseT connections to terminate. It is used as a part of a star network. The dumb hub has no intelligence and simply moves the electrical signals across all of the ports.

An "intelligent" hub can be configured to only allow certain connections to certain ports on the hub. The hub depends on knowing the correct hardware level address for the device, and which port on the hub it is attached to.

A repeater is a device that "copies" electrical signals from one network to another. The intent is to link two or more segments together. The downside of a repeater is that is retransmits the electrical noise as well as the signal.

Routers are devices that can connect a number of LANs. Routers use headers and a forwarding table to determine where packets go. They use ICMP to communicate with each other and configure the best route between any two hosts. Very little filtering of data is done through routers. Routers do not care about the type of data they handle. Routers work at the network layer (layer 3) of the OSI model.

Switches are devices that filter and forwards packets between LAN segments. Switches operate at the data link layer (layer 2) of the OSI Model and therefore support any packet protocol. LANs that use switches to join segments are called *switched LANs* or, in the case of Ethernet networks, *switched Ethernet LANs.*

Gateways sit between a client application, such as a Web browser, and a real server. It intercepts all requests to the real server to see if it can fulfill the requests itself. If not, it forwards the request to the real server.

Packet Sniffers

A packet sniffer is a program that can record, monitor and analyze all network packets that travel past a given network interface. It can help troubleshoot network problems, bottlenecks and mine sensitive information such as Credentials from unencrypted Login Session's. A sniffer can also be used for both legitimate or illegitimately to capture data being transmitted on a network.

Network Availability

Single Points of Failure

Single points of failure are a very common mistake in networks and should be identified and redundancy should be built in. An example would be a single firewall or single router. It is important to have multiple paths between routers and to use dynamic routing protocols such as Open Shortest Path First (OSPF).

RAID

Redundant array of Inexpensive Drives (RAID) help provide fault tolerance against hard drive crashes and helps to improve system performance (See figure 2.8):

RAID Level 0	Fast, stripes data across all disks, No redundancy
RAID Level 1	Mirrors data across multiple disks, when one fails data is available on others, good for small capacity applications
RAID Level 2	Bit interleaves data across multiple disks with parity information using a Hamming code. This is not used in production.
RAID Level 3	Byte level parity, stripes data across multiple drives, good for large data transfers
RAID Level 4	Block level parity, stripes data across multiple drives, good for large data transfers
RAID Level 5	Stripes data and parity information at a block level across all drive arrays, Read and writes and done concurrently, spare drives replace failed drives.
RAID Level 7	Array functions as one virtual disk, uses parity protection, still functions if disk fails

Figure 2.8- RAID

Tape Backup

Tape backup is very important for protecting or restoring lost or corrupted data. There are three methods of selecting files:

- Full backup- this is a complete archive of every file.
- Differential backup- only copies files that have been changed since the last full backup was performed.
- Incremental backup- this is when you only copy files that have recently been added or changed.

There are four technologies for tapes:

- DLT- digital linear tape has the highest capacity and a high transfer rate, but is the most expensive.
- 8 mm- these tapes have the high capacity rates, high transfer rates and medium cost
- DAT- Digital audio tape has low capacity, low transfer rates and a medium cost
- QIC- has a medium capacity, medium transfer rates and a low cost

Other media available is optical media such as a Write-Once-Read Many (WORM) drive, Zip drives, and jaz drives.

Data Transmission Control Methodologies

There are a number of different methods to protect the data while in transit on a network. It is important to protect the confidentiality and integrity of the information. Protecting the integrity of the information may even be more important. It is possible to check for modification or loss of the data by using any of the following methods.

Hash totals

Hash totals identify errors and omissions in the information, A hash algorithm provides a hexadecimal checksum of the data. This is stored in a record prior to transmission, and then sent to the remote computer with the data. The remote system can then compute the checksum, and if it agrees with the value that was calculated before transmission, the information arrived intact.

Record sequence checking

Record sequence checking is when a sequence number is attached to the data prior to transmission. When the data is received at the remote end, the sequence number is checked and then evaluated to see if all data has been received.

Transmission logging

Transmission logging is built into the front-end communications program. It is responsible for recording all data sent and received by the system. This can provide an audit trail, and is often done on the host. However, depending upon the communications program in use, it may be possible to also perform this task at the client end.

Transmission error correction

Transmission error correction is when there are extensive controls built into the communications program to find and correct errors in the transmission.

Secured Computing: A CISSP Study Guide, Copyright 2001

Retransmission controls

Retransmission controls are used to detect and prevent the duplicate transmission of data. The front-end communications program detects that duplicate data has been sent.

Email Security

The biggest email threats consist of dangerous attachments, impersonation, eavesdropping, mail bombing and harassing emails. One can protect them against this by scanning emails for virus's, executables and macros. Digital signatures will help thwart an impersonation and encryption will stop any eavesdropping.

Suggested controls for email are message origin authentication, secure access management, proof of delivery, proof of submission, non-repudiation, content labeling, and encryption.

Fax Security

The best way to secure a fax transmission is to use a fax encryption, bulk data link encryption, activity logs and exception reports.

Fax encryptors and bulk data link encryption are examples of technical controls over fax machines. Activity logs and exception reports are management controls over Fax machines

Secure Voice communications

Voice mail systems are computer systems with their own input, storage, retrieval and transmission capabilities. They are either PBX or PC based. Phone system attacks are hard to trace but you can monitor a trace if you know what you are doing.

Suggested controls for secure voice transmission are call detail recording, use switch security features, review telephone bills, block remote calling after business hours, install strong password management, block unassigned access codes, change systems administrative passwords regularly, monitor PBX options and settings.

Secured Computing: A CISSP Study Guide, Copyright 2001

Test Your Knowledge

1. IP sec uses what key management protocol?
    - A. Triple DES
    - B. ISAKMP/Oakley
    - C. ROT3
    - D. Diffie-Hellman

2. The three major TCP/IP risks are: TCP/IP is Easy to hack, easy to tap into and _____ ?
    - A. Very hard to hack
    - B. Easy to eavesdrop
    - C. Uses to much bandwidth
    - D. Uses too little bandwidth

3. What Network layer does a router fall under?
    - A. Layer 1
    - B. Layer 2
    - C. Layer 5
    - D. Layer3

4. _____ is the most commonly used cable type today, and transmits up to ___ Mhz?
    - A. Cat3, 100Mhz
    - B. Cat 1, 10 Mhz
    - C. Cat 5, 10 Mhz
    - D. Cat 5 100 Mhz

5. _____ is used for transmissions over long distances, downlinks, and backbones, and is very useful in an environment subject to electrical interference?
    - A. 100baseFX
    - B. 10BaseT
    - C. 100BaseTX

Secured Computing: A CISSP Study Guide, Copyright 2001

D. 10baseFX

6. True or False: The ring topology is the easiest to implement, but the most expensive to put in?
    A. True
    B. False

7. What are the three main network topologies?
    A. Ring, Bus, Circle
    B. Ring, Bus, Star
    C. Star, pentagon, extended star
    D. Extended star, linear bus, circle

8. BOOTP falls at what layer of the OSI model?
    A. Application
    B. Presentation
    C. Data Link

9. What layer of the OSI does IP work at?
    A. Application
    B. Presentation
    C. Data Link
    D. Network

10. _____ is the most common used cable time?
    A. Cat1
    B. Cat 3
    C. Cat 5
    D. Cat 10

11. _____ embeds information in a data frame that allows devices to control data flow and correct errors.
    A. SDLC
    B. HDLC
    C. DLCE
    D. MSDE

Secured Computing: A CISSP Study Guide, Copyright 2001

12. _____stripes data and parity information at a block level across all drive arrays, Read and writes and done concurrently, spare drives replace failed drives?
    A. RAID 2
    B. RAID 3
    C. RAID 5
    D. RAID 7

13. SKIP is a Type II block cipher with a block size of __ bits and key size of __ bits.
    A. 64,64
    B. 64, 80
    C. 80,64
    D. 64,128

14. What are the two Ipsec encryption modes?
    A. Tunnel and Transport
    B. Transport and Session
    C. Session and Tunnel
    D. Tunnel and Session

15. Phone calls are very easy to trace, true or false?
    A. True
    B. False

16. When all data is captured and analyzed at all communication layers this describes what?
    A. Stateful Inspection
    B. NAT
    C. Packet Filtering
    D. Stateless Inspection

17. _____ circuits are established on demand and terminated when the transmission is complete
    A. Switched Virtual Circuits
    B. Permanent Virtual Circuits
    C. Temporary Circuits
    D. Transient Circuit

Secured Computing: A CISSP Study Guide, Copyright 2001

18. _____ applies access controls when a TCP or UDP connection is established. Once the connection has been made, packets can flow freely between the hosts without further checking?
    A. Circuit level gateway
    B. Packet filter
    C. Stateful inspection
    D. Orions Gateway

19. _____ is a short-distance communications interface that is commonly used to interconnect routing and switching devices on local area networks with the higher-speed lines of a WAN?
    A. HSSD
    B. ISDN
    C. HSSI
    D. VoIP

20. _____ a standard for packet-switching networks that was approved by the ITU in 1976?
    A. X.10
    B. X.25
    C. ISDN
    D. Token Ring

21. The _____ mode encrypts both the header and the payload of the packet in IPsec?
    A. Tunnel
    B. Transport
    C. Transient
    D. Tuple

22. True or False, LAN topologies can never be mixed?
    A. True
    B. False

Answers: 1.B, 2.C, 3.D, 4.D, 5.A, 6.B, 7.B, 8.A, 9.D, 10.C, 11.B, 12.C, 13.B, 14.A, 15.B, 16.A, 17. A, 18.A, 19.C, 20. B, 21.B, 22.B

Secured Computing: A CISSP Study Guide, Copyright 2001

References

Information in this chapter was referenced from the following sources:

1. *Computer Security Handbook, Third edition, Arthur E, Hutt et al. 1995 John Wiley & Sons Inc.*

2. *Information Security Management Handbook, 4th edition, Harold F. Tipton, et al. 2000, Auerbach Publications.*

3. *RFC 2828*

4. *RFC 2196 Site Security Handbook, RFC 2196, author B. Fraser, 1997*

<u>Notes</u>

Domain 3

Security Management Practices

Security Management Practices

Security management entails the identification of an organization's information assets and the development, documentation, and implementation of policies, standards, procedures and guidelines, which ensure confidentiality, integrity, and availability. Management tools such as data classification, risk assessment, and risk analysis are used to identify the threats, classify assets, and to rate their vulnerabilities so that effective security controls can be implemented.

Definitions

Authorization — An access or privilege that is granted by management to access information based on the individual's access rights. A management and preventative control that helps determine if a subject is trusted to act for a specific purpose, like reading a file.

Accountability - The ability to assure individual accountability of classified and sensitive information whenever a security policy is used.

Identification and authorization — This is the combination of something a user knows, and something that they have which would be stronger than any one of those alone.

Non-repudiation- An authentication that can be determined with a high degree to be genuine. It is a service in which those who are involved cannot deny that they have participated.

Privacy- The right of an individual to determine to what degree that individual is willing to disclose information about themselves in information that may be exchanged, and possibly compromised, among other individuals or organizations. This includes the right for these individuals and organizations to control the collection of that data as well how they distribute and store that information.

Secured Computing: A CISSP Study Guide, Copyright 2001

Security Management Concepts and Principles

The C-I-A Triad

The CIA triad (See figure 3.1) is the three concepts that information security is founded on. They stand for:

Confidentiality — the process of ensuring that no unauthorized person can access or modify information, or disclose that information.

Integrity — the process of ensuring that information is not modified while in storage or in transit. This ensures the accuracy of the information.

Availability — to make sure that the information is available to all authorized users when they need it.

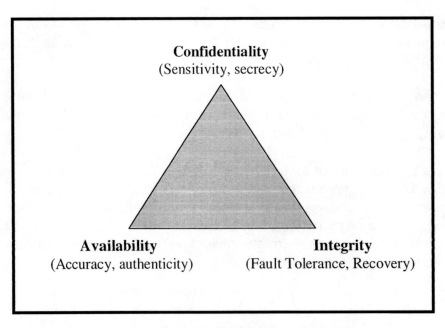

Figure 3.1- CIA Triad

Protection Mechanisms

Abstraction

Abstraction means to ignore or segregate details in order to focus on what is important for some purpose. This helps remove complexity and helps make designs and specifications easier to understand.

Data hiding

Data hiding is when each component reveals to other components only its external properties; the implementation and data are hidden. This is also called encapsulation, as there are barriers that prevent the access to the procedures and data of the component.

Layering

Layering is when abstractions may be used for a layered structure, where each layer uses abstractions provided by the layer below to create its own abstractions, which in turn are used by the layer above.

Encryption

Encryption is the process of turning data into an unintelligible form in such a way that the original data cannot be derived from the cipher text unless the use of the inverse decryption process. All sensitive and confidential information should be encrypted.

Change/Control Management

Modifications to hardware and software are necessary in the life cycle of an information system because of the changes in the internal operations of an organization, competition, new technology, and possible regulatory requirements. Requests for change should be documented on a standard change request form and should include the following information:

- Request date
- Description and reason for the change
- Business case for the change
- Name of person requesting the change

Secured Computing: A CISSP Study Guide, Copyright 2001

- Contact person
- Proper management approvals

Change requests should be tracked from the time submitted to the time of implementation and completion. There are times when certain processes need to bypass the normal change request process, such as small minor changes or changes of an emergency manner. When these changes are made the management should approve them in advance, change forms should still be filled out after the fact for audit trails of the change, and any types of shortcuts should be followed up with to go through the formal process.

Data Classification Schemes

The idea behind classification is to put the policies and information in a classification scheme according to its sensitivity to loss or disclosure. The benefits of data classification are:

- Helps identify sensitive information
- Shows an organizations commitment to security
- May be required by law

Data is broken down into four major sensitivity classification schemes: sensitive, confidential, private, and public. The owners of the information (personal or organizational) determine the sensitivity scheme, and management should review that.

Sensitive

These are restricted items that need more than ordinary precautions to be taken to protect that data from modification or deletion. This could include financial documents and/or regulatory actions.

Confidential

This applies to the most sensitive business information intended for view only within the company. These documents are exempt from public view under the Freedom of Information Act and federal law. If information could affect the company's stockholders, adversely impact the company or cause damage to the national security of a country it should definitely be considered confidential.

Private

This applies to personal information that should only stay within the company. Any unauthorized disclosure of this information could adversely harm the company or an individual. Examples could be Human Resource information.

Public

This classification is for all the other information that does not apply to the previous three mentioned. This information may not be authorized to be released, but if it were it would not cause harm to the customers, employees or the company.

Government Classifications

Government classifications include Unclassified, secret, top secret, confidential and sensitive but unclassified.

Unclassified

Requires no protection against unauthorized disclosure. Can be released publicly.

Secret

Applied to information that if released could compromise national security and *cause serious damage*.

Top Secret

Applied to information that if released would compromise national security and be expected to put the country in *extremely grave danger*. Highest sensitivity.

Confidential

This information is of a sensitive manner that could have potential damage to a company.

Secured Computing: A CISSP Study Guide, Copyright 2001

Sensitive but Unclassified (SBU)

Information that would not compromise the security of the government but is still sensitive. Examples might be test questions, investigation manuals, data containing internal advice and candidates for promotions.

Military Data Classifications

Military data classification data schemes can include all of the above as well as Sensitive but Unclassified, unclassified and declassified. These are determined by each organization.

Sensitive but Unclassified (SBU)

Information that would not compromise the security of the government but is still sensitive. Examples might be test questions, investigation manuals, data containing internal advice and candidates for promotions.

Unclassified

This would include any data that is neither sensitive nor classified.

Declassified

This is usually done as an administration procedure to reduce the security of certain data. Usually used when the information is no longer in use or ready for public view.

Commercial/business classification

Commercial or business classification data schemes can include all of the above. These are determined by each organization.

Proprietary- competitive information.

Privileged- this can be to conform to the law.

Private- this can be any information on an individual like HR records.

Secured Computing: A CISSP Study Guide, Copyright 2001

When classifying information there are eight things that need to be considered: value, age/useful life, authorization, custody, reproduction, logging, marking and labeling, and filing and safekeeping.

- *Value* — what is the information worth to the company? How much would it cost to reproduce if it was lost? What would the consequences be if this information found its way to a competitor, or on the front page of the newspaper?

- *Age/Useful Life* — how old is this information? When will its useful lifetime be reached?

- *Authorization* — who is authorized to see this information? Who is authorized to allow declassification?

- *Custody* — Who will have custody of this information? How will they determine if the requesting user is entitled access?

- *Reproduction* — Can this material be copied? If so, how will distribution be controlled?

- *Logging* — Should records be kept regarding who has the material, was it returned or destroyed? Was it copied?

- *Marking and Labeling* — How will the classified information be labeled and marked to show the classification?

- *Filing and Safekeeping* — How will the information be protected in storage? Does it require the use of encryption or special locking mechanisms?

The classification program must also address a security awareness program, and how the classification and handling of information will be provided to employees.

Distribution of classified information can be done through a court order, an executive level approval in a corporate environment or through governmental contracts.

Employment Policies and Practices

There are eight major practices that need to be exercised by management when dealing with employees: background checks, employment agreements, hiring and termination practices, job descriptions, roles and responsibilities, separation of duties, least privilege, and job rotation.

Secured Computing: A CISSP Study Guide, Copyright 2001

Background Checks

Once an employee is being seriously considered there should already be an established list that can checked. This may include previous employment, marriage records, military records, personal bankruptcy, education and court actions. These types of checks need to be done based on the sensitivity level of the individual's potential position. These can include: reference checks, military checks, law enforcement records, drug testing, lie detector test (depending on state law), and educational records.

Employment Agreements

Typically required when a new employee joins an organization or takes a more sensitive position. The person agrees that they understand the security policy and the sanctions for any violation of that policy. It is important to get the person to sign the agreement as a clear indication that the employee read, agreed and understood the document.

Hiring and Termination Practices

The method in which an organization hires its personnel is the foundation of a good security program. Using good screening and a practical means for assessing someone can help to find the type of person you are looking for.

Termination of an employee can happen through a death, retirement, or a firing. If the termination happens under negative circumstances then it is best that person be escorted to their desk to collect their belongings and then to leave immediately by escort. There should be a checklist which describes the forms to be filled out and should include the following

- Surrendering keys, badges or proximity cards

- An exit interview

- Returning all company materials

- Change passwords

- Change Locks

Secured Computing: A CISSP Study Guide, Copyright 2001

- Delete all access privileges

Job Description

It is important to have clear job descriptions for all areas in the department. These can provide clear statements of the authority and responsibility of the job.

Roles and Responsibilities

Perspective employees should have a clear understanding of the role that they will play as well as the role of others in the organization.

Separation of Duties

This refers to dividing roles up so that one individual cannot cause harm to a critical process. This is critical in a security program. Examples would be having more than one person responsible for issuing checks in a financial department. When the security program is a part of the IT operations the program often lacks independence, has minimal authority and lacks management attention.

Least Privilege

This refers to only granting users the accesses that they need to perform their job function. This does not mean that employees have little access; some employees have significant access, if it is necessary for their job responsibility.

Job Rotation

Allowing individual to experience different roles in an organization makes a person well rounded. This helps to educate employees as well as keep them interested and fresh on new technologies.

Policies, Standards, Guidelines, and Procedures

Lets start off distinguishing the difference between Policies, Standards, Guidelines, and Procedures (See figure 3.2):

Policies

A policy is a high-level statement of beliefs, goals and objectives and the general means for their attainment for a specific subject area. They help to set strategy for the standards, guidelines and procedures. There are four main policy types:

Senior management policy

This helps define the standards, guidelines and procedures for an organization and to inform users the importance of information security.

Regulatory policies

Some governing body requires these policies. This may be a regulatory or a federal requirement. These are typically very specific policies and require much detail.

Advisory policies

Advisory policies are "suggested" but not mandatory. This is the where most policies fall under.

Informative policies

These policies are meant to inform the constituents of certain information. They are not meant for public consumption, but it will not be harmful if it was.

Standard

A standard is a mandatory activity, action, rule or regulation designed to provide policies with the support structure and specific direction they require to be effective. They are often expensive to administer and therefore should be used judiciously.

Guideline

A guideline is a more general statement of how to achieve the policies objectives by providing a framework within which to implement procedures. Where standards are mandatory, guidelines are recommendations.

Secured Computing: A CISSP Study Guide, Copyright 2001

Procedure

A procedure spells out the specific steps of how the policy and supporting standards and how guidelines will be implemented. A procedure is a description of tasks that must be executed in a specific order.

Baseline

A baseline is a method of implementing security mechanisms and products. They are platform unique and should be implemented throughout the organization.

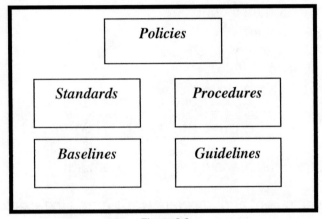

Figure 3.2

Risk Management

Risk management is the process of identifying, controlling, and eliminating or minimizing uncertain events that may affect system resources. It includes risk analysis, cost-benefit analysis, selection, implementation and test, security evaluation of safeguards, and an overall security review.

Risk management determines the value of the data, what protections exist already, and how much more protection is needed. The results of these activities contribute to a certification decision, which provides the information on which a Designated Approving Authority (DAA) can base an accreditation.

Certification is the process of verifying the technical and non-technical security features that are sufficient for a systems mode of operation. These features are compared to a specific set of security requirements. Accreditation is the declaration by the DAA that the system is approved to operate in a particular security mode using a pre-selected set of safeguards.

The risks that IT professionals can fall victim to include the following:

- Improper use of technology
- Repetition of errors
- Translation of user needs into technical requirements
- Inability to control technology
- Equipment failure
- Incorrect data entry
- Concentration of data
- Inability to react quickly

Principles of Risk Management

There are four general areas for risk management:

- Risk assignment and transfer- Transferring the risk to others, this would include buying insurance or co-insurance.

- Risk rejection- ignoring the risks altogether.

- Risk reduction- installing the necessary precautions to guard against a risk.

- Risk acceptance- accepts the risk as the cost to protect that risk would outweigh or cost more, than the risk itself.

When managing risk one needs to be concerned with three things:

- Risk assessment- includes assessing the scope and methodology, collecting and analyzing data and interpreting those results.

- Risk mitigation- is selecting safeguards, accepting residual risk and implementing controls and monitoring effectiveness.

Secured Computing: A CISSP Study Guide, Copyright 2001

- Uncertainty analysis- is to look at a model, data and assumptions for validity.

Risk Analysis Evaluation Functions are the evaluation functions that help to:

- Delay loss, reduced productivity, income, extra expense, and license penalties
- Delay damage/service outage
- Fraud via EDP
- Altered or omitted data- application or file tampering
- Unauthorized disclosure of EDP data -accidental, intentional, and malicious attacker
- Physical theft –petty theft, insider, breaking & entering, armed robbery

The Basic Risk Analysis Steps

1. Estimating the potential losses, threat classification and analysis.
2. Analyze the threats to assets.
3. Define the annual loss expectancy. There are two types of risk analysis for potential losses, Quantitative and qualitative:

   - Quantitative risk analysis attempts to assign an independently objective numeric value to components of the risk assessment and to the assessment of potential losses.
   - Qualitative Risk Analysis does not attempt to assign numeric values to the components of the analysis. Rather, it is scenario oriented to identify the types of problems that can occur, the development of a scenario, working through the scenario to determine the outcome and then ranking the seriousness of the threat and sensitivity of the assets. This is less subjective that quantitative analysis, and lends itself to the application of analysis tools and fuzzy logic.

Cost/Benefit Analysis

After one has done a risk assessment it is then important to do a cost/benefit analysis. Determine the Annual Loss Expectancy (ALE) this combines the potential for loss and probability and becomes a guide to determine which security measures should be focused on and how much to spend to reduce the associated risk.

> *ALE* is calculated as $I \times F = ALE$
> *Where* I *is the single loss expectancy and* F *is the probability or annual rate of occurrence.*

Threats & Vulnerabilities

Threats are a circumstance or event that has the potential to cause harm to a person or a thing. Threats can occur naturally or unnaturally. Three things make up a threat: Capability, motivation and willingness to cause the threat. (See figure 3.3)

Vulnerability is a weakness in a system that could be exploited to violate system security policy.

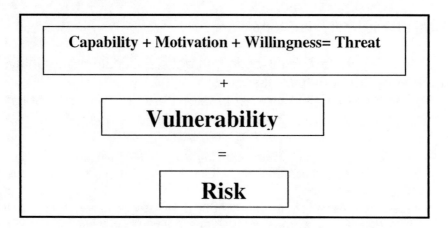

Capability + Motivation + Willingness= Threat

+

Vulnerability

=

Risk

Figure 3.3 - Threats and vulnerabilities

The threats to IS Security include:

- Unauthorized access
- Hardware failure
- Utility failure
- Natural disasters
- Loss of key personnel
- Human errors
- Neighboring hazards
- Tampering

- Disgruntled employees
- Emanation/Radiation interception
- Safety of personnel

Threat Classifications

There are four classifications (See figure 3.4) that can be summed up in a matrix. When considering this matrix, it is important to focus time and resources on the high loss/high events and then ignore low loss/low events.

High loss per event High frequency of occurrence	High loss per event Low frequency of occurrence
Low loss per event High frequency of occurrence	Low loss per event Low frequency of occurrence

Figure 3.4 - Threat classifications

Philosophy of Due Care in Regards to Risk Analysis

The approach of due care is an important one. Even if the organization gets caught in a problem, they may not be held fully responsible or liable. Should the organization be able to demonstrate that it took the appropriate cautions and used controls and practices that are generally used and meet the commonly desired security control objectives, used methods that are considered for use in well-run computing facilities, used common sense and prudent management practices and the organization will be said to have operated with due care, as any other informed person would.

Countermeasures

Countermeasures are tools and techniques used to address vulnerabilities. For example, if you want to reduce the risk of a break-in at your home, you will install an alarm system, which is an example of a countermeasure.

There are several selection principles with regard to countermeasure selection. These include:

Cost Effectiveness

When you are trying to determine if a particular countermeasure is cost effective, you must consider the cost of the countermeasure itself, the costs to support it, and ongoing maintenance costs. In addition, it is necessary to include the human intervention cost. For example, if you choose to install a door alarm. How much does it cost you to have someone to respond to that alarm 24 hours a day?

Override and Failsafe Defaults

Each of the countermeasures must have some sort of shutdown/failsafe capability. It should default to lack of permission, yet still allow for the safety of personnel.

Least Privilege

Here the countermeasure operates by providing only the minimal amount of information to the user in order for them to function effectively.

Enticement/Entrapment

The vulnerability is made to be attractive for the attacker who already had intentions to attack. Entrapment is when the vulnerability is made to be attractive for someone that may not have intended to attack, but tempted by the ease of the attack. This countermeasure is unethical and should be avoided.

Independence of Control and Subject

This countermeasure controls and/or constrains the subject into only doing what is permitted based upon certain factors.

Universal Countermeasure

This is done to all subjects in an area to minimize the exceptions to the countermeasure.

Isolation, Economy and least common mechanisms

This minimizes the dependencies on common systems to implement the safeguards. Here the countermeasures must work totally independent of each other.

Instrumentation

This monitors the countermeasure for proper function and reports on failures to perform as expected and identifies attacks.

Acceptance and Tolerance by Personnel

Management and the users must be willing to accept and tolerate the constraints imposed by the countermeasure. If they do not, they will find a way to work around the countermeasure, thereby eliminating any value.

Sustainability

The more automatic the operation, the more sustainable the countermeasure is over a longer period of time.

Audit ability

It must record actions taken by personnel and be verifiable. Auditors should be involved in the design and implementation.

Accountability

Assign at least one person to take ownership of the countermeasure, and its implementation within the organization. The operation of the countermeasure should be associated directly with that employee's performance.

Reaction and Recovery

The operation of the countermeasure when activated must be evaluated. For example, the asset must not be destroyed (so don't use dynamite to protect your bank vault), don't cause personnel to panic by placing them in a situation they cannot control or interact with.

Secured Computing: A CISSP Study Guide, Copyright 2001

Residual and Reset

Once the countermeasure has been activated, the asset must be as protected as it was before, and the asset must continue to be protected as the countermeasure is reset.

Vendor Trustworthiness

Review the past performance of the vendor and their products. This includes trade journals, product reviews, and seeking experience with the product/service through client references.

Multiple Functions

If the countermeasure has the ability to provide several operations and functions, and then base the evaluation of the primary function supported.

Data/Information worth

There are three considerations for information worth. These are:

- Cost to develop/acquire and maintain the information
- Value to owners, custodians, users and adversaries
- Cost and value in the real world

Roles and Responsibilities

Computer security is the responsibility of everyone, but there are certain roles that can be defined:

Senior Management

The success of the organization ultimately resides with these individuals. They decide on the policy, goals and direction of the organizations security policy.

Security management

These are the individuals who manage the organization on a day-to-day basis. This group helps to organize how security will fit in with other areas of the organization.

Secured Computing: A CISSP Study Guide, Copyright 2001

IS/IT Function

These are the people that are responsible for a specific function within systems. They will help to provide the appropriate security and technical controls for their specific area.

Supporting Functions

The supporting functions are the areas that support the IS/IT environment. This could include disaster recover/business continuity planning, a quality assurance group, physical security and auditing.

Users

There are two types of users to consider, the users of the information and the users of the actual computer systems. The information users are responsible for letting management know what their needs are for the protection of their information. The computer users are responsible for reporting security problems.

Security Awareness

Having a great security plan and all the procedures in place is only as good as the people who use it. If employees are not aware of the policies and how they can contribute to them, they are useless. Many employees will not take the time to read over the security policies and therefore a security awareness program can help to make employees aware of the organizations security goals and policies.

There are several elements to security awareness. The first thing an organization needs is the implementation of the proper policies, procedures and guidelines. In addition, having a specialized team to deal with these issues is the best way to implement it. Also be able to classify assets according to their value is also a key element. Finally the need for separation of duties will help to eliminate the potential for one individual to have complete control of a business process, this helps eliminate the potential for error and temptation on personnel.

In addition to these key elements there are several goals that the security awareness program should try to attain. These include:

Secured Computing: A CISSP Study Guide, Copyright 2001

Modify behavior

Eliminating errors and omissions can greatly reduce the computer related losses in an organization. This will eliminate many of these through training and education of the employee as well as help reduce unauthorized activity, as employees will understand they are accountable and the penalties for such actions.

Accountability

It is important to have employees prove knowledge of a program by signing a policy that states that they have read and agree with that policy.

Training

This is to teach people the skill they need to do their jobs more securely. This would include what they should do and how they should do it.

Education

This is more than basic security training and is designed for the professionals whose jobs require security expertise.

Implementation

An effective security awareness program will include proper planning, evaluation and maintenance.

Security Management Planning

The security function needs to have the proper plans to manage that function properly. To effectively do this there are three areas that need to be considered: General security plans, System security plans and Basic computer security practices.

General security plans would include having a security policy to help provide a foundation for the security program, a mission statement, long-term strategies, a compliance program and the proper liaisons for sharing of information and having security considered in the organization.

System security plans are to help provide an overview of security requirements of the network and to describe what types of precautions are in place, or planned to be out into place. In addition to help define the responsibilities and expected behaviors of individuals who access the computer systems.

Basic computer security practices are the actions that all organizations should take. This would include:

- Having a computer security policy as well as the procedures to implement it.
- Contingency planning
- Incident response team
- Screening of the personnel
- Data classifications
- Risk analysis
- Protective measure baseline
- Appropriate security requirements

Secured Computing: A CISSP Study Guide, Copyright 2001

Test Your Knowledge

1. Which of the following is the preliminary step you should take when doing security planning?

    A. Establish objectives
    B. List planning assumptions
    C. Create a timeline
    D. Get buy in from middle management

2. _____ analysis attempts to assign an independently objective numeric value to components of the risk assessment and to the assessment of potential losses?

    A. Quantitative

    B. Relative

    C. Qualitative

    D. Quality based

3. What formula describes ALE?

    A. Single loss occurrence X Annualized rate of expectancy
    B. Single loss expectancy X annualized rate of occurrence
    C. Total sum expectancy of loss – Annualized rate of return
    D. Single loss expectancy X single rate of occurrence

4._____ is where each component reveals to other components only it external properties, the implementation and data are hidden.

    A. Data hiding
    B. Data layering
    C. Data encryption
    D. Data instantiation

Secured Computing: A CISSP Study Guide, Copyright 2001

5. What are the three government classifications?

A. Secret, Top secret and Unclassified
B. Classified, Confidential and Secret
C. Classified, Secret and Top Secret
D. Classified, Top Secret and Classified

6.What makes up the CIA triad?

A. Classified Information Authority
B. Confidentiality, intimidation and Authenticity
C. Confidentiality, Integrity and Authorization
D. Confidentiality, Integrity and Availability

7. A countermeasures that must have shutdown capability describes what?

A. Emergency power off
B. Override and failsafe defaults
C. Least privilege
D. Status clustering

8.Which is the proper order:

A. Policies, guidelines, procedures
B. Policy, procedure, guideline
C. Guidelines, policy, procedure
D. Procedures, Guideline, policy

9.It is important to focus time and resources on _____ frequency and ignore _____ frequency.

A. High loss/high, low loss/low
B. High loss/low, medium loss/high
C. Low loss/low, high loss/high
D. High loss/low, low loss/high

10.Commercial and business classifications only include Proprietary, Privileged and private?
       A. True
       B. False

Secured Computing: A CISSP Study Guide, Copyright 2001

11.Which of these is NOT a threat to IS security?
   A. Unauthorized access
   B. Hardware failure
   C. Utility failure
   D. Natural disasters
   E. Fusion

12.Which one is illegal?
   A. Entrapment
   B. Enticement

13.Selecting safeguards, accepting residual risk and implementing controls and monitoring effectiveness best describes?
   A. Risk management
   B. Risk mitigation
   C. Uncertainty analysis
   D. Risk assessment

14.Computer security is the responsibility of?
   A. Everyone
   B. No one
   C. Management
   D. Executives

15.True or False: Privacy is the right of an individual to determine to what degree that individual is willing to disclose information about themselves in information that might be exchanged, and possibly compromised, among other individuals or organizations.
   A. True
   B. False

Answers: 1.A, 2.A, 3.B, 4.B, 5.C, 6.D, 7.B, 8.B, 9.A, 10.B, 11.E, 12.A, 13.B, 14A, 15.A

References

Information in this chapter was referenced from the following sources:

1. Computer Security Handbook, Third edition, Arthur E, Hutt et al. 1995 John Wiley & Sons Inc.

2. *Information Security Management Handbook, 4th edition, Harold F. Tipton, et al. 2000, Auerbach Publications.*

3. *RFC 2828*

4. *RFC 2196 Site Security Handbook, RFC 2196, author B. Fraser, 1997*

5. *Security in Computing, Second edition, Charles P. Pfleeger, 1997 Prentice Hall*

<u>Notes</u>

Domain 4

Applications and Systems Development Security

Applications and Systems Development Security

Applications and systems development security refers to the controls that are included with in systems and applications software and the steps used in their development. Applications refer to agents, applets, software, databases, data warehouses, and knowledge-based systems. These applications may be used in distributed or centralized environments.

Definitions

Distributed computing environment (DCE)- Open Group's integration of a set of technologies for application development and deployment in a distributed environment. Security features include a Kerberos based authentication system, GSS API interface, ACL-based authorization environment, delegation, and audit

Database management system (DBMS)- A computer system whose main function is to facilitate the sharing of a common set of data among many different users.

Reference monitor- an access control concept that refers to an abstract machine that mediates all accesses to objects by subjects.
A reference monitor should be complete, isolated, and verifiable.

Client- A system entity that requests and uses a service provided by another system entity, called a 'server'. Usually, the requesting entity is a computer process, and it makes the request on behalf of a human user. In some cases, the server may itself be a client of some other server.

Application Issues

Distributed Environment

Organizations today are unable to stay with single vendor homogenous systems and are turning towards a multi-vender heterogeneous distributed system. Distributed computing environments (DCE) are a framework for building and running distributed environments. With enterprise systems growing manual management of these systems is extremely difficult and has lead to more automated approaches to managing a distributed computer environment.

All distributed systems should meet five major requirements: Interoperability, Portability, transparency, extensibility, and security.

- Interoperability- this is getting vendors to talk with each other and communicate and share information. Systems and components need to interoperate and have a common environment.
- Portability- the ability to have software that at the source code level can be moved between different systems to different vendors. Interfaces are needed to enhance portability of managed objects.
- Transparency- this is the ability to keep the application and its processes invisible to the end user. There are different aspects of transparency, which include access failure, transaction transparency, migration and location. Transparency must be selective for management, as they will have needs to access certain information.
- Extensibility- the systems must be able to adapt to various management polices and allow introduction of new resources to manage and new ways to manage those resources.
- Security- authorization, authentication and access controls are a must. The management system needs to provide the necessary levels of integrity, security and reliability. This would include the proper alarms, audit trails and authentication.

One definition of client/server (See figure 4.1) applications is that it is distributed between the client that requests services and the server that provides those services. This is true in the sharing of hardware, the roles that each can play, the risks they share and the distribution of their functionality.

Client/Server Functions

Client	Server
Front-end programs	back end programs
User initiated	client initiated
GUI interface	no user interface
No direct access to data	Returns data to the user
Runs batch jobs	Places data in the database

Figure 4.1 - Client Server Functions

Secured Computing: A CISSP Study Guide, Copyright 2001

JAVA and ActiveX

Java and ActiveX are two systems that let people attach computer programs to Web pages. These are systems because they allow Web pages to be more interactive and dynamic. However there are some serious security implications involved with Java and ActiveX because they can cause potentially hostile programs to be automatically downloaded and run on your computer, just by visiting some Web page. Both Java and ActiveX take measures to protect your from this risk.

Java was developed by JavaSoft, a division of Sun Microsystems. Java is supported by both of the major browsers, Microsoft Internet Explorer and Netscape Navigator. Microsoft developed ActiveX. It is supported in Microsoft's Internet Explorer, and an ActiveX plug-in is available for Netscape Navigator.

The Java and Active X platforms are both used in a distributed computing environment and are based on the idea that the same software should run on many different kinds of computers. We will start off with a discussion of Java and the move on to Active X.

Java technology-based software is on the Internet and on enterprise networks in interactive programs called "applets". An Applet is a small program that is downloaded and executed from applet-enabled browsers; this would include active X and Java applets. In general, applets loaded over the Internet are restricted from reading and writing files on the client file system, and from making network connections other than to the originating host. In addition, applets loaded over the Internet are prevented from starting other programs on the client, are not allowed to load libraries, or to define native method calls. If an applet could define native method calls, that would give the applet direct access to the underlying computer.

There are other kinds of Java technology-based software: programs written in the Java programming language that can run directly on your computer (without requiring a browser), or on servers, on large mainframe computers, or other devices.

Java's security model is to tightly control the environment that applets can run in. This concept is called a "sandbox" which creates a safe environment for applet processing. However there have been many bugs discovered in Java that allow applets to escape this sandbox and cause damage. The main danger in Java comes from the complexity of the software that implements the sandbox. Since this is a complicated technology it is more likely to break down than simple technology, and several breakdowns have been known to happen.

The average person does not have the time or the desire to examine Java and look for implementation errors. So one hopes that it was done right. When Java security does break down, the potential consequences are just as bad as those of an ActiveX problem: a hostile program can come to your machine and access your data at will.

ActiveX security relies entirely on human judgment. ActiveX programs come with digital signatures from the author of the program and anybody else who chooses to endorse the program. Once your browser has verified the signatures, it tells you who signed the program and asks you whether or not to run it. At that point you can both accept the program and let it do whatever it wants on your machine, or you can reject it completely. ActiveX security relies on you to make correct decisions about which programs to accept. If you accept a malicious program, you made the choice and you could be in trouble.

Even more dangerous is when the program is signed by someone you don't know anything about, but you accept it anyway. You'd really like to see what this program does, but if you reject it you won't be able to see anything. So you go ahead and accept it and take your chances. The problem is that even if the risk of accepting one program is fairly low, time after time it starts to add up. The only way to avoid this scenario is to refuse all programs, no matter how fun or interesting they sound, except programs that come from a few people you know well. But this is not very practical.

Plug-ins have the same security model as ActiveX. Plug-ins are a method for adding code to your browser, when you download a plug-in, you trust it to be harmless. This depends entirely on what the plug-in or program does. Many plug-ins such as Macromedia's Shockwave or Sun's Safe-Tcl are actually completely general programming systems, just like Java. By accepting a plug-in like this, you're trusting that the plug-in program has no security-relevant bugs. As we have seen with Java, systems that are meant to be secure often have bugs that lead to security problems.

Secured Computing: A CISSP Study Guide, Copyright 2001

With ActiveX, the same person or company makes this problem worse if you click the box that accepts all programs signed. While one program may be secure, another one may have a bug. This problem even applies to code written by your own company for internal use. If you wanted to be ultra-secure then you could allow only the only plug-ins with general-purpose functionality. All of the warnings about ActiveX programs apply to plug-ins too.

In conclusion the advantages of Java over ActiveX are that you can put only partial trust in a program, while ActiveX requires either full trust or no trust at all. And a Java-enabled browser could keep a record of which dangerous operations are carried out by each trusted program, so it could be easier to reconstruct what happened if anything went wrong. Finally, Java offers better protection against accidental damage caused by buggy programs.

Com/Dcom

COM (Component Object Model) is Microsoft's framework for developing and supporting program component object. It is geared towards providing similar capabilities to those defined in Common Object Request Broker Architecture (CORBA). COM provides the underlying services of interface negotiation, life cycle management, licensing, and event services (putting one object into service as the result of an event that has happened to another object).

Distributed Component Object Model (DCOM) is a set of Microsoft concepts and program interfaces in which client program object can request services from server program objects on other computers in a network. DCOM is based on the Component Object Model (COM), which provides a set of interfaces allowing clients and servers to communicate within the same computer. DCOM can also work on a network within an enterprise or on other networks besides the public Internet.

Local/Non-Distributed Environment

In a local/non-distributed environment the applications are located in one location. This is done through either a traditional application system or non-database system or through a Database management application system (DBMS).

A local/non-distributed environment can be made up of a centralized or decentralized environment (See figure 4.2). A centralized environment is where all of the work is performed in one place. In a decentralized environment each department or function performs its own data processing work.

Centralized V.S.	Decentralized
Central control	local control
Comparative cost advantages	low cost for hardware and software
Centralized database	end user control over system
Loss of employee motivation	lack of career path development
Restrictive procedures	difficulty implementing standards

Figure 4.2 - Centralized VS Decentralized

Traditional application systems (Non Database)

The traditional non-database systems may or may not include database technology. Program logic and data formats are closely related; therefore any changes or redesigns can introduce problems. The coordination with other applications is lessened and the physical machines and their capabilities are what the factors of design are dependent on.

The traditional approach is still highly effective where data may need to be processed daily or in batch files, where large amounts of data need to be handled without delay, records, reporting and processing functions are limited, predictable and unlikely to change and updating of computer equipment is not expected for some time.

The places that would not work well with the traditional environment would be when conditions call for you would have very short development time, the data element are similar across departments and must be shared for economical reasons and the need for large amounts of programming assistance is needed.

Database Management Systems (DBMS)

Data base security is based on the concern of keeping data a secret. In this case secrecy refers to making sure only authorized users have access. Database Management Systems (DBMS) is software that maintains databases and provides access to them. A DBMS would be more beneficial than the traditional approach when the functions are in fluctuation and the important elements are uncertain, there is a short development time and when substantial programming assistance is unavailable.

Both traditional relational DBMS security models and Object orientated (OO) database models use one of two control policies to protect information in multi-level systems. These would be the use of Mandatory access controls (MAC) and discretionary access controls (DAC).

MAC controls secure information through security labels, sometimes referred to as classification levels. MAC policies tend to be more secure, but are also more rigid. DAC policies many times are included in the MAC policies to help to help overcome these issues.

Relational DBMS (RDBMS) access typically uses the traditional views and structured query language (SQL) GRANT and REVOKE statements.

There are Object orientated DBMS (OODBMS) security models that have been designed. Among these models are the ORION authorization model, Data hiding model, and the SODA model. An object is meant to represent a concept in the real world. Each object belongs a single class. A class is viewed as having two parts, a *structure* and a *behavior*. The structure is the instance variables and the methods of the class define its behavior. Classes are encapsulated entities, and the public methods for each class provide the user interface to that class, hiding the implementation details. Classes can be either "base" or "derived". Derived classes inherit from one or more base classes. The set of classes in OODB are organized into a class hierarchy and the schema of each class includes the schema of all of its super classes.

Data Warehouse

The purpose of a data warehouse is data analysis and information retrieval. It is the process of extracting operational data into informational data and taking that information and putting it in a central data store or warehouse.

Data Mining

A class of database applications that look for trends or anomalies in a group of data without knowledge of the meaning of the data. Data mining software can help companies find customers with common interests. Many time you here this term used incorrectly as to describe software that presents data in new ways. True data mining software doesn't just change the presentation, but actually discovers previously unknown relationships among the data.

Metadata

Meta data is data about data.

Inference

This is when authorized information enables a user to infer something about information that is not authorized. An inference problem occurs if a user with low-level access is able to draw conclusions about high-level information. There are three types of means that allow inference, called inference channels:

- Deductive channels- these allow formal deductive proof of high data to be derived from low data.
- Abductive channels- these are channels in which through the assumption of low-level axioms a deductive proof becomes possible.
- Statistical channels- these exist when the likelihood of the users knowing these low level axioms can be determined.

Aggregation

This is similar to inference. This is when a user receives many items of similar data and is able to determine sensitive information from these that would not be able to determined from just a few of the items. Data Aggregation occurs when smaller pieces of information are assembled together to provide the "big picture". The risk is that through data collection techniques, a person who is authorized to have some of the information may be able to discern more than what they should from the information. A good countermeasure is to maintain strong separation of duties and a "need to know" approach. Job rotation can be beneficial.

Secured Computing: A CISSP Study Guide, Copyright 2001

Data Information Storage

It is very important to understand the various types of data storage available and what they do.

Primary Memory

Primary memory (Random Access Memory, or RAM), which is volatile but not portable. This is the computer's main memory that is directly accessible by the CPU. This is a volatile storage medium, meaning that the contents of the physical memory are lost when the power is removed.

Secondary Storage

Secondary storage includes hard drives, magnetic tape, CD-ROM, DVD drives, floppy disks, punch cards and paper tape. Secondary storage devices are usually accessed via some kind of controller. This contains registers that can be directly accessed by the CPU like main memory. Reading and writing these registers can cause the device to perform actions like reading a block of data off a disk or rewinding a tape. Programs and data stored in secondary storage must first be loaded into main memory before the processor can use them.

Real Storage

This is where a program has been given a definite storage location in memory and direct access to a peripheral device.

Non-volatile

Storage medium that is not directly accessible to the processor. Memory directly accessible to the processor includes main memory, cache and the CPU registers.

Sequential access media

Any volume that is accessed in a sequential manner, as opposed to a random manner. In ADSM, volumes are accessed sequentially if they reside in a device class other than DISK.

Secured Computing: A CISSP Study Guide, Copyright 2001

Volatile storage

A storage device in which the contents are lost when power is removed.

Virtual Storage

This is extending the physical amount of primary storage by using secondary storage to hold the memory contents. In this way, the operating can run programs larger than the available physical memory.

Random Storage

This is the computer's primary working and storage area. It is addressable directly by the CPU and stores application or system code in addition to data.

Knowledge Based Systems

Knowledge based systems, more commonly known as artificial intelligence (AI), is software that tries to emulate the way people reason and solve problems. Many disciplines are involved in AI such as expert system technology and operations research. In addition AI is enabling technology for neural networks, fuzzy logic, and expert systems.

Neural network technology is based on the way that the neurological connections of the human brain are believed to work in problem solving, identifying patterns and learning. These systems will be particularly good for identifying intricate patterns as in intrusion detection, risk management, and forecasting of activities.

Fuzzy logic is designed on parallels more closely related to how humans think than on absolute values. It uses set theory, which is a mathematical notion that elements have partial membership in a set. It is used in information where there is an uncertainty about a certain characteristics of data. This works well in insurance and financial risk assessment applications.

Expert systems are computer programs that help to solve problems that are normally handled by human experts. The system stores knowledge about problems and when an example of that problem is presented, then it uses that stored knowledge to find the solution.

Secured Computing: A CISSP Study Guide, Copyright 2001

Covert Channels and Buffer Overflows

Covert Channel

A covert channel is a communications channel that violates normal communications channels. In other words you are communicating in an unauthorized way.

Covert Storage Channel

A covert storage channel is a communications path that writes to storage by one process and allows reading of that information through another, less secure, channel.

Covert Timing Channel

A covert timing channel is when one process signals to another process by modulating its own system use.

Buffer Overflow

A buffer overflow is what happens when you try to put more data into a buffer of a program than it can handle. This may be due to a mismatch in the processing rates of the producing and consuming processes or because the buffer is simply too small to hold all the data that must accumulate before a piece of it can be processed. Good programming checks for overflows on each character and stops accepting data when the buffer is filled.

Security Control Architecture

There are several things that need to be considered when looking at security control architecture and security architecture in general. Domain six focuses on security architecture in much more detail. In this section we will look at some security controls available in security architecture.

Process Isolation

Process isolation is where each process has its own distinct address space for its application code and data. In this way, it is possible to prevent each process from accessing another process' data. This

Secured Computing: A CISSP Study Guide, Copyright 2001

prevents data leakage, or modification to the data while it is memory. It also allows the system to keep track of the relevant information when it needs to switch from one process to another.

Least Privilege

Like its counterpart in the function role, the concept of least privilege means that a process has no more privilege than what it really needs in order to perform its functions. Any modules that require "supervisor" or "root" access that is complete system privileges are embedded in the kernel. The kernel handles all requests for system resources, and permits external modules to call privileged modules when required.

Hardware Segmentation

Hardware segmentation specifically relates to the segmentation of memory, both virtual and real, into segments. This is a protection feature. The kernel allocates the required amount of memory for the process to load its application code, its process data, and its application data. The system prevents user processes from being able to access another processes allocated memory. It also prevents user processes from being able to access system memory

System High

System high is the highest security level by a system at a particular time or in a particular environment. A system high security mode is a mode of operation in which system hardware and software is only trusted to provide discretionary protection between users.

A system that operates in system high mode operates at the same level as the highest information stored within. For example, if the highest information is classified "Top Secret", the system and all users who have access must be cleared for "Top Secret" access. This operation include the need to know principle, as not all users, even though they have clearance, will not need to know all of the information contained on the system.

Secured Computing: A CISSP Study Guide, Copyright 2001

Security Kernel

The security kernel can be a software, firmware or hardware component in a trusted computing base that implements the reference monitor. Implementing the security kernel as a software approach is the more traditional method. The use of specialized hardware is an option. Finally, the use of a separation kernel, which completely isolates the security functions from the primary kernel, is also an option.

Development Life Cycle

Development life cycle includes the conceptual definition, the functional requirements definition, system functional design review, preliminary design review, code design review, hardware integration and software development.

Security Control Architecture

Security control architecture focuses on the platform specific security criteria including a risk assessment and system software control that are reviewed between the definition and design phases, and again during the certification and acceptance phases.

System Integrity

System integrity is an attribute of the system relating to the successful and correct operation of computing resources to prevent unauthorized modification of the information.

Database Integrity

Database integrity centers on the preservation of data's meaning and completeness. The database determines how the information will be represented while it is stored in the database, and the correspondence between the data and what the database entry represents.

Operating System Integrity

Operating system integrity is the complete assurance that under all conditions, a system is based on the logical correctness and reliability of the operating system.

Secured Computing: A CISSP Study Guide, Copyright 2001

System Confidentiality

System confidentiality discusses access controls that allow only authorized users access to the system using good passwords, either one-time or strong reusable type, and the detection of either storage or timing covert channels.

Reference Monitor

The reference monitor an access control concept that refers to an abstract machine that mediates all accesses to objects by subjects. The reference monitor is invoked on every request for access to an object, there can be no exceptions, and this is called *completeness*. There must be no path that can bypass the reference monitor. A reference monitor should be complete, isolated and verifiable. In addition it should be small enough to be subjected to analysis and tests to ensure that it is correct, this is known as *verifiability*.

System Development Controls

System Life Cycle Phases

The systems life cycle phases the best way to ensure good security, if it is planned through out. It is the process by which systems analysts, software engineers, programmers, and end-users build information systems and computer applications. There are seven basic principles:

1. **Project initiation**
   This is when you get a conceptual definition of what you are trying to do and do the initial research.

2. **Functional design and analysis**
   Define the functional requirements and the specification for the systems environment.

3. **System design specification**
   This is the review of the functional design, code and specification errors.

4. **Software development**
   This is the programming and documentation.

Secured Computing: A CISSP Study Guide, Copyright 2001

5. **Installation**
   Installing the hardware needed. Testing that hardware.

6. **Maintenance support**
   This is where the fine-tuning, modifications and changes take place.

7. **Revisions and Replacement**
   Any major modifications or total replacement happens at this stage.

Configuration Management

Configuration Management applies to technical and administrative direction and surveillance to identify and document the functional and physical characteristics of a configuration item, control changes to those characteristics; record and report change processing and implementation status, and verify compliance with specified requirements.

There are four main features associated with configuration management:

1. Configuration identification is identifying what function and physical characteristics an item has and documenting that information.

2. Configuration status accounting is recording any changes to the configuration process.

3. Configuration control is to issue versions to configuration items as they are updated.

4. Configuration auditing is controlling the quality of the configuration management procedures.

Certification & Accreditation

Certification is the process of performing a comprehensive analysis of the security features and safeguards of a system to establish the extent to which the security requirements are satisfied.

The certification process considers the system in its operational environment. This means the security mode of operation, specific users, what training the users will receive, the applications and their data sensitivity, system and facility configuration and location, and its intercommunication with other systems are all considered during the certification process.

Accreditation is the official management decision to operate a system. Certificate proves it is capable, while accreditation means that we will run it. The accreditation specifies the security mode it will work in, countermeasures, threats, and stated vulnerabilities. The accreditation is for a stated period.

Primary Causes of Programming Environment Security Problems

The following is a list of common security problems in the programming environment:

- Minimum Management Commitment to Security & Control management must create an environment where they demonstrate full support for the security program and policies. They must provide the resources and time required to build security into the program in the first place. Management must also ensure that their programmers understand the organization's data classification scheme and handle both electronic and physical information appropriately.

- Anti-Security Work Habits of Programmers– Programmers generally have poor work habits. These include being pack rats, and keeping a copy of every piece of information they touch. This includes copies of previous programs, debugging sessions and test cases. Programmers will often use live data to test the operation of their program because they can easily check it against the existing system. However, the program is not exercised with bad data, and so no one knows how it will operate with bad data.

- Programmers often co-operate with their peers to assist in solving a problem, and will share access information including passwords to help get a project done.

- Work Environment Design & Implementation – the work environment posses some other challenges. For example, the lack of control in the physical workspace and lack of secure storage is a problem for many programmers. In addition, programs are developed on systems that are also used for live/production activities. This leaves that system open to attack (such as DoS) when it fails.

- Even worse is that the source code for the applications and the production test data are all stored on a machine that a lot of people have access to. This places the code and data in danger.

Management can address the problems discussed previously by ensuring that there is a corporate policy statement in effect. This policy statement must require a risk analysis be done prior to a new service being placed into operation. The policy must stress information is a valuable asset, and impose sanctions for improper handling of the corporate information. For this to be effective, the employees must have a real understanding and acknowledge their agreement with the requirements.

Management must provide an ongoing security awareness program for all employees to keep them informed about their responsibilities. Training for those specific functions in how to implement security would be beneficial. Finally, the system development life cycle must include security components up front. Security is much too difficult to retrofit into the application.

The programmers can also aid in address the causes by agreeing to control their use and misuse of computing resources. They must agree to use and support the corporate access control procedures and protect sensitive data.

This means they will comply with the classification procedures and encrypt sensitive information, avoid testing with live data, and destroy or degauss storage media before disposal.

Security Problems Caused by Decentralization

The decentralization or outsourcing of data processing personnel has caused a number of different problems to come to the surface. These include:

Secured Computing: A CISSP Study Guide, Copyright 2001

- **Hiring non-professional DP personnel** – this causes high error rates and omissions due to inadequate training. The lack of resources within this structure means that security gets dropped.

- **Internal control deficiencies** – there is inadequate separation of duties, audit trails are not examined on a regular basis. User management issues including account suspension and password changes fail to occur when expected. This alone may be enough to compromise a system.

- **Uncertain backup and recovery procedures** – with the DP function outsourced, there is likely confusion regarding the backup and recovery procedures, with one group thinking it happened one way, when it is another. This problem exposes the company to data loss through a missed backup, or an inappropriately applied backup.

Modes of Operation

Most systems operate with only two modes: user mode and supervisor or privileged mode. These are very general, and can be strengthened by adding additional granular protection. The most outer ring has the lowest privilege level, and each interior ring increases in privilege level until you reach the center. This has the highest privilege level. In this manner, the process can increase and decrease its privilege level by moving from one protection ring to the other. This model also allows for data or information hiding in order to protect data that may be in place at a different level. It also means that a process cannot access information that is at a higher privilege level than it is.

Integrity levels

When we are talking about integrity controls they will apply to the operating system, hardware and database. For an operating system we are referring to the reliability and correctness of it. As far as hardware we are referring to the logical completeness of the hardware that implements the protection mechanisms. And finally we want the database to be consistent. Integrity models can be attained through the use of encryption, anti-virus software, logical and physical access controls, security awareness training, digital signature and system backups to name a few.

Secured Computing: A CISSP Study Guide, Copyright 2001

Service Level Agreements (SLA)

A service level agreement is the need to define the set of user service levels, which include the volume of transactions, processing windows, response times and batch job turnarounds. It is best to define exact maximum and minimum numbers for each objective.

Test Your Knowledge

1. _____ is an access control concept that refers to an abstract machine that mediates all accesses to objects by subjects?
   - A. Monitor systems
   - B. Reference monitor
   - C. System High mode
   - D. DAC

2. A _____ channel is a communications path that writes to storage by one process and allows reading of that information through another, less secure, channel.
   - A. Covert operation
   - B. Covert
   - C. Covert storage
   - D. Electromagnetic

3. Accreditation is the process of performing a comprehensive analysis of the security features and safeguards of a system to establish the extent to which the security requirements are satisfied. T/F?
   - A. True
   - B. False

4. _____ is based on the way that the neurological connections of the human brain are believed to work in problem solving, identifying patterns and learning.
   - A. Fuzzy Logic
   - B. Neural network Technology
   - C. Expert systems
   - D. Knowledge based systems

5. What makes up secondary storage?
   - A. Hard drives, magnetic tape, CD-ROM, DVD drives
   - B. RAM, VRAM
   - C. Zip drives and CDRW only
   - D. Optical WORM drives

6. The security kernel can be a software, firmware or hardware component in a trusted computing base that implements the reference monitor? T/F
   - A. True
   - B. False

Secured Computing: A CISSP Study Guide, Copyright 2001

7._____ a class of database applications that look for trends or anomalies in a group of data without knowledge of the meaning of the data?
   A. Data Tree
   B. Data Mining
   C. Meta data
   D. Sequential tuning

8. _____ this is when authorized information enables a user to infer something about information that is not authorized?
   A. Interference
   B. Data Mining
   C. Scavenging
   D. Inference

9. Java's security model is to tightly control the environment that applets can run in. This concept is called a _____?
   A. Secure area
   B. Sandbox
   C. Playbox
   D. Segregated module

Answers: 1.B, 2.C, 3.B, 4.B, 5.A, 6.A, 7.B, 8.A, 9.B

Secured Computing: A CISSP Study Guide, Copyright 2001

References

Information in this chapter was referenced from the following sources:

1. Computer Security Handbook, Third edition, Arthur E, Hutt et al. 1995 John Wiley & Sons Inc.

2. *Information Security Management Handbook, 4th edition, Harold F. Tipton, et al. 2000, Auerbach Publications.*

3. *RFC 2828*

4. *RFC 2196 Site Security Handbook, RFC 2196, author B. Fraser, 1997*

5. *Security in Computing, Second edition, Charles P. Pfleeger, 1997 Prentice Hall*

NOTES

Domain 5

Cryptography

Cryptography

The cryptography domain deals with the principles, means, and methods of disguising information to insure its confidentiality, integrity and authenticity. Cryptography helps support the CIA triad of Confidentiality, Integrity and Authentication. It does this through cryptographical algorithms that are extremely hard to break, thus giving an individual or organization the ability to allow information to be only in the hands of the intended. It can be used to make a hash of a document that will show that it was not modified. It can also allow non-repudiation of information, which in some instances in more important than the confidentiality.

In this chapter we will take a look at the uses of cryptography, cryptographic concepts, methodologies and practices, private/public key algorithms, PKI, implementations and finally types of attacks.

Definitions

Cryptanalysis- The mathematical science that deals with analysis of a cryptographic system in order to gain knowledge needed to break or circumvent the protection that the system is designed to provide.

Cryptographic algorithm - An algorithm that employs the science of cryptography, including encryption algorithms, cryptographic hash algorithms, digital signature algorithms, and key agreement algorithms.

Cryptography- the principles, means, and methods for rendering information unintelligible, and for restoring encrypted information to intelligible form.

Cryptology-The science that includes both cryptography and cryptanalysis, and sometimes is said to include steganography.

Steganography -Methods of hiding the existence of a message or other data. This is different than cryptography, which hides the meaning of a message but does not hide the message itself. An example of a steganographic method is 'invisible' ink.

Uses of Cryptography

In today's world cryptography is more than encryption and decryption. We use authentication in our everyday lives from the PIN number entered at the ATM to the signature on important documents. Cryptography provides mechanisms for such procedures. A digital timestamp binds a document to its creation at a particular time, while a digital signature binds a document to the owner of a particular key. These cryptographic mechanisms can be used to control access to a shared disk drive, confidential files and even pay-per-view TV channels.

The many uses of cryptography are growing everyday. The main areas include, Identification & authentication, secure communications, and e-commerce.

Identification

Identification is the process of verifying someone's or something's identity. When you sign legal documents you will be asked for a driver's license to verify your identity. This same process can be done electronically using cryptography.

Authentication

Authentication is similar to identification, in that they both allow an entity access to resources, but authentication is broader because it does not necessarily involve identifying a person or entity. Authentication merely determines whether that person or entity is authorized for whatever is in question.

Non-repudiation

Non-repudiation is an authentication that is of such high assurance that it can be asserted to be genuine. This way someone involved in a transaction or communication cannot deny his or her involvement. This can be done with the use of digital signatures.

Secure Communication

Secure communications is probably what most think of when cryptography is mentioned. Individuals can communicate privately without fear of others

Secured Computing: A CISSP Study Guide, Copyright 2001

having access to that communication. While secure communications have been around for a long time, key management has prevented it from becoming everyday. With the development of public-key cryptography, there are tools that exist to create a large network of people who can communicate securely with one another even if they had never communicated before.

Electronic Commerce

In the last few years e-commerce has exploded into the marketplace and is comprised of online banking, online brokerage, and Internet shopping, to name a few. The problem is that when entering a credit card number on the Internet leaves one open to fraud. One cryptographic solution to this problem is to encrypt the credit card number when it is entered on-line; another is to secure the entire session. These are typically done through an HTTPS or SSL session. When a computer encrypts this information and sends it out on the Internet, it is a scrambled meaningless string of text to a third party viewer. The web-server receives the encrypted information, decrypts it, and goes ahead with the sale without any fear that the credit card number slipped into the wrong hands. The more we see the growth of e-commerce the more that we will see the role of encryption grow.

Cryptographic Concepts, Methodologies, and Practices

Plaintext is when all of your data is in unscrambled form, normal text that you would read in the newspaper or a book.

Ciphertext is that data in a Scrambled form. The original message is called a plaintext. The disguised message is called ciphertext.

Enciphering data is the act of scrambling that data with a cryptographic algorithm. The act of encryption, more specifically enciphering, is the transformation of data into a form that is not viable to read with out the appropriate knowledge, the key. Its purpose is to ensure privacy by keeping information hidden from anyone for whom it is not intended, even those who have access to the encrypted data.

Deciphering would be to unscramble that data into readable form. Decryption or to decipher is the reverse of encryption. It is the transformation of encrypted data back into an intelligible form.

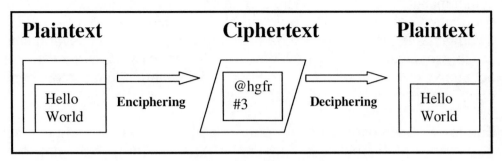

Figure 5.1 – Encryption Process

Encryption and decryption generally require the use of some secret information, referred to as a key. For some encryption mechanisms, the same key is used for encryption and decryption, private keys, and for other mechanisms the keys used for encryption and decryption are different, public key.

Cryptanalysis is the reverse of cryptography. It is the science of violating authentication schemes, cracking codes and breaking cryptographic protocols. In order to design a strong encryption algorithm or cryptographic protocol, it is recommended to use cryptanalysis to find and correct any weaknesses. This is why the most trusted encryption algorithms are the ones that have been made available to public scrutiny, like DES. One of the basic tenets of cryptology is that the security of an algorithm should not rely on its secrecy. If there is a weakness then cryptanalysis can help uncover and correct this.

A **cryptosystem** is usually a collection of algorithms that are labeled and are what we call keys. Encryption is based on factoring; therefore a longer key will provide better protection than a shorter key. However one must ensure that the algorithm being used is a strong cryptosystem. Every well-made cryptosystem has such a large key space that a brute-force attack is impractical. Of course with today's changing technology the impracticality of a brute force changes, what was difficult to crack many years ago is easier to crack today.

Link Encryption V.S. End-to-End Encryption

There are two basic types of encryption in networks, link and end-to-end. Link encryption encrypts all the data in a communications path. This would include the routing data, therefore it needs to decrypt and encrypt at every communication node. Link encryption is easy to implement and protects information between nodes by encrypting the entire packet. The disadvantages are that it must be encrypted and decrypted several times which can cause a latency problems. In addition, it is a security risk because it can be read at every point it is decrypted, if that system has been compromised.

End-to-end encryption is usually performed by the end user and encrypts all data except the routing information as it passes through the network. Therefore in end-to-end encryption the data is encrypted and decrypted only at the end points, which overcomes the problems we have with link encryption.

Symmetric and Asymmetric Algorithms

Symmetric algorithms are called by many names; but single key and secret key is the most common. Both the sender and the receiver share the same key, therefore the key must be decided on before hand. Symmetric keys have a computational efficiency advantage (10-100 million bits/sec.) that rivals asymmetric keys. The most popular secret-key cryptosystem in use today is known as DES, the Data Encryption Standard. IBM developed DES in the middle 1970's and it has been a Federal Standard ever since 1976. Which will be replaces slowly by AES starting in 2001. Other popular algorithms include IDEA, blowfish and RC4.

The strengths of symmetric key are there speed, strength (when a large key is used) and their availability (there are many algorithms available). The main weaknesses are that the same key is used to encrypt and decrypt. Also, It is not scalable with the more users that you have and it has limited security such as no repudiation and authentication.

Asymmetric algorithms, known as public keys use two asymmetric keys, one to encrypt and the other to decrypt. Computationally these keys are much slower than symmetric keys, with a speed around a few thousand bits/sec., because it has a difficulty factoring a product of 2 large prime numbers. The RSA public-key cryptosystem and the Digital Signature Algorithm (DSA) are the most popular forms of public-key cryptography.

The primary advantage of public-key cryptography is increased security and convenience, as private keys never need to be transmitted or

Secured Computing: A CISSP Study Guide, Copyright 2001

revealed to anyone. Another advantage is they can provide non-repudiation through digital signatures.

A big disadvantage of public-key cryptography for encryption is speed. The best solution is to combine public and secret-key systems in order to get both the security advantages of public-key systems and the speed advantages of secret-key systems. Another disadvantage of public-key cryptography is that it is vulnerable to impersonation, even if users' private-keys are not available. A successful attack on a certification authority (CA) will allow an attacker to impersonate whomever he or she chooses by using a public-key certificate from the compromised authority to tie a key of the adversary's choice to the name of another user.

Public key cryptography is not meant to replace asymmetric cryptography. In general, public-key cryptography is best suited for an open multi-user environment and symmetric for personal file encryption.

Block and Stream Ciphers

Block Ciphers Operate on fixed size blocks, for most block ciphers, the size is 64 bits, of plain text. In the coming years the block size will increase to 128 bits as processors become more sophisticated. Block ciphers are more suitable for implementation in software to execute on general-purpose computers. A single error can damage the entire block of data.

A stream cipher is a symmetric encryption algorithm that is very fast, much faster than any block cipher. While block ciphers operate on large blocks of data, stream ciphers typically operate on smaller units of plaintext, usually bits and generates what is called a keystream. Encryption is accomplished by combining the keystream with the plaintext.

Hash functions

The main role of a cryptographic hash function is in the provision of message integrity checks and digital signatures. It is used to condense an arbitrary length message to a fixed size. Hash functions are generally faster than encryption or digital signature algorithms, it is typical to compute the digital signature or integrity check to some document by applying cryptographic processing to the document's hash value, which is small compared to the document itself.

Secured Computing: A CISSP Study Guide, Copyright 2001

A good hash function should be a one-way function, should be computationally infeasible to attack, and resist key clustering. Examples of hash functions include MD4, MD5, RSA message digest, SHA and HAVAL.

Key Management

Key management is crucial and helps protects against key destruction, keys that are lost as well as stolen. The following steps, when followed, can help in key management:

- Key management must be fully automated for key discipline and secrecy
- No key should be in the clear outside of the cryptographic device, for secrecy and known plaintext attack resistance
- Choose keys randomly from entire key space
- Key encrypting keys must be separate from the data keys
- Infrequently use keys with long life
- The more a key is used, the more likely a successful attack and the greater the consequences

Key recovery

One of the barriers to the widespread use of encryption in certain contexts is the fact that when a key is somehow "lost", any data encrypted with that key becomes unusable. Key recovery is a general term encompassing the numerous ways of permitting "emergency access" to encrypted data. Key recovery permits recovery of lost or damaged keys without need to store or escrow them with a third party.

Key Escrowed Encryption

Key escrow is a controversial subject because encryption is so strong that many governments are unable to get at certain information in efforts to lawfully perform electronic observation. So to meet the needs of the US government they have adopted the Escrowed Encryption Standard (EES). This allows for individuals and organizations to use strong encryption, but allows the government when legally authorized to do so. Key escrow is one method of key recovery, though you do not see it used much.

Fair Public Key Cryptosystems

The object of a fair public key cryptosystem is similar to an escrowed key system. The keys are separated into parts and held by different escrow agents, thus no one-escrow agency has the full key.

Export Issues regarding Encryption

Cryptography is export-controlled for several reasons. Strong cryptography can be used for criminal purposes or even as a weapon of war. During wartime, the ability to intercept and decipher enemy communications is crucial. Therefore strong cryptography is usually classified as an export-controlled commodity, just like tanks and missiles.

In the United States export issues are based on the 1943 law designed to stop Nazi Germany and Japan from obtaining U.S. technology. In 1996 this was updated as the Export Administrations Regulations (EAR).

<u>Ciphers</u>

Substitution Cipher

Substitution cipher when each character of the plaintext is substituted for another character of ciphertext. The receiver inverts the substitution on the ciphertext to recover the plaintext. An example would be the "Caesar cipher". In which each plaintext characters are replaced by the character three to the right of modulo 26 ("A" is replaced by "D", "B" is replaced by "E", and so on...

Polyalphabetic Ciphers

A polyalphabetic cipher is made up of multiple simple substitution cipher. It uses different alphabets to defeat frequency analysis. An example with 3 alphabets below:

a b c d e f g h i (normal alphabet)
g h y l................ (1st alphabet)
w s d e.............. (2nd Alphabet)
g b h p ...... (3rd Alphabet)

Transposition Cipher

Transposition ciphers are when the plaintext remains the same, but the order of characters is shuffled around. An example of would be as follows:

- Position of letters permuted.
- Message broken into 5-character groups
- Letters rearranged

don't give up the ship (Message)
1234512345123451234512345 (Groups of 5)
3512435124351243512435124 (The key)
n'dtoiv egp tu shhe i p (Ciphertext)

Concealment Ciphers

Concealment Ciphers is when the true letters of plaintext is hidden/disguised by a device or algorithm. An example would be to divide the message using one word at a time, having it appear as the 6th word in every sentence. Example:

- Message: "**Sell Now**"
- Message in concealment: I do not really want to **SELL** this, I don't need the money **NOW**"

Steganography

Steganography serves to hide secret messages in other messages or images so that the secret message is concealed in the other item. Generally the sender writes a harmless message and then conceals a secret message on the same piece of paper. We see this a lot with images and it is extremely hard to detect.

One-Time-Pad

An on-time pad is unbreakable by exhaustive search (brute force). It is a large set of truly random letters and is used only once for one key. The sender sends the message and then destroys the pad and the receiver does the same thing. One-time pads are used in very high security, low bandwidth channels. The main disadvantage is that the key length needs to be the same size as the data being sent or enciphered.

Secured Computing: A CISSP Study Guide, Copyright 2001

Cryptographic Algorithms

DES Encryption

Data Encryption Standard (DES) is the most common private key encryption standard and was developed by IBM in the early 1970s. It has been the de facto industry standard for cryptography systems and is the world's most commonly used encryption mechanism. It was adopted as a Federal Information Processing Standard (FIPS) in 1977 and as an American National Standard (ANSI X3.92) in 1981.

The DES algorithm is a 64-bit circulating block cipher based on a symmetric key. The keys are based on a 64-bit vector consisting of 56 information bits and 8 parity bits. The 56 bit keys used are for encrypting and decrypting the information, referred to as the active key. The algorithm uses 16 rounds to produce a cipher block, which will have no resemblance to the original input data. DES uses what is called round by round encryption for a given key, which means that the out depends on every bit of the input and every bit of the active key. The three major elements of DES are S-boxes, the key schedule and the permutations and E operator.

What are parity bits?
A bit indicating whether the sum of a previous series of bits is even or odd. Parity bits can detect unintentional modifications to data.

S- boxes

S-boxes are non-linear substitution tables that ensure that the algorithm is not linear.

The key Schedule

The key schedule helps mix up the 48 bits of the 56 bit key so that each of the 16 rounds forms a different 48 bit key.

Secured Computing: A CISSP Study Guide, Copyright 2001

The permutations and E Operator

The role of permutation or "P" is to mix the data bits so that they cannot be traced back to the S-boxes. The E operator expands a 32-bit input to a 48-bit output that is added mod two to the round.

The four modes of the DES algorithm:

- Electronic codebook (ECB) is a 64-bit data block of ciphertext that is encrypted independently of any other block. Each ciphertext block corresponds to one plaintext block just like in a codebook. This is usually the highest performance mode, but suffers under the problem that when the same pattern appears, it is always encrypted the same.

- Output Feedback (OFB) is a DES generated stream that is XORed with a message stream and simulates a one-time pad.

What is XOR?

The *XOR (exclusive-OR)* acts in the same way as the logical "either/or." The output is "true" if either, but not both, of the inputs are "true." The output is "false" if both inputs are "false" or if both inputs are "true." Another way of looking at this circuit is to observe that the output is 1 if the inputs are different, but 0 if the inputs are the same.

- Cipher Feedback (CFB) generates a stream of random binary bits combined with plain text, and then it generates a cipher with the same number of bits. Part of the cipher text is then fed back to form part of the next message.

- Cipher Block Chaining (CBC) is similar to ECB, except that each encrypted block is XORed with the previous block of ciphertext. Thus, identical patterns in different messages will be encrypted differently, depending upon the difference in previous data.

Triple DES

Triple DES (See figure 5.2) is simply another mode of the DES operation. It takes three 64-bit keys, for an overall key length of 192 bits. In Stealth, you simply type in the entire 192-bit (24 character) key rather than entering each of the three keys individually. Then Triple DES breaks the user provided key into three sub keys, padding the keys if necessary so they are each 64 bits long. The procedure for encryption is exactly the same as regular DES, but it is repeated three times, hence the name Triple DES. The data is encrypted with the first key, decrypted with the second key, and finally encrypted again with the third key.

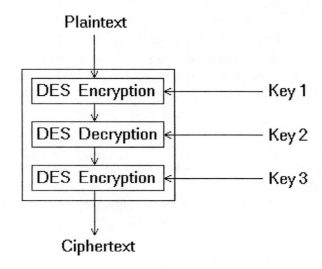

Figure 5.2 - Triple DES

ADVANCED ENCRYPTION STANDARD (AES)

The Advanced Encryption Standard (AES) will be a new Federal Information Processing Standard (FIPS) Publication that will specify a cryptographic algorithm for use by U.S. Government organizations to protect sensitive information. NIST also anticipates that the AES will be widely used on a voluntary basis by organizations, institutions, and individuals outside of the U.S. Government. NIST has selected Rijndael as the proposed AES algorithm.

The AES will specify three key sizes: 128, 192 and 256 bits. In decimal terms, this means that there are approximately:

$$3.4 \times 10^{38} \text{ possible 128-bit keys;}$$

$$6.2 \times 10^{57} \text{ possible 192-bit keys; and}$$

$$1.1 \times 10^{77} \text{ possible 256-bit keys.}$$

When you compare this with DES, which is 56 bits long, there are on the order of 10^{21} times more AES 128-bit keys than DES 56-bit keys.

Rijndael

The Rijndael algorithm is the new AES algorithm. It helps resist against attacks and has a more simplistic design than other ciphers. It uses an iterated block cipher with variable block lengths. These block lengths are chosen at 128, 192 or 256 bits.

RSA

RSA is an algorithm for asymmetric cryptography, invented in 1977 by Ron Rivest, Adi Shamir, and Leonard Adleman. The difficulty of breaking RSA is believed to be equivalent to the difficulty of factoring integers that are the product of two large prime numbers of approximately equal size.

RSA can be used to generate digital signatures, encrypt messages, and provide key management for DES, RC2, RC4 and other secret key algorithms. RSA performs the key management process, in part, by encrypting a secret key for an algorithm such as DES, RC2, or RC4 with the recipient's public key for secure transmission to the recipient. This secret key can then be used to support private communications.

Kerberos

Kerberos is a secure method for authenticating a request for a service in a computer network. Kerberos was developed in the Athena Project at the Massachusetts Institute of Technology (MIT). The name is taken from Greek mythology; Kerberos was a three-headed dog that guarded the gates of Hades. Kerberos lets a user request an encrypted "ticket" from an authentication process that can then be used to request a particular service from a server. The user's password does not have to pass through the network. Read RFC 1510 for a more detailed discussion on kerberos.

Skipjack

Skipjack is the encryption algorithm designed by the NSA. It uses an 80-bit key to encrypt 64-bit blocks of data. Skipjack is said to be more secure than DES in the absence of any analytic attack since it uses 80-bit keys. By contrast, DES uses 56-bit keys.

The Clipper Chip

The Clipper chip is a tamper resistant hardware chip designed by the NSA that uses the skipjack algorithm and contains a unique 80-bit unit key, which is escrowed in two parts at two escrow agencies; both parts must be known in order to recover the key. In addition, there is a serial number and an 80-bit key; the latter is common to all Clipper chips. The chip is manufactured so that it cannot be reverse engineered; this means that the Skipjack algorithm and the keys cannot be recovered from the chip. The disadvantage of the clipper chip is that it uses too weak a key at 80 bits and it has not been put under much public scrutiny.

HMAC

Hash Message Authentication Code (HMAC) is a secret-key algorithm. HMAC provides data integrity and origin authentication through a digital signature produced by a keyed hash function. Message Digest version 5 (MD5) algorithm is a hash function that can produce a 128-bit value. Secure Hash Algorithm (SHA) is a hash function that can produce a 160-bit value. By virtue of its increased bit value, HMAC SHA is more secure than HMAC MD5 but requires a slightly longer processing time.

MD5

Message digest algorithm 5 (MD5) is a message digest algorithm that digests a message of arbitrary size to 128 bits. MD5 is a cryptographic checksum algorithm. The message undergoes 4 rounds of transformation.

Secured Computing: A CISSP Study Guide, Copyright 2001

DSA

Digital signature algorithm (DSA) is an asymmetric cryptographic algorithm that produces a digital signature in the form of a pair of large numbers. This algorithm uses a private key to sign a message and a public key to verify the signature. It is a standard proposed by the U.S. Government.

ISAKMP

Internet Security Association and Key Management Protocol (ISAKMP) is an Internet IPsec protocol. It negotiates, establishes, modifies, and deletes security associations. It also exchanges key generation and authentication data, independent of the details of any specific key generation technique, key establishment protocol, encryption algorithm, or authentication mechanism.

SHA

Secure hash standard (SHA) is a message digest algorithm that digests a message of random size to 160 bits. SHA is a cryptographic checksum algorithm.

Elliptic Curve Cryptosystems (ECC)

Victor Miller and Neal Koblitz first proposed elliptic curve cryptosystems (ECC) independently in the mid-1980s. It uses an algebraic system defined on points of an elliptic curve to provide public-key algorithms. There are several advantages to using ECC:

- Highest strength/bit of public key systems
- Big saving over other public key systems
- Computation
- Bandwidth
- Storage
- Bandwidth reduced
- Short signature and certificates
- Fast encryption and signature speed
- Hardware and software
- Ideal for very small hardware implementations
- Used in smart cards

Secured Computing: A CISSP Study Guide, Copyright 2001

- Encryption and digital signatures stages separable to simplify export

Pretty Good Privacy (PGP)

Phil Zimmerman created Pretty Good Privacy. It converts a pass phrase into a bit stream. It uses the International Data Encryption Algorithm (IDEA) for symmetric encryption with DES as an option. It uses RSA for public key encryption. It is based on a trust model.

PGP adopts a trust approach in its architecture. There is no central authority, which everybody trusts, but instead, individuals sign each other's keys and progressively forming a web of individual public keys interconnected by links formed by this signatures. For example, Alice signs Bob's public-key certificate, which she knows is authentic. Bob then forwards his signed certificate to Carol who wishes to communicate with Bob privately. Carol, who knows and trusts Alice as an introducer, finds out, after verification, that Alice is among Bob's certificate signer (Bob could have more than one signature on his certificate to make it more widely acceptable). Therefore, Carol can be confident that Bob's public key is authentic. However, had Carol not known or trusted any of Bob's signers, including Alice, she would have been skeptical about the authenticity of Bob's public-key. Bob would have to find another introducer whom Carol trusts to sign bob's public-key certificate.

El Gamal

The El Gamal algorithm is an unpatented, public key algorithm used for both digital signatures and encryption. It was the first algorithm suitable for both digital signatures and encryption unencumbered by patents. El Gamal relies on the difficulty of discrete logarithms in a finite field. The algorithm is based on the problem of exponentiation.

Digital Signatures

Digital signatures are an authentication tool to verify a messages origin and a sender's identity. It is typically created through the use of a hash function and a private signing function. Authentication is any process through which one proves and verifies certain information. Sometimes one may want to verify the origin of a document, the identity of the sender, the time and date a document was sent and/or signed, the identity of a computer or user, and so on. A digital signature is a cryptographic means through which many of these may be verified.

To sign a message a sender computes a digest of the message using a public hash function. The hash is applied to the sender's private key, which creates a digital signature. The signature is attached to the message.

The receiver receives the message and computes a digest of the message. Then applies the senders public key to the digest and the signature, and if they match, identifies the sender.

The Digital Signature Standard (DSS) was proposed by NIST in 1991 and uses the secure hash algorithm (SHA) condensing the message to 160 bits. The key sizes range from 512-1024 bits.

This Digital Signature Algorithm (DSA) standard is appropriate for applications requiring a digital rather than written signature. The DSA digital signature is a pair of large numbers represented in a computer as strings of binary digits. The digital signature is computed using a set of rules and a set of parameters such that the identity of the signatory and integrity of the data can be verified. The DSA provides the capability to generate and verify signatures.

Diffie Hellman

Diffie Hellman was the first public key algorithm ever developed. It is still very popular and recommended for key exchange. Its advantage over RSA, the most widely used public key algorithm, is that Diffie Hellman is a negotiated key generation while RSA is a master/slave key generation. It is vulnerable to Man in the middle attacks. The patent ran out in 1997.

Diffie and Hellman developed the Diffie-Hellman key agreement protocol, also called exponential key agreement, in 1976. The protocol allows two users to exchange a secret key over an insecure medium without any prior secrets. The protocol depends on a discrete logarithm problem for its security. The Diffie-Hellman key exchange is vulnerable to a *middleperson attack*. In this attack, an opponent intercepts someone public value and sends their own public value to the intended recipient. This vulnerability is due to the fact that Diffie-Hellman key exchange does not authenticate the participants. Possible solutions include the use of digital signatures and other protocol variants.

Public Key Infrastructure (PKI)

Public-key infrastructure (PKI) uses a combination of software, encryption technologies, and services that enables organizations to protect the security of their communications and business transactions on the Internet.

PKI integrates, digital certificates, public-key cryptography, and certificate authorities into total network security architecture. A typical enterprise's PKI encompasses the issuance of digital certificates to individual users and servers; end-user enrollment software; integration with corporate certificate directories; tools for managing, renewing, revoking certificates; and related services and support.

PKI helps to protect information in several ways:

- **Support for non-repudiation.** Digital certificates validate their users' identities, making it nearly impossible to later repudiate or deny a digitally "signed" transaction, such as a purchase made on a web site.
- **Authorize access.** PKI digital certificates replace easily guessed and frequently lost user IDs and passwords to streamline intranet login security.
- **Authenticate identity**. Digital certificates issued as part of PKI will allow individual users and organizations to confidently validate the identity of each party in an Internet transaction.
- **Verify integrity**. A digital certificate ensures that the message or document the certificate "signs" has not been changed or corrupted in transit online.
- **Ensure privacy.** Digital certificates protect information from interception during Internet transmission.
- **Authorize transactions.** With PKI solutions, your enterprises can control access privileges for specified online transactions.

Digital certificates

Digital certificates are electronic files that act like a kind of online passport. They are issued by a trusted third party, called a certificate authority (CA).

Secured Computing: A CISSP Study Guide, Copyright 2001

The CA verifies the identity of the certificate's holder. They are tamper-proof and cannot be forged.

Digital certificates do two things:

1. They authenticate that their holders - people, web sites, and even network resources such as routers - are truly who or what they claim to be.
2. They protect data exchanged online from theft or tampering.

There is two types of digital certificates that are important when building secure web sites: server certificates and personal certificates.

Digital certificates employ the more advanced public key cryptography system, which does not involve the sharing of secret keys. Rather than using the same key to both encrypt and decrypt data, a digital certificate uses a matched pair of keys that uniquely complement each other. When a message is encrypted by one key, only the complementary key can decrypt it.

Certificate Authority

A certificate authority (CA) is an entity that issues digital certificates and verifies them between the data items in a certificate. In addition, the CA creates user keys. Certificate users depend on the validity of information provided by a certificate. Therefore, a CA should be someone that the certificate users trust, and holds an official position created and granted power by a government, a corporation, or some other organization. Certification authorities may themselves have a certificate that is issued to them by other certification authorities. The highest certification authority is called the root CA.

Two Models for PKI Deployment

There are two different approaches to building an enterprise PKI:

- **Deploying an integrated PKI platform**–this uses the combination of enterprise-controlled and operated PKI software/hardware, compatibility with popular applications, and the certificate processing services and infrastructure of a high-availability, high-security PKI backbone—with shared liability and independently audited business processes.

- **Purchase standalone PKI software:** and create a standalone PKI service—where the enterprise alone assumes 100% responsibility for provisioning all the surrounding technology, including systems, telecommunications, and databases, in addition to providing physical site security, Internet-safe network configurations, high-availability redundant systems, disaster recovery, PKI specialists, viable PKI legal practices, and financially safe PKI liability protection;

Key Distribution and Management

The proper management of cryptographic keys is essential. Ultimately the protection of the keys is the level of security you have for your system and/or enterprise. They need to be protected from unauthorized use and modification. Key management involves the procedures and protocols through the lifecycle of the keys, this would include generation of the keys, distribution, storage, entry, use, recovery, destruction and archiving.

Some of the controls over cryptographic keys would include:

- Split knowledge procedures- this is similar to separation of duties, as one person alone does not have all the knowledge or access to the keys to cause damage. The knowledge and access is distributed.
- Zeroization- a method of erasing electronic data by altering the contents so that recovering the data is not possible.
- Zero Knowledge proof- this is when one party can reveal something to a second party without revealing any additional information.
- Avoidance controls- the separation of threats from assets and assets from threats.

Secured Computing: A CISSP Study Guide, Copyright 2001

Application and Network Based Protocols

SSL

An Internet protocol, originally developed by Netscape Communications, Inc., that uses connection-oriented end-to-end encryption to provide data confidentiality service and data integrity service for traffic between a client (often a web browser) and a server, and that can optionally provide peer entity authentication between the client and the server. SSL uses the DES encryption algorithm and is the most popular way to make secure connection on the WWW.

DNSSEC

Domain Name Server Security and was designed to secure distributed name services.

GSSAPI

GSSAPI is Generic Security Services API and provides a generic authentication, key exchange and encryption interface for different systems and authentication methods.

HTTPS

HTTPS is an Internet protocol for providing client-server security services for HTTP communications. S-HTTP supports choice of security policies, key management mechanisms, and cryptographic algorithms through option negotiation between parties for each transaction. S-HTTP supports both asymmetric and symmetric key operation modes. S-HTTP attempts to avoid presuming particular trust models, but it attempts to facilitate multiply rooted hierarchical trust and anticipates that principals may have many public key certificates.

SET

Secure Electronic Transaction is a protocol developed jointly by MasterCard International and Visa International and published as an open standard to provide confidentiality of transaction information, payment integrity, and authentication of transaction participants for payment card transactions over unsecured networks, such as the Internet.

Secured Computing: A CISSP Study Guide, Copyright 2001

PEM

Privacy Enhanced Mail is an Internet protocol to provide data confidentiality, data integrity, and data origin authentication for electronic mail. PEM encrypts messages with DES in CBC mode, provides key distribution of DES keys by encrypting them with RSA, and signs messages with RSA over either MD2 or MD5. To establish ownership of public keys, PEM uses a certification hierarchy, with X.509 public-key certificates and X.509 CRLs that are signed with RSA and MD2. PEM is designed to be compatible with a wide range of key management methods, but is limited to specifying security services only for text messages and, like MOSS, has not been widely implemented in the Internet.

S/MIME

S/MIME (Secure Multi-Purpose Internet Mail Extensions) is a secure method of sending e-mail that uses the Rivest-Shamir-Adleman encryption system. S/MIME is included in the latest versions of the Web browsers from Microsoft and Netscape and has also been endorsed by other vendors that make messaging products. RSA has proposed S/MIME as a standard to the Internet Engineering Task Force IETF. An alternative to S/MIME is PGP/MIME, which has also been proposed as a standard.

IPSEC

Internet Protocol Security (IPsec) is a standard for security at the network or packet-processing layer of network communication. IPsec is especially useful for implementing virtual private network (VPN) and for remote user access through dial-up connection to private networks. A big advantage of IPsec is that security arrangements can be handled without requiring changes to individual user computers.

IPsec provides two choices of security service: Authentication Header (AH), which essentially allows authentication of the sender of data, and Encapsulating Security Payload (ESP), which supports both authentication of the sender and encryption of data as well. The specific information associated with each of these services is inserted into the packet in a header that follows the IP packet header. Separate key protocols can be selected, such as the ISAKMP/Oakley protocol.

Secured Computing: A CISSP Study Guide, Copyright 2001

Smart cards

Smart cards are small electronic devices about the size of a credit card that contains electronic memory, and possibly an embedded integrated circuit (IC). Smart cards containing an IC are sometimes called Integrated Circuit Cards (ICCs). Smart cards have processing capability and are tamper resistant. The user PIN is secretly stored in the cards memory and provides two-factor authentication. To use a smart card, either to pull information from it or add data to it, you need a smart card reader, a small device into which you insert the smart card.

Memory Only Cards

Memory only cards come with fixed logic for encryption. They are usually a magnetic stripe on a card. If used with a password or PIN provide two-factor authentication. They are easy to counterfeit.

Tokens

In security systems, a small device the size of a credit card that displays a constantly changing ID code. A user first enters a password and then the card displays an ID that can be used to log into a network. Typically, the IDs change every few minutes or so.

WAP

The wireless application protocol is spreading quickly and security of it is a concern. WAP uses the wireless transport layer security protocol (WTLS) for security.

WTLS has three classes of security:
- Class 1-Anonymous authentication

- Class 2-Server authentication, the server authenticates to the client only

- Class 3-Two way authentication, both the server and the client authenticate.

Secured Computing: A CISSP Study Guide, Copyright 2001

Methods of Attack

The following are several attacks that can take place against secret key algorithms:

Brute force attack

This is the type of attack that tries every possible combination of keys and passwords in an attempt to break the cryptosystem. Two ways to help this is to change keys often and use keys higher than 128 bits.

The time it takes to brute force a key is important. For example if your system is testing 1000 keys per second it would take 300,000,000 years to crack it, but only 17.6 days to crack a 40 bit key. This is why key length is important.

Man in the Middle Attack

This is when the information is encrypted on one end and decrypted on the other and the results are matched in the middle.

Chosen Plaintext Attack (CPA)

CPA is when a cryptographic device is loaded with a hidden key and the input of any plaintext is allowed to see the output.

Known Plaintext Attack (KPA)

Some past plain text and matching ciphertext are known. A known-plaintext attack is one in which the cryptanalyst obtains a sample of ciphertext and the corresponding plaintext as well.

Differential Cryptanalysis Attack

Looks at pairs of plaintext and pairs of ciphertext. This attack is dependent on the structure of S-boxes as in DES.

Related Key Attack

Chooses the relation between a pair of keys, but does not choose the keys themselves.

Ciphertext Only Attack (COA)

A ciphertext-only attack is one in which the cryptanalyst obtains a sample of ciphertext, without the plaintext associated with it. This data is relatively easy to obtain in many scenarios, but a successful ciphertext-only attack is generally difficult, and requires a very large ciphertext sample.

Chosen Text Attack (CTA)

A Crypto device loaded with a hidden key provided and input of the plaintext or ciphertext allowed to see the other. A chosen-plaintext attack is one in which the cryptanalyst is able to choose a quantity of plaintext and then obtain the corresponding encrypted ciphertext.

The Birthday Attack

This attack is a key clustering attack that happens when two different keys generate the same cipher text from the same plaintext.

Secured Computing: A CISSP Study Guide, Copyright 2001

Test Your Knowledge

1. _____ chooses a piece of cipher text and attempts to obtain the corresponding decrypted plaintext.
   - A. Chosen plaintext attack (CPA)
   - B. Chosen Cipher text attack (CCA)
   - C. Cipher text only attack (COA)
   - D. Known plaint text attack (KPA)

2. _____ is the weakest form of authentication and is an ANSI X9.9 standard.
   - A. DES
   - B. MAC
   - C. Digital signatures
   - D. MD5

3. _____ attacks rely on block ciphers exhibiting a high degree of mathematical structure.
   - A. Differential crypto
   - B. Algebraic Crypto
   - C. Linear Crypto
   - D. Differential linear crypto

4. _____ is a protocol developed jointly by MasterCard International and Visa International for payment card transactions over unsecured networks, such as the Internet?

   - A. IPsec
   - B. SET
   - C. SSL
   - D. Fortezza

5. _____ is a method of erasing electronic data by altering the contents so that recovering the data is not possible.

   - A. Erasure
   - B. Zeroization
   - C. Duplexing
   - D. Degaussing

Secured Computing: A CISSP Study Guide, Copyright 2001

6.Secure hash standard (SHA) is a message digest algorithm that digests a message of random size to ___ bits?

    A. 128
    B. 160
    C. 256
    D. 1024

7. Message Digest version 5 (MD5) algorithm is a hash function that can produce a ___-bit value?

    A. 128
    B. 160
    C. 256
    D. 1024

8. _____ are non-linear substitution tables that ensure that the algorithm is not linear

    A. Ciphers
    B. Linear boxes
    C. S-boxes
    D. Sanders Box

9. _____ is a key clustering attack that happens when two different keys generate the same cipher text from the same plaintext.

    A. Cluster attack
    B. Birthday attack
    C. Man in the middle attack
    D. Salami attack

10._____ are electronic files that act like a kind of online passport. They are issued by a trusted third party, called a certificate authority (CA). The CA verifies the identity of the certificate's holder.

    A. Digital Signatures
    B. Digital Passports
    C. Digital Certificates
    D. PKI

Secured Computing: A CISSP Study Guide, Copyright 2001

11. An Internet protocol that uses connection-oriented end-to-end DES encryption to provide data confidentiality service and data integrity service for traffic between a client and a server?

A. SET
B. SSL
C. Triple DES
D. Fortezza

12.DES has how many usable bits?

A. 56
B. 48
C. 128
D. 1024

Answer: 1.C, 2.B, 3.B, 4.B, 5.B, 6.B, 7.A, 8.C, 9.B, 10.C, 11.B, 12.B

Secured Computing: A CISSP Study Guide, Copyright 2001

References

Information in this chapter was referenced from the following sources:

1.IPsec The new Security Standard for the Internet, intranets, and Virtual Private Networks, Naganand Doraswamy et al., 1999 Prentice Hall

2.RSA Laboratories' Frequently Asked Questions About Today's Cryptography, Version 4.1, Copyright © 1992-2000 RSA Security Inc.

Notes

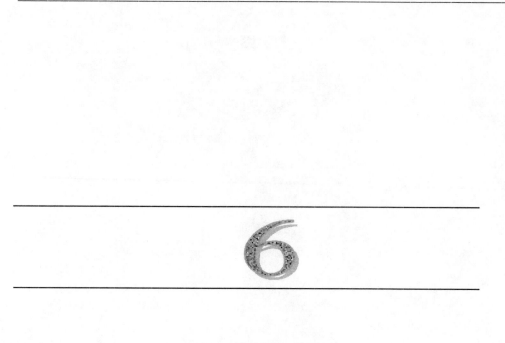

Domain 6

Security Architecture and Models

Security Architecture and Models

The security Architecture and Models domain contains the concepts, principles, structures and standards used to design, implement, monitor and secure, operating systems, equipment, networks, applications and those controls used to enforce various levels of Confidentiality, integrity and availability.

Definitions

Security architecture-A plan and set of principles that describe the security services that a system is required to provide to meet the needs of its users, the system elements required to implement the services, and the performance levels required in the elements to deal with the threat environment.

Security model-A schematic description of a set of entities and relationships by which a specified set of security services are provided by or within a system.

Trusted computing base (TCB)- The totality of protection mechanisms within a computer system, including hardware, firmware, and software, the combination of which is responsible for enforcing a security policy. The totality of protection mechanisms within a computer system -including hardware, firmware, and software - the combination of that is responsible for enforcing a security policy.

Principles of Common Computer and Network Architecture and Design

Architecture is the general term for referring to the structure of a computer system or network. This includes the entire structure and the details needed to make it functional. We will do a quick review over the basics of computer and network terminologies that you need to have a clear understanding of. You should understand: hardware, firmware and software.

Hardware

Hardware is considered to be objects that you can physically touch, like keyboards, disk drives, display screens, printers, and boards. In contrast, software is untouchable.

CPU

The central processing unit (CPU) is made up of four parts: a control unit, arithmetic unit, logic unit, and a storage unit. The control unit coordinates activities during execution of programs. The arithmetic and logic units have the most influence on cost versus performance than the other CPU components. It performs many functions including data transfer, decision-making, and arithmetic. Finally the storage unit (memory) stores the instructions and data needed by the CPU for currently used programs.

There are several addressing schemes that you need to aware of, which include:

- Virtual address- combines primary and secondary storage to provide an address space that is larger than physically exists.
- Base address- this is the address used as the origin in the calculation of other addresses.
- Absolute address- this is the address that identifies a location without the use of the base address or being a base address itself.

Firmware

Firmware is software that has been programmed onto read-only memory (ROM). Firmware is best described as a combination of software and hardware. ROMs, PROMs and EPROMs that have data or programs recorded on them are firmware.

Software

There are four main components to software operating systems: process management, input/output device management, memory management and file management.

Secured Computing: A CISSP Study Guide, Copyright 2001

Machine types

A <u>Multi-tasking system</u> is one that is capable of running two or more tasks in a parallel performance. Many systems give the appearance of multi-tasking because of the small amount of real time that the process is actually running in the CPU.

A <u>Multi-programming systems</u> – allows for the interleaved execution of two or more programs on a processor.

<u>Multi-processing</u> – simultaneous execution of two or more programs by a processor. This can also be done through parallel processing of a single program by two or more processors in a multi-processor system.

<u>Multi-processor</u> – A Computer that has two or more processors that all have common access to main storage.

Single State vs. Multi State Machines

A Single state machine is capable of only processing one security level at one time. A multi-state machine can process 2 or more security levels at any given time, without the risk of corrupting one or more of those levels.

OSI Seven Layer Model

Refer to Domain 2 (Chapter Two).

Protection mechanisms

In the principle of least privilege involves each process only having access to the minimum information, memory, peripherals that it requires access to.

Separation of duties is the term applied to people. Separation of privilege is the term used to indicate that two or more mechanisms must agree to unlock a process, data or system component. In this way, there must be agreement between two system processes to gain access.

Accountability is being able to hold a specific person, individual or user responsible for their actions. To hold a person accountable, it must be possible to uniquely and effectively identify and authenticate them.
The concept of least privilege means that a process or program only allows enough privilege than what it really needs in order to perform its functions.

System Security techniques

There are three main techniques that can be used for system security. These access controls fall under preventive, corrective and detective controls.

Preventive Controls

Preventive controls are meant to minimize the occurrence of unauthorized use in a system. This would include the use of passwords, dial back modems, least privilege, systems development life cycle (SDLC), access rights and permissions and security rules to name only a few.

Corrective Controls

Corrective controls can help to provide information, procedures and instructions for correcting irregularities that have been detected. Examples include backup of data, incident handling, contingency planning and audit trails.

Detective Controls

Detective controls are meant for detecting an error or possible unauthorized use. These include both automated and manual tools and techniques. Some examples of detective controls are audit trails, checksums, surveillance and virus scanners.

Principles of Common Security Models, Architectures, and Evaluation Criteria

Open Systems and Closed Systems

Closed systems are of a proprietary nature. They use specific operating systems and hardware to perform the task, and generally lack standard

Secured Computing: A CISSP Study Guide, Copyright 2001

interfaces to allow connection to other systems. The user is generally limited in the applications and programming languages available.

An open system on the other hand, is based upon accepted standards and employs standard interfaces to allow connections between different systems. It promotes interoperability and allows the user to have full access to the total system capability.

Bell-LaPadula Confidentiality Model

As discussed in Domain One the Bell-LaPadula (BLP) model is a confidentiality-based model for information security (See figure 6.1). It is an abstract model that has been the basis for some implementations, most notably the Department of Defense (DoD) Orange Book. The model defines the notion of a secure state, with a specific transition function that moves the system from one security state to another. The model defines a fundamental mode of access with regard to read and write, and how subjects are given access to objects.

The secure state is where only permitted access modes, subject to object are available, in accordance with a set security policy. In this state, there is the notion of preserving security. This means that if the system is in a secure state, then the application of new rules will move the system to another secure state. This is important, as the system will move from one secure state to another.

The BLP model identifies access to an object based upon the clearance level associated with both the subject and the object, and then only for read-only, read-write or write-only access. The model bases access upon two main properties. The simple security property, or secure state property, is for read access. It states that an object cannot read material that is classified higher than the subject. This is called "no read up". The second property is called the *star property or *-property* and relates to write access. The subject can only write information to an object that is at the same or higher classification. This is called "no write down" or the confinement property. In this way, a subject can be prevented from copying information from one classification to a lower classification.

Secured Computing: A CISSP Study Guide, Copyright 2001

Bell-LaPadula Confidentiality Model SECRECY: Read Down and Write Up			
"SECRECY"	Simple Security READ Access	Star Property WRITE Access	Strong Star Property READ/WRITE Access
HIGHER	Prohibited Reading secrets	Okay WRITE UP	Prohibited
SAME	Okay	Okay	Okay
LOWER	Okay READ DOWN	Prohibited Divulging secrets	Prohibited

Figure 6.1 - Bell-Lapadula

While this is a good thing, it is also very restrictive. There is no discernment made of the entire object or some portion of it. Neither is it possible in the model itself to change the classification (read as downgrade) of an object.

The BLP model is a discretionary security model as the subject defines what the particular mode of access is for a given object.

Biba Integrity Model

Biba was the first attempt at an integrity model (See figure 6.2). Integrity models generally are different than the confidentiality models. Biba has not been used much as it does not directly relate to a real world security policy. The Biba model is based upon a hierarchical lattice of integrity levels. The elements of which are a set off subjects and a set of passive, information repository objects. The purpose of the Biba model is to address the first goal of integrity, which is to prevent unauthorized users from making modifications to the information.

The Biba model is the mathematical dual of BLP. Just as reading a lower level may result in the loss of confidentiality for the information, reading a lower level in the integrity model may result in the integrity of the higher level being reduced.

Like the BLP model, Biba makes use of the ss-property and the *-property, and adds a third one. The ss-property states that a subject cannot access/observe/read an object of a lesser integrity. The *-property states that a subject cannot modify/write-to an object with a higher integrity. The third property is the invocation property. This property states that a subject cannot send messages (i.e. logical requests for service) to an object of a higher integrity.

Biba Integrity Model

Biba			
Reverse of Bell-LaPadula			
ACCURACY: Read Up and Write Down			
"ACCURACY"	Simple Integrity READ Access	Integrity *-Property WRITE Access	Invocation Property SERVICE Request
HIGHER	Okay READ UP	Prohibited You contaminate it	Prohibited
SAME	Okay	Okay	Okay
LOWER	Prohibited Get contaminated	Okay WRITE DOWN	Okay

Figure 6.2 - Biba Model

Clark-Wilson Integrity Model

Unlike Biba, the Clark-Wilson model addresses all three integrity goals:

- Preventing unauthorized users from making modifications
- Maintaining internal and external consistency
- Preventing authorized users from making improper modifications.

The Clark-Wilson model is designed to rely upon a well-formed transaction, which is a transaction that has been ordered and controlled enough as to be able to keep the internal and external consistency requirements.

Noninterference, State Machine, Access Matrix, Information Flow and Lattice Models

The _Non-Interference Model_ is based upon a system where the commands that are being executed by one set of users have no effect on what a second set of users is observing.

Secured Computing: A CISSP Study Guide, Copyright 2001

The *State Machine Model* is an abstract mathematical model that uses state variables to represent the system state at any given time. The transition function defines how the system moves from state to state using these variables. BLP is based upon the state machine model.

The *Access Matrix model* is a simple and intuitive model that assigns rights to subjects and objects. This model is also based upon the state machine model. This model identifies the access modes (read, write, etc) for each object that a subject can access. For each subject, there is one row in the matrix that defines the access modes for each object.

The *Information Flow model* is a variation of the access control model, in that it is based upon information flow and not access controls. This model makes it easier to look for cover channels and is often implemented in a lattice format.

Dorothy Denning developed the lattice access control model. This mathematical structure of a lattice allows it to easily represent the different security levels. Every pair of elements has a greatest lower bound and a lowest upper bound. Every resource is also associated with one or more classes within the matrix. The classes are stemmed from the military designations. A subject that is in the same or higher class can use objects that are in a particular class.

Trusted System

A trusted system is defined as a system that by virtue of having undergone sufficient benchmark testing and validation, can be expected to meet the user's requirements for reliability, security and operational effectiveness with specific performance characteristics.

NSA/NCSC Rainbow Series

The term "Rainbow Series" comes from the fact that each book is a different color. The main book (upon which all other expound) is the Orange Book. It is important to know what the different rainbow series books define and discuss. They are an excellent resource for security management:

NCSC-TG-003 [Orange Book]
A Guide to Understanding Discretionary Access Control in Trusted Systems

NCSC-TG-001 [Tan Book]
A Guide to Understanding Audit in Trusted Systems

NCSC-TG-002 [Bright Blue Book]
Trusted Product Evaluation - A Guide for Vendors

NCSC-TG-004 [Aqua Book]
Glossary of Computer Security Terms

NCSC-TG-005 [Red Book]
Trusted Network Interpretation [Version 1 7/31/87]

NCSC-TG-015 [Brown Book]
A Guide to Understanding Trusted Facility Management

NCSC-TG-017 [Light Blue Book]
A Guide to Understanding Identification and Authentication in Trusted Systems

NCSC-TG-019 [Blue Book]
Trusted Product Evaluation Questionnaire

NCSC-TG-021 [Lavender/Purple Book]
Trusted Database Management System Interpretation

NCSC-TG-022 [Yellow Book]
A Guide to Understanding Trusted Recovery

NCSC-TG-027 [Turquoise Book]
A Guide to Understanding Information System Security Officer Responsibilities for Automated Information Systems

NCSC-TG-028 [Violet Book]
Assessing Controlled Access Protection

NCSC-TG-029 [Blue Book]
Introduction to Certification and Accreditation

NCSC-TG-030 [Light Pink Book]
A Guide to Understanding Covert Channel Analysis of Trusted Systems

Information System Evaluation Standards

There are three major criteria efforts, the TCSEC, ITSEC, and the common criteria effort.

The TCSEC, or Trusted Computers System Evaluation Criteria were written to establish a metric for trust, identify built-in security features, and specify security requirements.

The ITSEC, or Information Technology Security Evaluation Criteria, were designed to harmonize international security criteria, and were built on experience that had been accumulated over time. It was an international effort driven primarily by the European Community.

The "Common Criteria" was based upon the work derived from both the TCSEC and ITSEC efforts. It was intended to form the framework for specifying new security requirements and to enhance existing development and evaluation criteria while preserving their fundamental principles.

TCSEC

The TCSEC identified that there are level of security within the criteria. These levels established how much of the security was implemented by the system (DAC vs. MAC), defined object labels (a requirement for MAC), subject identification and protected audit information. It also defined a mechanism to make sure that the requirements were enforced by the system and how it must be protected from tampering.

- An object is defined as something that is being accessed. For example, an object could be a file, a directory, a device or a process.

- A subject is something that is accessing an object. For example, a user, or a process can be a subject.

- Labels are used to identify the classification/categorization that is attached to an object or subject.

The TCSEC has four major areas of classification for systems (See figure 6.4).

Finally, it is important to remember that TCSEC was focused on confidentiality issues.

ITSEC

Developed by Germany, France, the Netherlands and Britain in 1991, ITSEC was to bring government and commercial requirements into one document. Unlike TCSEC, ITSEC was focused on providing more than confidentiality in the model. It also more clearly separated the functionality required, from the level of assurance that the system should be evaluated for.

For functionality, there are for three levels of ITSEC security features:

- Security objectives
- Security enforcing functions
- Security mechanisms

These corresponding roughly to policies, services and mechanisms. Assurance has two levels:

Correctness - deals with the correctness of the implementation, development process, documentation and operational procedures.

Effectiveness of the TOE (Target of Evaluation) has 6 elements to consider:

1. Are the security functions provided suitable to counter the threats?

2. Do the individual functions and mechanisms work together to provide an effective whole?

3. How well can the security mechanisms survive a direct attack?

4. Will it be possible in practice to exploit any design or implementations weaknesses found during evaluation?

5. Will it be possible in practice to exploit operational vulnerabilities found during evaluation?

6. How easy to use are the security functions?

Secured Computing: A CISSP Study Guide, Copyright 2001

Minimal	D	No Security Features
Discretionary Protection	C1 – Discretionary Security C2 – Controlled Access Protection	Identification and Authentication Discretionary Access Controls Object Reuse Audit Security Testing System Architecture (process isolation)
Mandatory Protection	B1 – Labeled Security Protection B2 - Structured Protection B3 – Security Domains	Labels Mandatory Access Controls Design Specification and Verification Covert Channel Analysis Trusted Facility Management Configuration Management Security Testing (penetration testing) System Architecture (software engineering) Trusted Recovery
Verified Protection	A1 – Verified Design	Design Specification and Verification (formal verification) Trusted Distribution Covert Channel Analysis (formal covert channel analysis)

Figure 6.4 - TCSEC Classifications

While the TCSEC is focused on confidentiality, ITSEC brings integrity and availability into the picture. There are seven assurance classes from E0 to E6 (See figure 6.5).

The ITSEC, or Information Technology Security Evaluation Criteria, was designed to harmonize international security criteria, and were built on experience that had been accumulated over time. It was an international effort driven primarily by the European Community.

Common Criteria Effort

The Common Criteria (CC) for Information Technology (IT) Security Evaluation is a standard for evaluating security features of computer products and systems and to resolve the differences among the TCSEC, ITSEC and Canadian CTCPEC and replace them.

Assurance Rating	Explanation
E0	Inadequate assurance. (It fails to meet level E1).
E1	Informal description of Target of Evaluation's (TOE) architectural design. TOE satisfies functional testing.
E2	E1+ informal description of detailed design. The testing evidence has been evaluated. There is configuration control and an approved distribution procedure.
E3	E2+ source code and/or drawings have been evaluated. The testing evidence of security mechanisms has been evaluated.
E4	E3+ a formal model of security policy; semiformal specification of security enforcing functions, architectural and detailed design.
E5	E4 + close correspondence between detailed design and source code/drawings
E6	E5+ formal specification of security enforcing functions and architectural design; consistency with formal security policy model.

Figure 6.5 - ITSEC Classifications

There are three Parts of the CC:

> **Part 1** introduces the CC. It defines general concepts and principles of IT security evaluation and presents a general model of evaluation.
>
> **Part 2** contains a catalog of well defined and understood security functional requirements that are intended to be used as a standard way of expressing the security requirements for IT products and systems. The catalog is organized into classes, families, and components.
>
> **Part 3** contains a catalog that establishes a set of assurance components that can be used as a standard way of expressing the assurance requirements for IT products and systems.

The CC is used in two general ways:

- As a standardized way to describe security requirements for IT products and systems; and
- As a sound technical basis for evaluating the security features of these products and systems.

Trusted Computing Base (TCB)

The Trusted Computing Base is considered to be the totality of protection mechanisms within a computer system, including hardware, firmware, and software, in which the combination of these are responsible for enforcing a security policy. A TCB consists of one or more components that together enforce a unified security policy over a product or system. The ability of a Trusted Computing Base to correctly enforce a security policy depends solely on the mechanisms within the TCB and on the correct input by system administrative personnel of parameters (e.g. a user's clearance) related to the security policy.

Objects and Subjects

Objects are a passive entity that contain or receive information. Having access to an object implies that you have access to the information it contains.

Subjects are active entities that cause information to flow among objects or changes in systems state.

Tokens, Capabilities and Labels

Token based authentication increases security. It requires a user to carry a physical token that the system recognizes as belonging to an authorized user. These tokens contain and integrated circuit that can store information. Token based systems help to reduce the threat of password guessing.

A capability is the representation of an objects address and a set of authorized types of access to that object. Implementation of these capabilities is through a capability list, similar to an access list, that lists a subjects access types for all objects.

Security labels are a designation assigned for a particular resource, like classifications. They are used for access controls, protective measures and indicated how the handling of that information should be handled. Unlike access controls and permission bits, security labels cannot ordinarily be changed.

Common Flaws in Security Architecture

Time of Check vs. Time of Use (TOCTOU)

TOCTOU is Time of Check to Time of Use. This is a class of asynchronous attacks that deal with timing differences. The value of the parameters is changed after they have been checked, but before they are used. This is very difficult to do, and should be prevented by applying task sequencing rules combined with encryption. An example would be if a print job for one user were exchanged with a print job for another user.

Fault Tolerance

A failure occurs when a module, component or system fails to operate as expected. Fault tolerance is the ability to continue operating in the event of a failure. The system should detect that a failure has occurred, report the failure and attempt to recover from it.

Secured Computing: A CISSP Study Guide, Copyright 2001

Covert Channels

A channel is the transfer path within a system for information. It is the means by which the path is connected. A covert channel is a communications channel that allows two cooperating processes to transfer information in a manner that violates the security policy, but not the access control.

A covert process involves the direct or indirect writing of a storage location by one process and the direct and indirect reading of the storage location by another process. This is limited to a finite resource that is shared by the two subjects.

The covert timing channel is where one process signals information to another by modulating its own use of systems resources in such a way that this manipulation affects the real response time observed by the second process.

Initialization and Failure Rates

Initialization is the process of clearing computer storage areas, addresses or memory in the beginning of a program or routine. It is best to initialize variables before their use.

Input and Parameter Checking

You need to check the program for validity, and input parameter checking. Checking for both input and output may be redundant.

Maintenance hooks and privileged programs

Maintenance hooks are just specialized instructions that allow for maintenance. Usually they allow entry into code at unusual points or with out the usual checks, so they are a serious computer risk if not taken out. Basically they are specialized back doors.

Privileged programs are programs that if not checked can cause damage to computer files. An example is IBM's Super Zap, which if left unchecked could destroy files.

Secured Computing: A CISSP Study Guide, Copyright 2001

Programming- techniques, compilers, API, library issues

There are many good programming techniques that help keep programs secure. Following are some you should know:

Controlled compiled libraries

This is the use of regression testing to verify compliance of the library functions with standard and expected behaviors.

Application Program Interface (API)

These are subroutines, calls and software interrupts which allow high-level programs make use of the lower level services and functions of another application, OS or driver.

Descriptive Identifier Names

This is using the appropriate names in code that will help to reduce the need for comments. This helps the code to avoid out dated comments.

Comments

Comments are best kept to a minimum in your code. Comment should identify the major data structures, purpose and input and outputs.

Single entry/exit points in subroutines

Each subprogram should only have one entry and exit point.

Electromagnetic Radiation

In 1974 the Industrial TEMPEST program was established. It was designed to specify standards for allowable levels on emissions for electronic devices, outline criteria for testing equipment and certify equipment that successfully meets the TEMPEST standard.

Tempest is based on the fact that electronic equipment transmits electromagnetic emanations through the air and through conductors. These emanations can be unique for different devices and the data on them interpreted.

Secured Computing: A CISSP Study Guide, Copyright 2001

Test Your Knowledge

1. _____ are subroutines, calls and software interrupts which allow high-level programs make use of the lower level services and functions of another application, OS or driver?
   - A. API
   - B. CGI
   - C. STD
   - D. HTML

2. _____ was designed to specify standards for allowable levels on emissions for electronic devices?
   - A. EMI
   - B. TEMPEST
   - C. EFI program
   - D. Standard Emanations Act

3. _____ are specialized instructions that allow for maintenance of the software by developers?
   - A. Back door
   - B. Maintenance hooks
   - C. Canon hook
   - D. Password

4. _____ is a class of asynchronous attacks that deal with timing differences?
   - A. TOCTOU
   - B. Snake attack
   - C. Maintenance hook
   - D. Sealed cipher attack

5. It is best to initialize variables after their use? T/F
   - A. True
   - B. False

6. Writing to storage by one process and reading by another of a lower security level is _____.
   - A. Covert storage channel
   - B. Strong * property
   - C. Covert timing
   - D. Lattice based access restriction

Secured Computing: A CISSP Study Guide, Copyright 2001

7. Match the following:
   - A. Bell-LaPadula
   - B. Biba
   - C. Clark & Wilson

   1. *-property A subject can   modify an object of a higher integrity level
   2. Invocation property
   3. Relies upon the well formed transaction
   4. Addresses all three integrity   goals

8. An abstract math model that state variables represent system state?
   - A. Non-interference model
   - B. State Matrix model
   - C. Access Matrix model
   - D. State Machine model

9. The totality of protection mechanisms within a computer system -including hardware, firmware, and software, describes?
   - A. TCBY
   - B. Trusted Computer Base
   - C. System Security
   - D. Secure State

10. _____is a simple and intuitive model that assigns rights to subjects and objects. This model is also based upon the state machine model?
   - A. Access Matrix model
   - B. Lattice model
   - C. State Machine Model
   - D. Biba Model

Answers: 1.A, 2.B, 3.B, 4.A, 5.F, 6.A, 7.A-1, B-2, C-3&4, 8.D, 9.B, 10.B

Secured Computing: A CISSP Study Guide, Copyright 2001

<u>Notes</u>

References

Information in this chapter was referenced from the following sources:

1. Computer Security Handbook, Third edition, Arthur E, Hutt et al. 1995 John Wiley & Sons Inc.

2. *Information Security Management Handbook, 4th edition, Harold F. Tipton, et al. 2000, Auerbach Publications.*

3. *RFC 2828*

4. *RFC 2196 Site Security Handbook, RFC 2196, author B. Fraser, 1997*

5. *Security in Computing, Second edition, Charles P. Pfleeger, 1997 Prentice Hall*

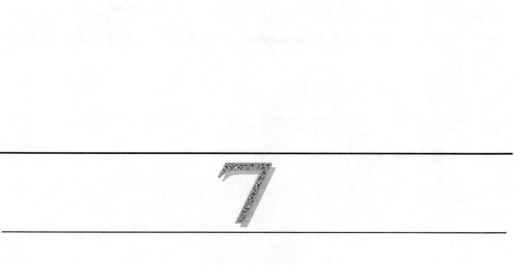

Domain 7

Operations Security

Operations Security

Operations security includes many areas. Many of these were discussed in other domains. We will attempt to only go over new points not discussed earlier in other domains.

Operations security is used to identify the controls over hardware, media, and the operators with access privileges to any of these resources. Audit and monitoring is the mechanisms, tool and facilities that permit the identification of security events and subsequent actions to identify the key elements and report the pertinent information to the appropriate individual, group, or process.

Definitions

Access Control Mechanisms are security safeguards designed to detect and prevent unauthorized access, and to permit authorized access in. Operations security uses access control mechanisms such as hardware and software, and procedures for access authorization.

Configuration management is the management of security features and assurances through control of changes made to a system's hardware, software, firmware, documentation, and test documentation throughout the development and operational life of a system. They help to protect against improper modification.

Computer facility is a physical structure that houses the data processing operations. The data processing area should be controlled by physical access controls to limit access to only those who are authorized; this is referred to as a closed shop.

Contingency Management establishes actions to be taken before, during, and after a threatening incident. This includes documented and tested procedures, ensures availability of critical systems and maintains the continuity of operations.

Contingency plan is the documented actions for emergency response, backup operations, and post-disaster recovery, maintained by an activity as a part of its security program that will ensure the availability of critical resources and facilitate the continuity of operations in an emergency situation. Also referred to as a "disaster plan" or "emergency plan."

Continuity of operations is the maintenance of essential data processing services after a major failure in a data center. Natural disasters or man made deliberate actions could cause these.

Security perimeter is a boundary where security controls protect assets. This usually will include a security kernel, hardware, trusted code and secure communication channels.

System High Security Mode is the mode of operation in which system hardware/software is only trusted to provide need-to-know protection between users. It is when all systems and peripherals are protected for the highest level of security of material in a system.

Administrative Management

Administrative management includes the operational procedures, data protection, physical facility protection and supplemental controls to establish acceptable levels of protection for these things.

Separation of Duties and Job Rotation

The object of separation of duties is to make sure no single individual has control over one single activity, procedure or control. The rotation of duties is used to interrupt opportunity to create collusion to subvert operation for fraudulent purposes and to cross train individuals.

Least Privilege

Least privilege is the principle that you allow users to only have enough access and privilege to do there job duties. This is considered a "need to know" type of access.

Operator and System Administrator Privileges

Operators are those who operate a computer and are what supports system operation from the operators console (keyboard). The Operators are responsible for the initial program loads, system backups, loading paper to printers, reset dates and times, and reassign ports.

Operators can potentially make unintended mistakes such as turning off logging, allow the storage space to fill up and lose the logging storage space, accidentally make changes to production data or not retain logs long enough.

Network Administrator processes include the startup and shutdown of servers, reset passwords, look at system logs, set file permissions, the boot sequence and what applications are installed.

Computer Operations Concepts

Recovery Procedures
Recovery procedures are actions to restore Data Processing capability after an outage or disruption. There are several recovery procedures that can be followed:

- Check Security Critical Files
- Get running in single-user mode
- Recover all files systems active at time of failure
- Restore missing/damaged files and database from most recent backup
- Reboot System

An operating systems response to failure can be classified into three general categories:

- System reboot
- Emergency system restart
- System cold start

Potential Abuses

There are always potential abuses that operations security needs to be aware of, these would include:

- Fraud- this could be a strange transaction that is rejected and the perpetrator handles those rejects.

Secured Computing: A CISSP Study Guide, Copyright 2001

- Interference with Operations- such as a Denial of service (DoS) attack.
- Conversion to personal use
- Unauthorized access and disclosure
- Audit trail/System log corruption

Input/Output Controls

Input Controls include the data counted, online transactions that are time stamped and recorded, data entered and data edited.

Output Controls are totals compared with input counts, ensure output reaches the proper people, restrict access to printed output storage areas, print heading and trailing banners with recipients names and locations, require signed receipt before releasing sensitive output and print "No output" with banners when report is empty.

Hardware Controls

Hardware controls are a very important part of operations security. Some hardware issues would include:

- Operator terminals
- Servers/Routers rooms
- Modem/Circuits rooms
- Magnetic media rooms/Cabinets

Change Control Management

Change control management authorizes changes to production systems, new applications; modify existing applications and removes old applications. It uses input from problem management to initiate changes. Security function can block a change or adversely affect security of applications/data.

Threats and Countermeasures to Media Library

The following are types of threats to media libraries:

- Errors and omissions: can be alleviated by a sound training and awareness program.

Secured Computing: A CISSP Study Guide, Copyright 2001

- Fraud and theft
- Employee sabotage
- Loss of physical and infrastructure support
- Malicious Hackers/Crackers
- Industrial espionage
- Malicious Code
- Foreign Government espionage

Trusted Recovery Process

Before allowing user access

- Reboot system
- Get running in single user mode
- Recover all file systems active at time of failure
- Restore missing/damaged files and databases from most recent backup
- Check security critical files

Protected resources are what operations security is trying to protect. These resources include:

- People
- Passwords and password files
- Source code
- Operating system software equipment
- Sensitive files
- Logs and audit trails

Secured Computing: A CISSP Study Guide, Copyright 2001

Test Your Knowledge

1. A data processing area using physical access controls to limit access to authorized personnel is called _____?
   A. Closed area
   B. Closed shop
   C. Security perimeter
   D. Secured facility

2. _____describes when systems and all peripherals are protected in accordance with requirements for highest security levels of material in system?
   A. High operation mode
   B. System high mode
   C. Super high mode
   D. Elevated high mode

3. What are the two most crucial ways in operations security to stop potential and current abuse?
   A. Separation of duties
   B. Audit everything that happens
   C. System high mode
   D. Log corruption
   E. Intrusion detection

4. Establishing a baseline violation count to ignore normal user error describes what?
   A. A Baseline
   B. A Profiling
   C. A Clipping level
   D. A Clipper Chip

5. Establishing actions to take before, during and after a threatening incident describes _____?
   A. Contingency management
   B. CPL
   C. Operations continuity
   D. Disaster recovery planning

Secured Computing: A CISSP Study Guide, Copyright 2001

6. What state should a program be in to execute privileged hardware instructions?
   A. Trusted
   B. Super user
   C. Supervisor
   D. Execute

7. Controlling modifications to system hardware, firmware and software is referred to as?
   A. Access control mechanisms
   B. Control settings
   C. Configuration system
   D. Configuration Management

8. Which of these does NOT describe risk analysis?
   A. Threat
   B. Repudiation
   C. Vulnerability
   D. Asset

9. Looking at the types of violations, where it is occurring and clipping levels describes?
   A. Operator privileges
   B. Violation analysis
   C. Anomaly analysis
   D. Auditing analysis

10. Having online transactions recorded and time stamped is what kind of control?
    A. Output control
    B. Transaction control
    C. Input control
    D. Communications control

11. _____ protects against design reliability threats?
    A. Tape backups
    B. Fault tolerance
    C. Inventory controls
    D. Check sum

Secured Computing: A CISSP Study Guide, Copyright 2001

12. Which of these is NOT a trusted recovery procedure?
    A. Reboot the system
    B. Restore missing/damaged files from most recent backup
    C. Check security-critical files
    D. Recover all file systems active at the time of failure
    E. All of the above
    F. None of the above
    G. Only A, B and C

13. An electrical device that can reduce magnetic flux density to zero on magnetic storage media is called?
    A. Disk striping
    B. Magnetic remanance
    C. Disk Wipe
    D. A deguasser

Answers: 1.B, 2.B, 3.A, B, 4.C, 5.A, 6.A, 7.A, 8.B, 9.B, 10.A, 11.C, 12.F, 13.D

References

Information in this chapter was referenced from the following sources:

1. Computer Security Handbook, Third edition, Arthur E, Hutt et al. 1995 John Wiley & Sons Inc.

2. *Information Security Management Handbook, 4th edition, Harold F. Tipton, et al. 2000, Auerbach Publications.*

3. *RFC 2828*

4. *RFC 2196 Site Security Handbook, RFC 2196, author B. Fraser, 1997*

Notes

Domain 8

Business Continuity Planning & Disaster Recovery

Business Continuity Planning & Disaster Recovery

Business Continuity Planning (BCP) and Disaster Recovery Planning (DRP) address the preservation of business when faced with a major disruption. BCP and DRP involve the preparation, testing and updating of specific actions to protect critical processes from the effect of major system and network failures.

The difference between BCP and DRP is as follows: If an event is major and very destructive the challenge would be to recover from that disaster and restore critical functions, have an emergency response plan and a computer back up plan, this is called disaster recovery. If the event is not major and is less destructive then the main idea is to continue support for the critical business functions to keep of the business operating and facilitates rapid recovery, this is referred to as business continuity planning.

A disaster can be defined as an unplanned catastrophic event that causes harm or damage or any event that can cause a business to lose the use of critical processes for a period of time. Remember that acts of God are not always the greatest disasters. Theft, errors, omissions, disgruntled employees and vandals are a very real threat.

Definitions

Recovery Planning is defined as the advance planning and preparation necessary to minimize loss and ensure continuity of the critical business functions of an organization.

Disaster Recovery Plan is defined as a comprehensive statement of consistent actions to be taken before, during and after a disaster.

Structured Walk-Through Test occurs when the functional representatives meet to review the plan in detail. This involves a thorough look at each of the plan steps, and the procedures that are invoked at that point in the plan. This ensures that the actual planned activities are accurately described in the plan.

Checklist test is a method of testing the plan by distributing copies to each of the functional areas. Each area reviews the plan and checks off

Secured Computing: A CISSP Study Guide, Copyright 2001

the points that are listed. This process ensures that the plan addresses all concerns and activities.

Simulation Test is where all operational and support functions meet to practice execution of the plan based on a scenario that is played out to test the reaction of all functions to various situations. Only those materials and information available in a real disaster are allowed to be used during the simulation, and the simulation continues up to the point of actual relocation to the alternate site and shipment of replacement equipment.

Parallel Test is essentially an operational test. In this test, the critical systems are placed into operation at the alternative site to see if things run as expected. The results can be compared with the real operational output and differences noted.

Full Interruption Test is when full normal operations are completely shut down, and the processing is conducted at the alternate site using the materials that are available in the offsite storage location and personnel that are assigned to the recovery teams.

Critical System is any system that has to run in order for the business to stay in business.

Business Continuity Planning

The primary objective of a Business Continuity Planning (BCP) is to enable an organization to survive a disaster and to reestablish normal business operations. In order to survive, the organization must assure that critical operations can resume normal processing within a reasonable time frame. Therefore, the goals of the Business Resumption Plan should be to:

- Identify weaknesses and implement a disaster prevention program;
- Minimize the duration of a serious disruption to business operations;
- Facilitate effective co-ordination of recovery tasks; and
- Reduce the complexity of the recovery effort.

Business Continuity Planning (BCP) depends upon a variety of technology including centralized and decentralized computing systems, specific support systems and communications systems. Some of these elements of Contingency Planning are:

- Contingency Planning Goals
- A statement of importance, priorities and organizational responsibility
- A statement of urgency and timing
- Vital Records Program -Ensuring the identification and protection of the organization's vital records.
- Emergency Response Procedures/Guidelines -This represents the set or prepared actions that are meant to cope initially with disruption.

For effective BCP to take place the following people must be involved:

- **Executive Management** -Executive management must provide consistent support throughout the planning process and must put the final approval on the business continuity plan.
- **Senior Functional Management -**It is the responsibility of these groups to identify and prioritize the mission-critical systems within the organization.
- **Central BCP Program Committee -**This committee is composed of coordinators representing all functional units within the organization that are involved in planning, implementing and monitoring BCP activities. This team should include an Information Security Task Force that is a group of people who have a major interest in Information Security for the organization. It should also include the corporate auditors due to legal and regulatory issues associated with BCP.

It is very important to understand that executives can be held criminally liable under many regulatory acts for not exercising due care and having the appropriate BCP and DRP plans. Some of the pieces of U.S. legislation and regulatory agencies that require organizations to take appropriate care in safeguarding their information include:

- Federal Financial Institution Examination Council
- Foreign Corrupt Practices Act of 1977
- Auditing Standards including SAS 30 and FCPA Compliance

Secured Computing: A CISSP Study Guide, Copyright 2001

- Defense Security Service
- Standards of Due Care
- Legal Precedence

Why plan?

BCP planning is very important when it comes to business. Just because you do not have a plan does not mean something will not happen. Many companies get faced with a disaster and pay dearly because they are not prepared. Also many legal and regulatory requirements give you no choice. US financial institutions are regulated at the federal level and are required to be prepared for events.

Disaster Recovery Planning

A disaster is defined as an interruption affecting a user operation significantly. Disaster Recovery Planning (DRP) is documents containing procedures for emergencies and a process to identify the critical computing resources in an organization.

Actions that must be taken in Disaster Recovery Planning (DRP) include but are not limited to recovering the data center, recovery of the business operations that depend upon computers, recovery of the business processes, and recovery of the business location

Preparing a full-scale disaster recovery plan can take many years. The problem is that you may not see any cost benefit from the plan, but if a disaster does happen it is well worth the money spent. The main objectives of Disaster Recovery Planning (DRP) are:

- To protect the organization if all or part off the computer services become unavailable;
- To provide a sense of security;
- To minimize the risk of delays to the business;
- To guarantee the reliability of standby systems;
- To provide a standard for testing the plan; and,
- To minimize the decision making during a disaster.

Secured Computing: A CISSP Study Guide, Copyright 2001

Recovery Planning Development

Recovery planning can be a complex process; it therefore requires redirection of valuable technical staff and information processing resources as well as the appropriate funding. In order to minimize the impact such an undertaking would have on scarce resources, the project for the development and implementation of disaster recovery and business resumption plans should be part of the organization's normal planning activities.

The proposed project methodology consists of eight separate phases, as described below.

Step 1 - Pre-Planning Activities/Project Initiation

Step 1 is used to obtain an understanding of the existing and projected computing environment of the organization.

Step 2 - Vulnerability Assessment and Definition of Requirements

Security and control within an organization is a continuing concern. It is preferable, from an economic and business strategy perspective, to concentrate on activities that have the effect of reducing the possibility of disaster occurrence, rather than concentrating primarily on minimizing impact of an actual disaster. This phase addresses measures to reduce the probability of occurrence.

Step 3 - Business Impact Assessment (BIA)

The Business Impact Assessment (BIA) Report identifies critical service functions and the timeframes in which they must be recovered after interruption. The BIA Report should then be used as a basis for identifying systems and resources required to support the critical services provided by information processing and other services and facilities.

Step 4 - Definition of Requirements

During this step, a profile of recovery requirements is developed. This profile is to be used as a basis for analyzing alternative recovery strategies. Identifying resources required to support critical functions identified in step 3 develop the profile. This profile should include hardware, software, documentation, outside support, facilities and personnel for each business unit. Recovery Strategies will be based on short term, intermediate term and long-term outages.

Step 5 - Plan Development

During this phase, recovery plans components are defined and plans are documented. This phase also includes the implementation of changes to user procedures, upgrading of existing data processing operating procedures required to support selected recovery strategies and alternatives, vendor contract negotiations (with suppliers of recovery services) and the definition of Recovery Teams, their roles and responsibilities. Recovery standards are also being developed during this phase.

Step 6 - Testing/Exercising Program

The plan Testing/Exercising Program is developed during this phase. Testing/exercising goals are established and alternative testing strategies are evaluated. Testing strategies tailored to the environment should be selected and an on-going testing program should be established.

Step 7 - Maintenance Program
Maintenance of the plans is critical to the success of an actual recovery. The plans must reflect changes to the environments that are supported by the plans. It is critical that existing change management processes are revised to take recovery plan maintenance into account. In areas where change management does not exist, change management procedures will be recommended and implemented. Many recovery software products take this requirement into account.

Step 8 - Plan Testing and Implementation

Once plans are developed, initial tests of the plans are conducted and any necessary modifications to the plans are made based on an analysis of the test results. The approach taken to test the plans depends, in large part, on the recovery strategies selected to meet the recovery requirements of the organization. As the recovery strategies are defined, specific testing procedures should be developed to ensure that the written plans are comprehensive and accurate.

Secured Computing: A CISSP Study Guide, Copyright 2001

Security Goals and their relationship to BCP and DRP

The Information Security goals are Confidentiality, Integrity and Available (See figure 8.1).

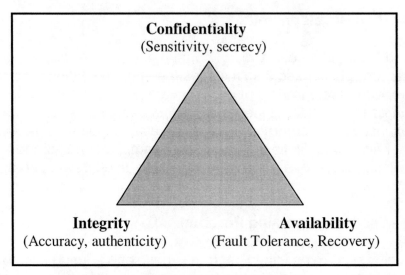

Figure 8.1 - CIA Triad

The intent is to continue to prevent accidental or intentional disclosure, modification destruction and denial. Throughout the planning and recovery process, the intent is to minimize the disaster impact as much as possible on these goals.

Dealing with Media

Dealing with media is always a sensitive area. The disaster recovery plan must include how the media is to handle the event during the disaster, in order to keep things under control. The Public affairs area of the company or the Chief security officer best handles this. The following are steps that need to be taken when dealing with the media:

- Establish a unified response for the organization
- Maintain a mailing list for larger audiences.
- Report your own bad news.
- Tell the story, quickly, easily and honestly.
- Determine in advance of that the appropriate approval and clearance processes are for the information that is to be conveyed.
- Make sure that the spokesperson is accessible to the media.

Secured Computing: A CISSP Study Guide, Copyright 2001

- Identify emergency press conference sites in advance.
- Record events as the crisis evolves.
- Review and update the crisis communications plans and documents on a regular basis so that information and the plan is relevant to the time frame and situation.
- Consider follow-up communications to allow for fair and impartial reporting of the event.

Organizational Placement of Planner

The organizational planner should be in a position within the organization to balance the needs of the corporation with the individual business units that would be affected. They must be able to review the corporation charter and viewpoint. They must have the knowledge of the business, which enables them to understand how the disaster can affect the corporation. They must have easy access to executive management and have the credibility and ability to influence senior management when there is a decision to be made.

Secured Computing: A CISSP Study Guide, Copyright 2001

Test Your Knowledge

1. The preparation for handling contingencies & disasters as well as the minimizing of disruption is:
   A. BCP
   B. Contingency planning
   C. DRP
   D. Contingency management

2. _____ describes procedure for emergency response, extended back up operations and post recovery?
   A. DRP
   B. BCB
   C. BCP
   D. BLT

3. The advance planning and preparations, which are necessary to minimize loss and ensure business continuity, is referred to as?
   A. Business continuity
   B. Disaster recovery
   C. Recovery Planning
   D. Recovery management

4. A system that has to run for an organization to stay in business is called?
   A. Core system
   B. Central system
   C. Critical system
   D. Mother system

5. True or False executives can be held criminally liable and face civil liability from stockholders for not using a standard of due care and having continuity plans in place?
   A. True
   B. False

6. Over 50% of real life threats in information security are caused by?
   A. Disgruntled employees
   B. Fire, water and electrical
   C. Outside threats
   D. Errors and Omissions

Secured Computing: A CISSP Study Guide, Copyright 2001

7. What is the correct order of recovery planning methodology?
    A. Project initiation, implementation, testing and maintenance, business impact statement, recovery strategy development, recovery plan development
    B. Project initiation, business impact statement, recovery strategy development, recovery plan development and implementation, testing and maintenance.
    C. Project initiation, implementation, testing and maintenance, business impact statement, testing and maintenance
    D. Implementation, testing and maintenance, business impact statement, Project initiation, testing and maintenance

8. Match the following with the proper definition:

    A. Recovery of the data center
       Business resumption planning
    B. Recovery of mainframe dependent operations
       Disaster recovery planning
    C. Recovery of business location and processes
    D. End-user contingency planning

9. Which of the following is NOT an objective of a DRP?
    A. Minimize the risk of delays
    B. Provide a standard for testing the plan
    C. Optimize decision making during a disaster
    D. Guarantee reliability of stand-by systems

10. Which two of the following DO NOT fall under the scope of DRP?
    A. End user contingency planning
    B. Business resumption planning
    C. Middle management level direction
    D. Contingency recovery modules
    E. Regular drills and testing

11. Policy statement, management letter, budget and planning are most crucial when supported by?
    A. Users
    B. Administrators
    C. Senior level executive management
    D. Middle management

12. Which of the following should NOT be done when dealing with media?
    A. Tell story quickly and honestly
    B. Should be by the company first
    C. Avoid accessibility to media during an event
    D. Establish a unified organizational response

13. A standard survey tool, used while identifying critical business units, that gathers input from most knowledgeable people is called _____?
    A. Criticality survey
    B. Vision survey
    C. Critical support survey
    D. Business criteria survey

14. A recovery time frame can best be described as:
    A. How long a critical system is going to take to get back up and running
    B. How long a system can be down for us to stay in business
    C. How long a system can remain up before effecting the business
    D. Loss impact

15. Identify which one of these is NOT a Vulnerability assessment step:
    A. Identify essential business functions
    B. Gather impact data
    C. Identifying the non-essential business applications impacted
    D. analyze and summarize impact

16. What type of site has no equipment, you must bring your own:
    A. Warm site
    B. Cold site
    C. Hot site
    D. Rolling hot site

17. A site that has everything but Mainframes is called;
    A. Warm site
    B. Hot site
    C. Rolling Hot site
    D. Cold site

Secured Computing: A CISSP Study Guide, Copyright 2001

18. Having an agreement with another organization, that uses similar equipment, to use some of their equipment in an emergency is called a:
    A. Mutual systems agreement
    B. Mutual aid agreement
    C. Alternate site agreement
    D. Rolling hot site

19. A subscription service, pertaining to BCP, is best described as:
    A. Commercial service available to provide back up in an emergency
    B. A service that is rendered on a monthly basis
    C. Sells you magazines

20. What type of plan gets the original facility back in operation?
    A. Disaster plan
    B. Hazard reduction plan
    C. Legacy recovery plan
    D. Restoration plan

21. What type of program helps to identify and correct life safety threats?
    A. Life issues plan
    B. Threat program
    C. Hazard reduction program
    D. DRP plan

22. Customized materials that gather quantitative and qualitative impact materials and are prepared for recommendations are called:
    A. Business impact analysis (BIA)
    B. Post Impact analysis (PIA)
    C. Recovery analysis
    D. System analysis

23. Detection, suppression and protection are preventative measures for what?
    A. Water
    B. Fire
    C. Systems
    D. Electrical

24. _____ is an example of environmental equipment:
    A. Power grid
    B. UPS
    C. HVAC
    D. Leaks

25. What testing type reviews a plan in detail, making sure all steps are addressed and accurately described:
    A. Full interpretation test
    B. Structured walk through test
    C. Parallel test
    D. Simulation

26. When the normal operations are shutdown and processing is conducted at an alternative site this is called?
    A. Hot site
    B. Full interpretation test
    C. Parallel test
    D. Structured walk through test

Answers:1.B, 2.A, 3.C, 4.C, 5.A, 6.D, 7.B, 8.A2, B3, C1, 9.C, 10.C, 11.C, 12.C, 13.A, 14.B, 15.C, 16.B, 17.A, 18.B, 19.A, 20.D, 21.C, 22.A, 23B, 24.C, 25.B, 26.B

References

Information in this chapter was referenced from the following sources:

1.Computer Security Handbook, Third edition, Arthur E, Hutt et al. 1995 John Wiley & Sons Inc.
2.Information Security Management Handbook, 4th edition, Harold F. Tipton, et al. 2000, Auerbach Publications.
3.RFC 2828
4.RFC 2196 Site Security Handbook, RFC 2196, author B. Fraser, 1997
5.Security in Computing, Second edition, Charles P. Pfleeger, 1997 Prentice Hall

Notes

Domain 9

Law, Ethics, and Investigation Domain

Law, Ethics, and Investigation Domain

The Law, Investigations, and Ethics domain addresses computer crime laws and regulations; the Investigative measures and techniques which can be used to determine if a crime has been committed and methods to gather evidence if it has; and the ethical constraints which provide a code of conduct for the security professional.

Definitions

Due Care- this is seen as a corporation/individual taking all commonly accepted security practices and applying them.

Criminal Law- Individual Conduct that violates the government laws that are enacted for the protection of the public.

Civil Law - This is also known as tort law. These are wrong doings against an individual or business that results in damage or loss. There is no prison time in civil law, but financial restitution is used to compensate the victim. Compensation typically consists of the actual damages to the victim in the form of: Attorney/legal fees, lost profits, and Investigative costs.

Punitive damages- Compensation in civil law may also consist of punitive damages. These are established by a jury, and are intended to punish an offender for their actions. The law establishes statutory damages that are paid to the victim.

Administrative Law- this is also known as regulatory law and establishes the standards of performance and conduct from government agencies to organizations.

Types of Laws

Trademark

A Trademark is any distinguishing character, name, logo or other symbol that establishes an identity for a product, service or organization.

Secured Computing: A CISSP Study Guide, Copyright 2001

Trademarks can be registered, meaning they have been filed in the appropriate jurisdiction. This prevents others from being able to use that trademark.

Patent

A Patent is an invention, that is documented and explained so that the patent office can verify its originality and to grant a patent. This patent is limited to the development and use of that design to the patent holder only for a specific period of time. The patent holder may then grant a license to others to the design information, typically for a fee.

Copyright

A Copyright allows an author to protect how the idea is expressed. An author does not generally have to file for copyright protection, as the law states that the copyright comes into force as soon as the idea is expressed in a tangible form. Many people will register their copyright through either a federal copyright registry.

Trade Secret

A Trade secret is proprietary information that a company or individual uses and has exclusive legal rights. This means that the company has ownership rights to its exclusive use of the information. A trade secret is specific proprietary information that meets specific criteria under the law. To qualify as a trade secret then, the information must conform to all three of these requirements (according to U.S. law):

- The information MUST be genuine.
- It must provide the owner competitive or economic advantages

The owner must take "reasonable" steps to protect that information.

U.S. LAWS

U.S. Federal Privacy Act of 1974

U.S. Federal Privacy Act of 1974 addressed the fact that there are many technological problems relating to privacy of information using technology.

Comprehensive Crime Control Act of 1984

Comprehensive Crime Control Act of 1984 was a US Federal Act that focused attention on the need to fight computer related crimes.

Medical Computer Crime Act of 1984

The Medical Computer Crime Act of 1984 was a result of the "414 gang" who broke into a New York Hospital's computer. This Act focuses on protecting information that uses computers and telecommunication devices that access medical records.

Computer Fraud and Abuse Act of 1986

The original act was very narrow in defining what was a computer crime. The act covered only
> (1) Classified defense or foreign relations information;
> (2) Records of financial institutions or credit reporting agencies;
> (3) Government computers.

Unauthorized access or access in excess of authorization became a felony on classified information and a misdemeanor for financial information. It also became a misdemeanor to access a government computer with or without authorization should the government's use of the computer be affected.

The amendments in 1986 clarified the law and added three new crimes:
> (1) Where use of a "federal interest computer" furthers an intended fraud;
> (2) Altering, damaging or destroying information in a federal interest computer preventing the use of the computer or information when this causes a loss of $1000 or more or

Secured Computing: A CISSP Study Guide, Copyright 2001

could impair medical treatment. (There was a further amendment to this.)

(3) Trafficking in computer passwords if it affects interstate or foreign commerce or permits unauthorized access to government computers.

Computer Security Act of 1987

The act states that the security and privacy of federal computer systems are in the public interest. It gives to NIST the computer security mission, including the development of standards. The Act requires that each U.S. Federal agency to provide its employees with training in computer security awareness and practice and to set up a security plan for each of its systems.

National Infrastructure Protection Act of 1996

The National Infrastructure Protection Act of 1996 amended the computer fraud and abuse act of 1986. It helped protect all U.S. government computers, referred to computers used in foreign commerce and punishes by felony anyone who causes damage.

Gramm – Leach – Bliley Act

Title V of the Gramm-Leach-Bliley Act, also known as the Financial Services Modernization Act, requires that banks and financial institutions ensure that customer information is protected from cyber criminals, and to provide detailed Security Policies to customers and regulators. This is the first law to mandate security policy in the electronic environment. This act recognizes by law that privacy policies are meaningless without security policies. The guidelines are to help ensure the security and confidentiality of customer records and information, protect against any anticipated threats or hazards to the security or integrity of these records, protect against unauthorized access to or use of these records or information that could result in substantial harm or inconvenience to a customer.

Secured Computing: A CISSP Study Guide, Copyright 2001

State Computer Crime Laws

All states have some computer related crime laws, with the exception of the state of Vermont. These laws vary in approach and definitions. The legislation continues to get more highly developed.

International Computer Crime Related Laws

There are some differences in laws from an international scope. Nations typically have different views regarding the seriousness of computer crime and how to interpret technology and crime issues. This sometimes leads to problems like what is illegal in one country is not illegal in another.

In addition, evidence rules generally differ in various legal systems, which posses other problems in the evidence collection approach. Added to this is the different technical capability of the various law enforcement units and things get more complicated. Finally, some governments may not wish to cooperate and assist each other in international cases. This means that the computer criminal may be "untouchable" by the country where the offence has occurred.

Most countries have some kind of computer related laws that can be enforced.

Canada

The Canadian government has Criminal Code: Section 342.1 section 430 (1.1)-section 326: copyright act: section 42. They also have Bill C-17, 1997. Canadian Laws are punishable up to ten years for unauthorized use/abuse.

European Union

The European Union has set for the European Union Computer Crime Directives that deal with search and seizure, technical surveillance, encryption and international cooperation.

Privacy Laws state that individuals should receive a report stating that there is data about them and it must ask permission if it is to given to a 3rd party. All data must be collected lawfully and only kept for a short period of

Secured Computing: A CISSP Study Guide, Copyright 2001

time and allow the opportunity for the individual to make corrections to that data.

BS 17799

BS 17799 was first published in February 1995 and is a comprehensive set of controls comprising best practices in information security. BS 7799 is intended to serve as a single reference point for identifying a range of controls needed for most situations where information systems are used in industry and commerce, and to be used by large, medium and small organizations. It was significantly revised and improved in May 1999 and became ISO17799 in December 2000. It is organized into ten major sections, each covering a different topic or area:

1. Business Continuity
2. Systems Access Control
3. System Development and Maintenance
4. Physical and Environmental Safety
5. Compliance
6. Personnel Security
7. Security Organization
8. Computer and Network Management
9. Asset Classification
10. Security Policy

Investigations

Evidence

As the evidence is gathered, it must be properly identified and marked so that it can be identified later as a piece of evidence found at the scene. The collection should be recorded in a logbook detailing the particular piece of evidence, who found it, where it was found, when it was found. The location must be specific to provide correlation later in court.

When you come to a computer that is still on the first thing to do is unplug it. If you were to shut it down by its normal processes you would find that the hard drive is written to and could erase, lose or damage some evidence you may find otherwise. You also want to take photographs of the cables wires and surrounding areas. Then make a bit-by-bit copy of the hard rive or other media using forensic software. Once you have the bit copy you can investigate it without any worry that the original evidence will change or be overwritten.

There are four sources of evidence:

- Oral
- Written
- Computer generated
- Visual or audio

The evidence life cycle has five stages:

1. **Collection and Identification**
   If possible mark the piece of evidence with your initials, Date and case number if known.
2. **Analysis** -examination or forensics of the evidence itself.
3. **Storage-** all evidence must be properly handled and prepared for storage. To protect the evidence from being damaged during transportation and storage prior to court. To protect the evidence for its return to the owner.
4. **Prevention** Once the evidence is properly preserved, it should be transported to a storage facility where it can be locked up and guarded until needed for a trial, or its return to its owner.
5. **Transportation-** this has several purposes: During the transportation of the evidence from storage to court, the same care as when it was first collected must be followed.
6. **Presented in Court**
7. **Returned to the Victim**

Hearsay Rule

A legal factor with computer-generated evidence is that it is considered hearsay. Hearsay evidence is that which is not gathered from the personal knowledge of the witness, but through another source. And Evidence is valued by the quality and competence of the source.

All business records are considered hearsay, because there is no way to prove that they in themselves are accurate, reliable and trustworthy in general. However, should the business documents be used regularly in business activity and presented by an individual who is competent in their formation and use, it may be possible to submit business documents as records. To do so, the corresponding witness must

    a) Have custody of the records in question on a regular basis;
    b) Rely on those records in the regular course of business;
    c) Know that they were prepared in the regular conduct of business.

Characteristics of Admissible Evidence

The concept of admissibility is based upon the following:

- Relevancy of evidence – meaning that the evidence must prove or disprove a material fact.
- Reliability of evidence – the evidence and the process to produce the evidence must be proven to be reliable.
- Foundation of admissibility- build trustworthy evidence through witnesses, the identification of the owner of the information, and document how the evidence is collected, and illustrates how errors are prevented and corrected if they occur.
- Legally Permissible- the evidence must have been collected using legal means.
    - Preservation of Evidence- all evidence must be properly handled and prepared for storage. This has several purposes:

    - Protection of the evidence for court
    - To protect the evidence for its return to the owner.
    - Once the evidence is properly preserved, it be locked up and guarded until needed for a trial, or its return to its owner.

Investigative Processes and Techniques

The steps in a computer crime investigation are:

    - A report is filed indicating that an event has occurred
    - A CERT/CSERT team reviews
    - Investigate the report to determine if a crime has occurred
    - Determine if Disclosure of the incident is required
    - Inform senior management

Secured Computing: A CISSP Study Guide, Copyright 2001

- Determine crime status
- When started, what occurred, source and operation
- Identify company elements involved
- Review security/audit policies and procedures
- Determine the need for law enforcement
- Protect chain of custody of evidence

Contacting Law Enforcement

Before calling in law enforcement, get approval from upper management. Some organizations do not want law enforcement involved in all computer crimes investigations. There are various reasons, including publicity, potential liability, and time involved. A major consideration may be the amount of time it might take to obtain search warrants and/or trap and traces orders. Check with your relevant federal, state or local authorities for an estimate.

Types of Surveillance

Surveillance generally falls into two categories: physical and computer. Physical surveillance is done at the time of the abuse through either Closed Circuit Television (CCTV), or after the fact through undercover operations.

Computer surveillance is accomplished passively through the use of audit logs, or actively using electronic monitoring tools including keyboard sniffing, line monitoring. To do this, you must have either a warrant or a statement in your security policy that informs users that they are being monitored, or that the corporation has the right to monitor.

Warrant Process in the U.S.

Obtaining a search warrant is required before an investigator can visit and search for information at a suspect's home or office. Before a warrant can be issued to a law enforcement officer, they must demonstrate probable cause, who is to be searched, where, and why.

Entrapment and Enticement

Enticement is the process of luring an illegal intruder to look at selected files. If the user downloads them, this could be used as evidence against

Secured Computing: A CISSP Study Guide, Copyright 2001

them. Entrapment is where someone induces a person to commit a crime that they were not previously contemplating.

Search and Seizure Rules and Procedures

Search and Seizure of computer evidence is often done quickly due to the nature of the evidence. The fact that it is online means that it can be easily erased without any trace of its existence. Computer evidence can be obtained through a seizure by several means:

- Voluntary or consent
- Subpoena
- Search warrant

A court issues the subpoena to an individual with the instructions to bring the evidence to court. A search warrant is issued to a law enforcement officer allowing them to take the equipment.

By seizing the equipment, it is possible to preserve the evidence, and once seized, the evidence must following the custody chain of evidence. This includes proper labeling and preservation of the evidence, and a log entry to show where it was taken from, who took it, and who has had contact with it since it was seized.

Types of Computer Crime

Military and Intelligence Attacks- this is when criminals or intelligence agents are after military and law enforcement files containing military data and/or investigation reports.

Business Attacks- businesses are reporting more and more information loss through competitive intelligence gathering and computer related attacks.

Financial Attacks- the more we see e-commerce and banking online we will see this area grow. Large corporations are often targeted to provide the hackers with the funds they need or want.

Secured Computing: A CISSP Study Guide, Copyright 2001

Terrorist attacks- this is being seen in the news as I write this. Terrorist groups are using online capabilities to assist in their bombing attacks, or attacking other sites and causing harm to another countries commerce.

Grudge Attacks- these are attacks to get back at someone or something because they hold a grudge against them. You will see this with disgruntled employees that plant logic bombs or delete data when they get fired.

"Fun" Attacks- Some people say they do it just for the fun of it. They do not mean to harm anyone and they do not use any of the information they may get a hold of, but it is still illegal.

Competitive Intelligence vs. Industrial Espionage

This category of computer crime includes international spies and their contractors who steal secrets from defense, academic, and laboratory research facility computer systems. It includes criminals who steal information and intelligence from law enforcement computers, and industrial espionage agents who operate for competitive companies or for foreign governments who are willing to pay for the information.

What has generally been known as industrial espionage is now being called competitive intelligence. As we know, a lot of information can be gained through "open-source" collection and analysis without ever having to break into a competitor's computer. This information gathering is also competitive intelligence, although it is not as ethically questionable as other techniques.

Incident Handling/Response

When you have an incident it is important that you are prepared to handle it both technically and procedurally. Incident response teams, many times called CSIRT, CERT or CIIT teams, will help to assume technical, physical and administrative control in an event. They will have the procedure and the technical savvy to respond to the situation. The following are the steps that need to take place in an incident:

The six steps:
Step 1: Preparation - preparation for the incident
Step 2: Identification -identifying the root

Secured Computing: A CISSP Study Guide, Copyright 2001

Step 3: Containment - containing the root cause
Step 4: Eradication - eliminating the root cause
Step 5: Recovery - recovering from the damage
Step 6. Lessons learned- what could be done differently in the future, what was done correctly?

Remember in an incident that it important to remain cal, take notes for everything done and make sure information is on a need to know basis.

The Incident response team should be made up of Computer security, legal, HR, public relations, auditing and others. The team should meet regularly and develop policy for the incident team.

Ethics

Common Ethical Fallacies

The Computer Game Fallacy- This is the view that what you do with a computer is not really wrong, it is like a game.

The Law Abiding Citizen Fallacy- As long as it does not break a law then I am OK. I can write a malicious program and give it to people, which is not illegal, but what they do with it has an impact on others.

The Candy from a Baby Fallacy- many computer crimes are very easy to do so they don't really seem wrong.

The Hacker Fallacy- This is based on the idea that they are just doing it for the experience or to learn from it.

The Free Information Fallacy- This is based upon the idea that information should be free and thus getting it by any means is OK.

ISC2 Code of Ethics

There is s fine line between ethical and unethical activities. What may be unethical does not even have to be illegal, depending upon the company and line of business you are in. However, it is generally agreed upon that any user who intentionally uses a computer to remove or disrupt services to other users, impact privacy, or conducts internet-wide experiments is generally being unethical.

Secured Computing: A CISSP Study Guide, Copyright 2001

"All information systems security professionals who are certified by (ISC)² recognize that such certification is a privilege that must be both earned and maintained. In support of this principle, all Certified Information Systems Security Professionals (CISSP's) commit to fully support this Code of Ethics. CISSP's who intentionally or knowingly violate any provision of the Code will be subject to action by a peer review panel, which may result in the revocation of certification.

There are only four mandatory canons in the code. By necessity such high-level guidance is not intended to substitute for the ethical judgment of the professional.

Additional guidance is provided for each of the canons. While this guidance may be considered by the Board in judging behavior, it is advisory rather than mandatory. It is intended to help the professional in identifying and resolving the inevitable ethical dilemmas that will confront him/her.

Code of Ethics Preamble:

- Safety of the commonwealth, duty to our principals, and to each other requires that we adhere, and be seen to adhere, to the highest ethical standards of behavior.
- Therefore, strict adherence to this code is a condition of certification.

Code of Ethics Canons:

- Protect society, the commonwealth, and the infrastructure.
- Act honorably, honestly, justly, responsibly, and legally.
- Provide diligent and competent service to principals.
- Advance and protect the profession.

The following additional guidance is given in furtherance of these goals.

Objectives for Guidance

- Give guidance for resolving good v. good and bad v. bad dilemmas.
- To encourage right behavior.
  - For example, teaching
  - Valuing the certificate

- o "Walking"
- Discourage certain common but egregious behavior.
  - o Crying wolf
  - o Consenting to bad practice
  - o Attaching weak systems to the public net
  - o Consorting with hackers

Protect society, the commonwealth, and the infrastructure

- Promote and preserve public trust and confidence in information and systems.
- Promote the understanding and acceptance of prudent information security measures.
- Preserve and strengthen the integrity of the public infrastructure.
- Discourage unsafe practice.

Act honorably, honestly, justly, responsibly, and legally

- Tell the truth; make all stakeholders aware of your actions on a timely basis.
- Observe all contracts and agreements, express or implied.
- Treat all constituents fairly. In resolving conflicts, consider public safety and duties to principals, individuals, and the profession in that order.
- Give prudent advice; avoid raising unnecessary alarm or giving unwarranted comfort. Take care to be truthful, objective, cautious, and within your competence.
- When resolving differing laws in different jurisdictions, give preference to the laws of the jurisdiction in which you render your service.

Provide diligent and competent service to principals

- Preserve the value of their systems, applications, and information.
- Respect their trust and the privileges that they grant you.
- Avoid conflicts of interest or the appearance thereof.
- Render only those services for which you are fully competent and qualified.

Secured Computing: A CISSP Study Guide, Copyright 2001

Advance and protect the profession

- Sponsor for professional advancement those best qualified. All other things equal, prefer those who are certified and who adhere to these canons. Avoid professional association with those whose practices or reputation might diminish the profession.
- Take care not to injure the reputation of other professionals through malice or indifference.

Maintain your competence; keep your skills and knowledge current. Give generously of your time and knowledge in training others.

* I would strongly recommend you to also read RFC 1087 on ethics.

Test Your Knowledge

1. What act addressed the fact that there are many technological problems relating to privacy of information using technology?
    A. Computer security Act of 1967
    B. U.S. Federal Privacy Act of 1974
    C. Privacy investigations law of 1986
    D. Comprehensive Crime Control Act of 1984

2. Which of the following is NOT listed in the ISC2 code of ethics to discourage certain common but egregious behavior?

    A. Crying wolf
    B. Consenting to bad practice
    C. Consorting with hackers
    D. Supporting privacy rights on the internet

3. _____ is proprietary information. That is, information that is used, made or marketed by one having the exclusive legal rights?
    A. Trademark
    B. Copyright
    C. Patent
    D. Trade secret

4. The first thing to due to a computer that needs to be investigated is to search the hard drive?
    A. True
    B. False

5. _____ was a result of the 414 gang and focuses on protecting information that uses computers and telecommunication devices that access medical records?
    A. Medical Computer Crime Act of 1984
    B. Medical information treaties, 1996
    C. Medical Access crime bill of 1998
    D. Medical Computer Crime bill of 1992

6. Enticement is the process of luring an intruder to look at selected files?
    A. True
    B. False

Secured Computing: A CISSP Study Guide, Copyright 2001

7. The wasting of computer resources is NOT considered unethical according to RFC 2828?
   A. True
   B. False

8. The most common attack will always come from the outside of the company?
   A. True
   B. False

9. What Act that amended the computer fraud and abuse act of 1986?
   A. The National Infrastructure Protection Act of 1996
   B. NIPC protection ACT
   C. Computer Security Act of 1987
   D. U.S. Federal Privacy Act of 1974

10. The United States is the only country with computer crime laws?
    A. True
    B. False

Answers: 1.B, 2.D, 3.D, 4.B, 5.A, 6.A, 7.B, 8.B, 9.A, 10.B

Secured Computing: A CISSP Study Guide, Copyright 2001

References

Information in this chapter was referenced from the following sources:

1. Computer Security Handbook, Third edition, Arthur E, Hutt et al. 1995 John Wiley & Sons Inc.

2. *Information Security Management Handbook, 4th edition, Harold F. Tipton, et al. 2000, Auerbach Publications.*

3. *RFC 2828*

4. *RFC 2196 Site Security Handbook, RFC 2196, author B. Fraser, 1997*

<u>Notes</u>

10

Domain 10

Physical Security Domain

Physical Security Domain

The physical security domain addresses the threats, vulnerabilities, and countermeasures that can be utilized to physically protect an enterprise's resource and sensitive information. These resources include people, the facility in which they work, and the data, equipment, support systems, media, and supplies they utilize.

Definitions

Fault tolerance-A method of ensuring continued operation through redundancy and diversity.

EPO- Emergency Power off

CCTV- Closed circuit Television (CCTV)

Administrative & Physical Controls

Administrative controls are the controls that facilitate facility management and planning. These would include emergency plans, personal access controls employee training and simulation testing.

Emergency procedures would include the following:

- Fire
- Bomb
- Evacuation and emergency plans
- Riots

In addition to the administrative controls identified above, the following physical controls should be implemented within the organization:

Secured Computing: A CISSP Study Guide, Copyright 2001

Personal Identification Systems

Universal Code/Card

May exist as a magnetic card stripe, magnetic dot, and embedded wire or proximity access.

Wireless keypad

The user identifies them self by depressing a series of keys on the keypad. The coded representation of the keys is then transmitted to a remote control device. (This type of device is prone to shoulder surfing, allowing someone else to see the code that is entered.)

Preset Code

The code is present in the device itself. A single button system, like a garage door opener would be capable of transmitting a single representation. Multiple button units store multiple codes.

System Sensing

Using this technology, the bearer has no action to take except to walk by a card reader. The card reader senses the card and takes the appropriate action. Some systems require a battery, while the RF field of the reader energizes other systems.

Passive devices

Theses systems contain no battery. They sense the electromagnetic field of the reader, and retransmit using different frequencies through tuned circuits in the portable device.

Field Powered Devices

These units contain active electronic circuits, code storage electronics, a digital sequencer, RF transmitter and a power supply. The power supply extracts power from the electromagnetic field supplied by the reader.

Transponders

These are fully portable two-way radio sets combining a radio transceiver, code storage, control logic and a battery. The reader transmits and the

Secured Computing: A CISSP Study Guide, Copyright 2001

portable unit receives the interrogating signal. When received, the portable unit responds by transmitting the coded data to the reader.

Facility Controls:

- Fences and Gates- the whole objective of perimeter protection is to deter intruders from selected areas. Fencing should be eight feet high in most secured areas and with three strands of barbed wire in very secure areas.

- Lighting in a parking lot or secured outside area is important. You want the lighting to be at the same height as the fence as to not block the view of a guard tower and to illuminate the area that the trespasser may be trying to penetrate. Lights in a parking lot should be 8' high with 2' candles.

Turnstiles/Mantraps

Can be used to deter tailgating into buildings and controlling access in and out of the building.

Closed circuit Television (CCTV)

CCTV can be used by guards to monitor several areas at once. The camera should have an automatic iris to adjust to lighting conditions. Tapes can be used to verify whereabouts of individuals during investigations.

Guards and Dogs

You can have many physical barriers in place, but without human intervention it is useless. Guards can help to check people enter the building, check credentials, reinforce the rules and monitor alarms systems, CCTV and personnel. Dogs can help to deter possible intruders.

Photo Identification

These help to clearly identify what the wearer looks like.

Biometric Controls

Biometric Access Controls use unique personal characteristics of an individual for authentication such as a fingerprint, iris scan or voice print. Biometric systems are measured through speed and throughput. The

Secured Computing: A CISSP Study Guide, Copyright 2001

standard is 5 seconds from authentication request by the user to the decision from the biometric system. This translates into a throughput speed of 6-10 per minute. Biometrics has not gained wide acceptance by users and organizations except in highs security areas. This has been mainly to do with the cost associated with implementation.

Biometrics have gained acceptance, as they are resistant to counterfeiting and generally reliable. However, there can be significant storage requirements to store the physical characteristics. Often people don't want to have elements of their physical being stored electronically due to the nature of the information and that some of the available metrics are viewed as generally intrusive.

System Type	Enrollment Time	Response Time	Accuracy (CER)
Fingerprints	<2 Min.	5-7 Sec.	5%
Hand Geometry	<2 Min.	3-5 Sec.	2%
Voice	<2 Min.	10-14 Sec.	10%
Retina Scan	<2 Min.	4-7 Sec.	1.5%
Iris Scan	<2 Min.	2.5-4 Sec.	0.5%

Figure 10.1 - Biometrics

From looking at the table above, the biometric with the lowest CER is the most accurate. This is the Iris scan. Notice that palm scanning is not the list as it is not assertive enough in its recognition. There are varieties of measurements available to distinguish between people. These include:

- Voice prints

- Finger prints

- Hand geometry

- Blood vein patterns (wrist/hand/eye)

- Retina scan

- Iris scan

- Keystroke recorders

Secured Computing: A CISSP Study Guide, Copyright 2001

- Signature readers

All of these systems have issues with accuracy. Accuracy is measured through three metrics:

False reject rate– percentage of authorized persons rejected as unidentified/unauthorized;

Failure to acquire – meaning that the biometric unit couldn't get enough information to decide;

False accept rate – percentage of imposters who are permitted entry.

The Crossover error rate, or CER, is that point where the percentage of false acceptances and false rejects is equal.

Other Access controls

Other Access control issues that need to be remembered are:

- Access control points- all entryways must be protected and able to handle visitors, delivery services and other unusual situations. In addition, internal entryways into sensitive areas should also be protected.

- Procedures-the access control procedures need to be able to address employees, employees from other company sites, employees who forget their ID, contractors, visitors (including logs and temporary ID), and service and maintenance personnel.

Physical Security Threats

Physical security threats include:
- Fire
- Water
- Earthquakes
- Toxic materials
- Explosions
- Personnel loss
- Sabotage

Secured Computing: A CISSP Study Guide, Copyright 2001

- Storms

Elements of Physical Security

The elements of physical security the following:

- <u>Fire</u>- having the appropriate sprinklers and extinguisher available.
- <u>Electrical</u>- having a power grid and uninterruptible power supply (UPS) available.
- <u>Water</u>- proper drainage. Detections controls for water leakage and floods.
- <u>Environmental</u>- having a HVAC in a good location and that is in proper working order as well as has a. EPO.

Facility Requirements

IS Processing Area

<u>Floor slab</u>- must be capable of a live load of 150-lbs/sq. ft. with a good fire rating.

<u>Raised Flooring</u> - The construction of the raised flooring must be grounded in order to reduce the likelihood of static discharges, and also in the event of an electrical failure, any current sent through the floor frame will be appropriately grounded. The surface of the floor must be of a nonconductive type to prevent electrical injuries.

<u>Walls-</u> the walls must be a floor to ceiling slab with a 1-hour minimum fire rating. Any adjacent walls where records such as paper, media etc. are stored must have a two-hour minimum fire rating.

<u>Ceiling</u>- the ceiling must have the same fire rating as the walls, be waterproof to prevent water leakage from above. Since it is part of the floor is above the ceiling, it must have an appropriate live load rate for the materials being stored above.

<u>Windows</u>- when installing either exterior or interior widows, the glass must be fixed in place, e.g. the window cannot open. It must be shatterproof and translucent.

<u>Doors</u>- the doors should be designed appropriately. Since most doorways open out to facilitate easy escape in an emergency, this places the door

221

Secured Computing: A CISSP Study Guide, Copyright 2001

hinges outside the doorframe. Appropriate care must be taken to protect the door hardware. The doorframe must be constructed to prevent the frame from being forced to open the door.

The fire rating must be equal to the walls where the door is placed, and have emergency egress hardware (panic bars, etc.) as appropriate. The lock mechanism on the door should fail open, in the event of an emergency, in order to facilitate escape. If the lock must fail closed, then a firefighter's key or some other emergency access must be available.

Air Conditioning- the AC units for the air must be dedicated to them, and controllable from within the area. It must be on an independent power source from the rest of the room, and have its own Energy power off (EPO). The AC unit must keep positive pressure in the room, in order to

force smoke and other gases out of the room. The air intakes must be protected to prevent tampering. Finally, the area must be monitored for environmental conditions to maintain the correct environment.

Electrical Power Protection- keeping the power on and stable is crucial whenever working in an IT center. Using UPS and backup generators and alternate feeders can do this.

It is important to understand the following power protection definitions:

- Blackout- is a total loss of power
- Brownout- is when voltage stays below normal for a prolonged period of time.
- Sag- this is a short period of low voltage
- Clean power- is the voltage that has no noise or fluctuations
- Fault- this is a momentary power out
- Inrush current- this is the initial jolt of power before it adjusts to normal.
- Ground- this is the connection from a circuit to the earth.
- Spike- is a momentary surge of high voltage
- Surge- is prolonged high voltage

Noise

Electromagnetic Interference (EMI) is created by the difference between three wires (hot, ground and neutral) and is caused by motors or lightening.

Radio Frequency Interference (RFI) is interference caused by other electrical components like fluorescent lighting and electric cables. It can cause damage to a CPU, data or other peripheral components.

The following is a list of some of the best ways to protect against noise:

- Use a Uninterruptible power supply (UPS)
- Do not start up many systems at one time
- Keep magnets away from computers and magnetic data
- Shield against electric motors
- Avoid fluorescent lighting
- Use grounded prong connections

Fire Classes and Controls

 Know the Fire Classes

There are three classes of fires:

- Class A -common combustibles, which can be put out with water/soda acid. Water is used to reduce the temperature of a fire

- Class B- liquid that can be suppressed with Halon and CO2

- Class C- electrical that can be suppressed with Halon and CO2

Halon is used to interfere with chemical reactions. The Montreal protocol of 1987 stopped the production of Ozone depleting substances, so new extinguishers use Halon Replacements, some of these are:

- FE13

- FM200
- PCF-410 & 218
- Argon

CO_2 is odorless and has no color. It removes oxygen, therefore it is very lethal and gas masks give no protection over this.

Smoke and gas can cause a lot of damage to your data. They travel at a faster rate than the heat or flame do.

Physical Access Controls

Restricted work areas are an additional need to help keep specific things safe. These areas would include a computer room, programmers work area, telephone closet, supplies storage area and data/document library. This will help to keep the confidentiality and integrity of these areas data to be safe.

Escort requirements/visitor controls are a necessity in any systems environment. This means that access in and out of the facility should be logged and recorded. This would include the visitation of vendors, sales people and guests in general. Individuals that are not employees should always be escorted while in the building.

Keys and combination locks are entrance door controls that will deny entrance to unauthorized individuals. They are less expensive and easier to maintain than having a guard. On the other hand, they are far less secure as there is no screening taking place, keys and combinations can be broken, picked or forged. Door control devices can be summarized as the following:

- Conventional key and lock set- these are inexpensive, work on most any door. The keys are easily duplicated and a key holder can enter and exit at any time.
- Pick resistant locks- these are much more difficult to pick, but can cost many times more than the average lock and key system.
- Electronic key systems- these are electronic encoded cards that actuate an electronic door strike. These can lock out users at specific time, record entry and exits. These are expensive.

Mechanical push button locks- these locks are difficult to break and are opened when the operator presses the correct combination. They are less expensive than electronic key systems, but do not log entry and exit.

Technical Controls

Objects used to prove the identity of a user through what they possess or have are called authentication tokens. There are two types of authentication tokens:

- Dumb cards- these are based on semiconductor technology. Data is stored on the tokens and is usually encrypted. The data cannot be decrypted without the password or PIN. An example is a magnetic stripe card.

- Smart Cards are also semiconductor technology, but with a small degree of processing capability. The microprocessor on the token can control access to data. You usually will still need a password or PIN to authenticate. The microprocessor acts as a gateway between the data and the host system providing a higher level of protection than a memory only token.

Environment/Life Safety

The candidate should have several items determined about him or her prior to their acceptance into the company. These items include:

Pre-employment:

- An employment history (provided by applicant)
- An education history (provided by applicant)
- Reference Checks

Post-Employment (as a condition of employment, promotion or transfer):
- Background investigation
- Credit checks
- Security clearances
- Ratings/supervision

Test Your Knowledge

1. Physical walls should have a firewall rating of?
    A. 1 hr.
    B. 1 ½ hrs
    C. 2 hrs.
    D. 3 hrs.
2. "EPO" stands for:
    A. Emergency power operator
    B. Emergency personnel officer
    C. Emergency Power off
    D. Environment protection officer
3. When you have prolonged outage below normal voltage, this describes?
    A. Blackout
    B. Brownout
    C. Fault
    D. Spike
4. When you have a momentary power outage, it is called?
    A. Blackout
    B. Brown out
    C. Fault
    D. Spike
5. The initial surge before adjustment to normal operation describes?
    A. Magnetic field
    B. Inrush current
    C. Peak rush
    D. Sag
6. A momentary period of low voltage is referred to as?
    A. Fault
    B. Spike
    C. Sag
    D. Lag

7. What detects and records frequency and amplitude changes?
    A. Altimeter
    B. Power line monitor
    C. Shielded line
    D. Flux capacitor

Secured Computing: A CISSP Study Guide, Copyright 2001

8. Prolonged high voltage is?
    A. Surge
    B. Spike
    C. Peak rush
    D. Poing
9. A line noise/disturbance superimposed on normal voltage is referred to as:
    A. RFI
    B. EMI
    C. Transient
    D. Magnetic field

10. _____ is caused by the difference between three wires (hot, neutral, ground)?
    A. EMI
    B. RFI
    C. EMS
    D. PMI
11. Static charge can increase greatly when?
    A. Relative humidity is too high
    B. Relative humidity is too low

12. A ____ class fire extinguisher suppresses with CO_2, soda acid and Halon?
    A. Class A
    B. Class B
    C. Class C
    D. Class AD

13. Match the extinguisher classes:
    A. A class   1. Liquid
    B. B class   2. Electric
    C. C class   3. Common combustibles
14. Which of these is not a Halon replacement?
    A. Argonite
    B. FM 200
    C. Integran
    D. Inergen

Secured Computing: A CISSP Study Guide, Copyright 2001

15. Ozone depleting substance controls were described on what protocol?
   A. Montreal protocol
   B. Miami Protocol
   C. CFC Protocol
   D. Halon 1301

16. Which Halon system requires an expensive pressure system?
   A. Halon 1301
   B. Halon 1304
   C. Halon 1201Halon 1211

17. Remaining information remaining after erasure is called:
   A. Data evidence
   B. Data Residue
   C. Data remanence
   D. Degaussation

18. Outside protective lighting should be:
   A. 6 ft high with 2 ft candles
   B. 8 ft high with 2 ft candles
   C. 10 ft high with 2 ft candles
   D. 8 ft high with 1 1/2 ft candles

19. A type I error is a:
   A. False reject rate
   B. False accept rate
   C. Crossover error rate

20. What describes the percent that a false rejection rate and false acceptance rate are equal:
   A. Type III
   B. CER
   C. COT
   D. Equalizer

21. An actual signature that is scanned into a system is called?
   A. Digital signature
   B. Digitized signature
   C. Digital infraction
   D. COT

22. Which of the following is not a space detective device?
    A. Passive infrared
    B. Photoelectric
    C. Microwave
    D. Ultrasonic
    E. Electro-interference

1. A   17. C
2. C   18. B
3. B   19. A
4. C   20. B
5. B   21. B
6. C   22. E
7. B
8. A
9. C
10. A
11. B
12. B
13. A3, B1, C2
14. C
15. A
16. A

References

Information in this chapter was referenced from the following sources:

1. Computer Security Handbook, Third edition, Arthur E, Hutt et al. 1995 John Wiley & Sons Inc.

2. Information Security Management Handbook, 4ᵗʰ edition, Harold F. Tipton, et al. 2000, Auerbach Publications.

3. RFC 2828

4. RFC 2196 Site Security Handbook, RFC 2196, author B. Fraser, 1997

5. Security in Computing, Second edition, Charles P. Pfleeger, 1997 Prentice Hall

NOTES

11

Methods of Attack

Methods of Attack

This chapter will briefly explain the types of attacks that you should be familiar with.

Definitions

Passive attack- this is a threat that just watches information cross a network wire and possibly siphons that information. There is no alteration of the data. Examples would be the sniffing of passwords, getting and reading someone else's email and data capturing. It is very difficult if not impossible to know when you have a passive attack

Active attacks – this is where the data is altered by the attacker to take advantage of a vulnerability in a system. These attacks are much easier to detect, as you see that something was altered.

Worms- Propagates new copies to other systems and executes unauthorized instructions. A self-contained program generally does not destroy data, but can prevent access to the system through consuming all available system resources.

Trap Door – an undocumented access path through a system. This typically bypasses the normal security mechanisms and can be used to plant any of the malicious code forms.

Flooding- type of attack on a network that is designed to bring the network to its knees by flooding it with useless traffic. Many DoS attacks, like the *Ping of Death* and *Teardrop* attacks, exploit limitations in the TCP/IP protocols.

Spamming- Electronic junk mail or junk newsgroup postings. Some people define spam even more generally as any unsolicited e-mail. Spam can eat up a networks bandwidth.

Secured Computing: A CISSP Study Guide, Copyright 2001

Sniffers- A program and/or device that monitors data traveling over a network. Sniffers can be used both for both legitimate network management and for stealing information off a network. Unauthorized sniffers can be extremely dangerous to a network's security because they are virtually impossible to detect and can be inserted almost anywhere. This would be a form of passive attacks.

Trojan Horse- A destructive program that masquerades as a benign application. Unlike viruses, Trojan horses do not replicate themselves but they can be just as destructive. One of the most insidious types of Trojan horse is a program that claims to rid your computer of viruses but instead introduces viruses onto your computer.

Brute force- brute force is exhausting all possible combinations of codes and words using computer software. This can be done using password crackers.

Denial of service (DoS attack)- results in a network being flooded with unwanted data or when a worm is spreading the network and takes control of the entire network.

Dictionary attacks- this is a brute force attack using a dictionary as the source of the guesses.

Spoofing- In a network when system A impersonates system B by sending B's address instead of its own. If system A trusts system B and system C spoofs system B, then system C can gain unauthorized access to system A.

Virus Types

Boot infector – moves or overwrites the boot sector with the virus code.

System infector – infects BIOS command other system files. It is often a memory resident virus.

General Application (COM/EXE) Infector – Infects any .exe or .com file, and if it is a memory resident virus, it infects each program as it is executed.

Secured Computing: A CISSP Study Guide, Copyright 2001

<u>Stealth virus</u> – It is capable of hiding from detection programs and installs a memory resident extension when it is executed.

<u>Multipart virus</u> - It is generally a file and master boot sector infector that is harder to find because its components are in several places.

<u>Self-garbling virus</u> – Hides from detection programs because most of its virus code is garbled. A small header program "degarbles" the virus code when run and then executes the virus code.

<u>Polymorphic virus</u> – this is also a self-garbling virus where the virus changes the "garble" pattern each time is spreads. As a result, it is also difficult to detect.

<u>Macro virus</u> – malicious code that is written in a macro language. Intended for applications that run specific macro languages, such as MS-Word.

Other Attacks

A man in the middle attack is one in which the attacker intercepts messages in a public key exchange and then retransmits them, substituting their own public key for the requested one, so that the two original parties still appear to be communicating with each other directly. The attacker uses a program that appears to be the server to the client and appears to be the client to the server. The attack may be used simply to gain access to the messages, or enable the attacker to modify them before retransmitting them.

Hidden code – this is undocumented program code that offers certain functions.

Interrupts – the attacker causes a program interrupt in order to take advantage of the trusted or elevated state during interrupt processing.

Logic bomb – code that is covertly inserted to operate when a specific event occurs.

Trap door – code inserted by the programmers to allow access to the system in the event of an authentication failure. This code allows the user

Secured Computing: A CISSP Study Guide, Copyright 2001

access to the system without having to authenticate to the security controls first.

Browsing attacks – the attacker searches through the available information without really knowing what they are looking for or the format it is in. They are simply "browsing".

Spoofing attacks – this occurs when an attacker masquerades as either a user or a computer to gain access to another system.

Exhaustive attacks – this involves trying to gain access to a system or to secret data by trying all known possibilities and checking for correctness.

Inference attacks – this involves reaching a conclusion about something based upon other information. For example, we can infer that a system is a UNIX system based upon observations made, but without specific confirmation.

Traffic analysis – This is the inference of information based upon the flow of information, including the presence of, the absence of, the amount and direction of, and the frequency. For example, an army may infer that the enemy based upon how much traffic there is, what direction it is in, and how often the traffic is sent may plan an attack.

Secret Key Algorithms Attacks

Brute force attack- this is the type of attack that tries every possible combination of keys and passwords in an attempt to break the

cryptosystem. Two ways to help this is to change keys often and use keys higher than 128 bits. The time it takes to brute force a key is important. For example if your system is testing 1000 keys per second it would take 300,000,000 years to crack it, but only 17.6 days to crack a 40 bit key. This is why key length is important.

Meet in the Middle attack- this is when the information is encrypted on one end and decrypted on the other and the results are matched in the middle.

Chosen plaintext attack (CPA) – a cryptographic device is loaded with a hidden key and the input of any plaintext is allowed to see the output.

<u>Known plaintext attack (KPA)</u>- Some past plain text and matching ciphertext known

<u>A known-plaintext attack</u> is one in which the cryptanalyst obtains a sample of ciphertext and the corresponding plaintext as well.

<u>Differential cryptanalysis attack</u>- looks at pairs of plaintext and pairs of ciphertext. This attack is dependent on the structure of S-boxes as in DES.

<u>Related Key attack</u>- chooses the relation between a pair of keys, but does not choose the keys themselves.

<u>Ciphertext Only Attack (COA)</u> A ciphertext-only attack is one in which the cryptanalyst obtains a sample of ciphertext, without the plaintext associated with it. This data is relatively easy to obtain in many scenarios, but a successful ciphertext-only attack is generally difficult, and requires a very large ciphertext sample.

<u>Chosen Text Attack (CTA)</u> Crypto device loaded with hidden key provided and input of plaintext or ciphertext allowed to see the other. A chosen-plaintext attack is one in which the cryptanalyst is able to choose a quantity of plaintext and then obtain the corresponding encrypted ciphertext.

<u>The birthday attack</u>- this is a key clustering attack that happens when two different keys generate the same cipher text from the same plaintext.

<u>Buffer overflow</u>- these attacks allow an attacker to execute code on a machine by putting too much information into undersized buffers in software. This also referred to as smashing the stack.

<u>SMURF attack</u>- software that mounts a denial-of-service attack ('smurfing') by exploiting IP broadcast addressing and ICMP ping packets to cause flooding. A smurf program builds a network packet that appears to originate from another address, that of the 'victim', either a host or an IP router. The packet contains an ICMP ping message that is addressed to an IP broadcast address, i.e., to all IP addresses in a given network. The echo responses to the ping message return to the victim's address. The goal of smurfing may be either to deny service at a particular host or to flood all or part of an IP network.

<u>Scavenging</u>- searching through object residue to acquire unauthorized data.

* I would strongly suggest you to look on the web at hacker tools and vulnerabilities to examine what they do.

Whatis.com Definitions

The following 20 definitions will also help you to further your studies for the CISSP. Whatis.com is a great resource to get technology terms.

Definitions copyrighted and used with permission of whatis.com (http://www.whatis.com) and TechTarget Inc. Over 3,500 definitions are provided in the book from Que Publishing, "The Whatis.com Encyclopedia of Technology Terms."

Distributed Denial-of-Service Attack

On the Internet, a distributed denial-of-service (DDoS) attack is one in which a multitude of compromised systems attack a single target, thereby causing denial of service for users of the targeted system. The flood of incoming messages to the target system essentially forces it to shut down, thereby denying service to the system to legitimate users.

A hacker (or, if you prefer, cracker) begins a DDoS attack by exploiting a vulnerability in one computer system and making it the DDoS "master." It is from the master system that the intruder identifies and communicates with other systems that can be compromised. The intruder loads cracking tools available on the Internet on multiple -- sometimes thousands of -- compromised systems. With a single command, the intruder instructs the controlled machines to launch one of many flood attacks against a specified target. The inundation of packets to the target causes a denial of service.

While the press tends to focus on the target of DDoS attacks as the victim, in reality there are many victims in a DDoS attack -- the final target and as well the systems controlled by the intruder.

Defense Message System

The Defense Message System (DMS) is a secure X.400-based e-mail system developed by the United States government in conjunction with industry partners to ensure safety for critical operations. Essentially an enhanced version of various commercial e-mail products, DMS was developed for the United States Department of Defense (DoD). DMS has replaced AUTODIN (automated digital network), the previous official DoD e-mail system as well as 45 separate e-mail systems that functioned within the DoD.

At the client level, DMS looks like a typical e-mail application and is designed to feature familiar user-friendly functionality, such as global X.500 Directory Service, and transmission support for digital files of any type and size. Security and delivery assurance mechanisms are approved by the National Security Agency (NSA) for information classified at all levels, up to and including those designated as top secret. Because sending message attachments between the unclassified and secret domains (known, respectively, as NIPRNET and SIPRNET) requires protection against leakage of classified information, DMS policies require that all organizational messages be signed and encrypted with Class IV

Secured Computing: A CISSP Study Guide, Copyright 2001

Public Key Infrastructure (PKI) protection through Fortezza, NSA's trademarked security products suite. Originally policies permitted organizational message attachments to be sent only from a low security domain to a high security domain, but security mechanisms (both technological and policy-based) are now in place to allow the information to flow in either direction.

DMS was designed to incorporate components from a variety of leading hardware and software vendors and to leverage the best current and emerging messaging technologies within the Defense Information Infrastructure (DII, a worldwide connectivity transport infrastructure). The DMS development program began in response to Joint Staff requirements for an integrated messaging service that could be accessed from any DoD location in the world, as well as by designated government users or contractors. DMS has been recommended to become the standard messaging system throughout the United States government.

Bucket Brigade

A bucket brigade attack is one in which the attacker intercepts messages in a public key exchange and then retransmits them, substituting their own public key for the requested one, so that the two original parties still appear to be communicating with each other directly. The attacker uses a program that appears to be the server to the client and appears to be the client to the server. The attack may be used simply to gain access to the messages, or enable the attacker to modify them before retransmitting them. The term derives from the bucket brigade method of putting out a fire by handing buckets of water from one person to another between a water source and the fire. Another name for the bucket brigade attack is the more accurately descriptive name, man-in-the-middle, based on the ball game where a number of people try to throw a ball directly to each other while one person in between them attempts to catch it.

Authentication, Authorization, and Accounting

Authentication, authorization, and accounting (AAA) is a term for a framework for intelligently controlling access to computer resources, enforcing policies, auditing usage, and providing the information necessary to bill for services. These combined processes are considered important for effective network management and security.

Secured Computing: A CISSP Study Guide, Copyright 2001

Authentication provides a way of identifying a user, typically by having the user enter a valid user name and valid password before access is granted. The process of authentication is based on each user having a unique set of criteria for gaining access. The AAA server compares a user's authentication credentials with other user credentials stored in a database. If the credentials match, the user is granted access to the network. If the credentials are at variance, authentication fails and network access is denied.

Following authentication, a user must gain authorization for doing certain tasks. After logging into a system, for instance, the user may try to issue commands. The authorization process determines whether the user has the authority to issue such commands. Simply put, authorization is the process of enforcing policies: determining what types or qualities of activities, resources, or services a user is permitted. Usually, authorization occurs within the context of authentication. Once you have authenticated a user, they may be authorized for different types of access or activity.

The final plank in the AAA framework is accounting, which measures the resources a user consumes during access. This can include the amount of system time or the amount of data a user has sent and/or received during a session. Accounting is carried out by logging of session statistics and usage information and is used for authorization control, billing, trend analysis, resource utilization, and capacity planning activities.

Authentication, authorization, and accounting services are often provided by a dedicated AAA server, a program that performs these functions. A current standard by which network access servers interface with the AAA server is the Remote Authentication Dial-In User Service (RADIUS).

Digital Signature Standard

Digital Signature Standard (DSS) is the digital signature algorithm (DSA) developed by the U.S. National Security Agency (NSA) to generate a digital signature for the authentication of electronic documents. DSS was put forth by the National Institute of Standards and Technology (NIST) in 1994, and has become the United States government standard for authentication of electronic documents. DSS is specified in Federal Information Processing Standard (FIPS) 186.
DSA is a pair of large numbers that are computed according to the specified algorithm within parameters that enable the authentication of the

signatory, and as a consequence, the integrity of the data attached. Digital signatures are generated through DSA, as well as verified. Signatures are generated in conjunction with the use of a private key; verification takes place in reference to a corresponding public key. Each signatory has their own paired public (assumed to be known to the general public) and private (known only to the user) keys. Because a signature can only be generated by an authorized person using their private key, the corresponding public key can be used by anyone to verify the signature.

A data summary of the information (called a message digest) is created through the use of a hash function (called the Secure Hash Standard, or SHS, and specified in FIPS 180). The data summary is used in conjuntion with the DSA algorithm to create the digital signature that is sent with the message. Signature verification involves the use of the same hash function.

Certificate Authority

A certificate authority (CA) is an authority in a network that issues and manages security credentials and public keys for message encryption. As part of a public key infrastructure(PKI), a CA checks with a registration authority (RA) to verify information provided by the requestor of a digital certificate. If the RA verifies the requestor's information, the CA can then issue a certificate.
Depending on the public key infrastructure implementation, the certificate includes the owner's public key, the expiration date of the certificate, the owner's name, and other information about the public key owner.

Dynamic Packet Filter

A dynamic packet filter is a firewall facility that can monitor the state of active connections and use this information to determine which network packets to allow through the firewall. By recording session information such as IP addresses and port numbers, a dynamic packet filter can implement a much tighter security posture than a static packet filter.
For example, assume that you wish to configure your firewall so that all users in your company are allowed out to the Internet, but only replies to users' data requests are let back in. With a static packet filter, you would need to permanently allow in replies from all external addresses, assuming that users were free to visit any site on the Internet. This kind of filter would allow an attacker to sneak information past the filter by making

the packet look like a reply (which can be done by indicating "reply" in the packet header).

By tracking and matching requests and replies, a dynamic packet filter can screen for replies that don't match a request. When a request is recorded, the dynamic packet filter opens up a small inbound hole so only the expected data reply is let back through. Once the reply is received, the hole is closed. This dramatically increases the security capabilities of the firewall.

Digital Silhouettes

Digital Silhouettes is the trademarked name that Predictive Networks has given to user profiles that are established through gathered click stream data and artificial intelligence (AI) processes. The profile, or cybersignature, is built from a mathematical analysis of an individual's interests as well as their keyboard and mouse activity.
A "fusion" algorithm composed of clickstream, keystroke, and mouse or pointer behavior is used to track recurring patterns. By examining the patterns over a long period of time, Digital Silhouettes is able to indentify a specific user (as opposed to device) and assign the user to one of over 140 demographic and content-related categories.

The selected demographics fall into the six major categories of gender, age, income, education, and race - all of which break down to subcategories. There are more than 90 content affinity subcategories, such as golf, pets, and car accessories, for example. Every time a user visits a Web site that is listed in an extensive Predictive Networks database, demographic and content characterization congruent with that site are added to the user's Digital Silhouette.

The more Web sites the user visits, and the longer the user is monitored, the more refined the Digital Silhouette will become. Useful statistics include average double-click intervals, ratio of double to single clicks, average mouse velocity and acceleration, and ratio of mouse to keyboard activity. Once the profile reaches a level of mathematical accuracy, participating content providers can target their marketing messages to individual Digital Silhouettes.

Predictive Networks claims that Digital Silhouettes are identified by randomly assigned and anonymous ID numbers. The company insists that

Personally Identifiable Information (PII) such as names, addresses, and other private information is not known to Predictive Networks. Because of the volume and sensitivity of data gathered, however, privacy issues have been raised about Digital Silhouettes.

Content Protection for Removable Media

Content Protection for Removable Media (CPRM) is a hardware-based technology designed to enforce copy protection restrictions through built-in mechanisms in storage media that would prevent unauthorized file copying.
Based on a technology called broadcast encryption that was developed by Amos Fiat and Moni Naar in 1993, the CPRM system would be used to incorporate digital tags into storage media, such as recordable CDs (CD-R, CD-RW) and flash memory cards for MP3 players.

CPRM was developed by 4C Entity, an industry consortium originally made up of Intel, IBM, Matsushita, and Toshiba. The system has been highly controversial, because it could be used not only with removable media, but as a part of every new hard drive produced as well. Technical Committee T13 (a coalition of companies that produce both flash memory and hard drives) considered adopting CPRM as an industry standard, but has since given approval to an alternative plan in development at Phoenix Technologies that would be used for other purposes - such as security mechanisms on removable media - in addition to copy protection.

Deniable Encryption

Deniable encryption is a type of cryptography that allows an encrypted text to be decrypted in two or more ways, depending on which decryption key is used. The use of two or more keys allows the sender, theoretically, to conceal or deny the existence of a controversial message in favor of a more benign decryption. For instance, a company may send an encrypted message to its high-level administrative staff whose key decrypts the message to read "We have no plans to change our business model", while the board of directors receives the same message that using its own key decrypts the same message to read "We are going bankrupt at this rate and need to let 20,000 people go, including high-level administrators". Deniable encryption is sometimes used for misinformation purposes when the sender anticipates, or even encourages, interception of a communication.

Carnivore

Carnivore is the Internet surveillance system developed by the U.S. Federal Bureau of Investigation (FBI), who developed it to monitor the electronic transmissions of criminal suspects. Critics, however, charge that Carnivore does not include appropriate safeguards to prevent misuse and might violate the constitutional rights of the individual.

Carnivore, a PC- or laptop-based application, is installed with an Internet service provider (ISP) to keep court-ordered tabs on a criminal suspect's e-mail and instant messages. The FBI says it cannot be enabled without help from the ISP. It works much like a commercial sniffer and other network diagnostic tools. The FBI says Carnivore has a unique ability to distinguish between communications that have been authorized for interception and those it does not have the right to search. For instance, Carnivore could be configured to intercept e-mail but not online shopping records.

Documents suggest that the FBI may have been working on a predecessor to Carnivore as early as 1996. But the FBI officially began the Carnivore project, under the name "Omnivore," in February 1997. It was proposed originally for a Solaris X86 computer. In June 1999, Omnivore was replaced by Carnivore running on a Windows NT-based system.

Carnivore's chief critic is the Electronic Privacy Information Center (EPIC), a public interest group dedicated to emerging civil liberties issues. The group sued and got the FBI to release background information on the system, although the Bureau refused to turn over Carnivore's source code. A private study conducted by the Illinois Institute of Technology Research Institute, which was commissioned by the U.S. Justice Department, found several shortcomings in Carnivore. For example, the system does not keep track of individual users, so any operator defaults to "administrator," leaving no audit trail. Also, the system lacks a feature that would require users to confirm that a court order was granted. The U.S. Congress is currently considering bills that would restrict the FBI's use of Carnivore.

Some security software vendors now claim to have developed alternatives to Carnivore. Carnivore could also lead to a rise in encryption software for Internet transactions, which would make such "sniffer" tools less effective.

Digital Certificate

A digital certificate is an electronic "credit card" that establishes your credentials when doing business or other transactions on the Web. It is issued by a certification authority (CA). It contains your name, a serial number, expiration dates, a copy of the certificate holder's public key (used for encrypting messages and digital signatures), and the digital signature of the certificate-issuing authority so that a recipient can verify that the certificate is real. Some digital certificates conform to a standard, X.509. Digital certificates can be kept in registries so that authenticating users can look up other users' public keys.

Integrity

Integrity, in terms of data and network security, is the assurance that information can only be accessed or modified by those authorized to do so. Measures taken to ensure integrity include controlling the physical environment of networked terminals and servers, restricting access to data, and maintaining rigorous authentication practices. Data integrity can also be threatened by environmental hazards, such as heat, dust, and electrical surges.
Practices followed to protect data integrity in the physical environment include: making servers accessible only to network administrators, keeping transmission media (such as cables and connectors) covered and protected to ensure that they cannot be tapped, and protecting hardware and storage media from power surges, electrostatic discharges, and magnetism.
Network administration measures to ensure data integrity include: maintaining current authorization levels for all users, documenting system administration procedures, parameters, and maintenance activities, and creating disaster recovery plans for occurrences such as power outages, server failure, and virus attacks.

Wireless LAN

A wireless LAN is one in which a mobile user can connect to a local area network (LAN) through a wireless (radio) connection. A standard, IEEE 802.11, specifies the technologies for wireless LANs. The standard includes an encryption method, the Wired Equivalent Privacy algorithm. High-bandwidth allocation for wireless will make possible a relatively low-cost wiring of classrooms in the United States. A similar frequency

Secured Computing: A CISSP Study Guide, Copyright 2001

allocation has been made in Europe. Hospitals and businesses are also expected to install wireless LAN systems where existing LANs are not already in place.

Using technology from the Symbionics Networks, Ltd., a wireless LAN adapter can be made to fit on a Personal Computer Memory Card Industry Association (PCMCIA) card for a laptop or notebook computer.

802.11

In wireless LAN (WLAN) technology, 802.11 refers to a family of specifications developed by a working group of the Institute of Electrical and Electronics Engineers (IEEE). There are three specifications in the family: 802.11, 802.11a, and 802.11b. All three specify the use of CSMA/CA (carrier sense multiple access with collision avoidance) as the path-sharing protocol.

The 802.11 and 802.11b specifications apply to wireless Ethernet LANs, and operate at frequencies in the 2.4-GHz region of the radio spectrum. Data speeds are generally 1 Mbps or 2 Mbps for 802.11, and 5.5 Mbps or 11 Mbps for 802.11b, although speeds up to about 20 Mbps are realizable with 802.11b. The 802.11b standard is backward compatible with 802.11. The modulation used in 802.11 has historically been phase-shift keying (PSK). The modulation method selected for 802.11b is known as complementary code keying (CCK), which allows higher data speeds and is less susceptible to multipath-propagation interference.

The 802.11a specification applies to wireless ATM systems and operates at radio frequencies between 5 GHz and 6 GHz. A modulation scheme known as OFDM (orthogonal frequency-division multiplexing) makes possible data speeds as high as 54 Mbps, but most commonly, communications takes place at 6 Mbps, 12 Mbps, or 24 Mbps.

Wireless

Wireless is a term used to describe telecommunications in which electromagnetic waves (rather than some form of wire) carry the signal over part or all of the communication path. Some monitoring devices, such as intrusion alarms, employ acoustic waves at frequencies above the range of human hearing; these are also sometimes classified as wireless.

The first wireless transmitters went on the air in the early 20th century using radiotelegraphy (Morse code). Later, as modulation made it possible to transmit voices and music via wireless, the medium came to be called "radio." With the advent of television, fax, data communication, and the effective use of a larger portion of the spectrum, the term "wireless" has been resurrected.

Common examples of wireless equipment in use today include:

Cellular phones and pagers -- provide connectivity for portable and mobile applications, both personal and business

Global Positioning System (GPS) -- allows drivers of cars and trucks, captains of boats and ships, and pilots of aircraft to ascertain their location anywhere on earth

Cordless computer peripherals -- the cordless mouse is a common example; keyboards and printers can also be linked to a computer via wireless

Cordless telephone sets -- these are limited-range devices, not to be confused with cell phones

Home-entertainment-system control boxes -- the VCR control and the TV channel control are the most common examples; some hi-fi sound systems and FM broadcast receivers also use this technology

Remote garage-door openers -- one of the oldest wireless devices in common use by consumers; usually operates at radio frequencies

Two-way radios -- this includes Amateur and Citizens Radio Service, as well as business, marine, and military communications

Baby monitors -- these devices are simplified radio transmitter/receiver units with limited range

Satellite television -- allows viewers in almost any location to select from hundreds of channels

Wireless LANs or local area networks -- provide flexibility and reliability for business computer users

Wireless technology is rapidly evolving, and is playing an increasing role in the lives of people throughout the world. In addition, ever-larger numbers of people are relying on the technology directly or indirectly. (It has been suggested that wireless is overused in some situations, creating a social nuisance.) More specialized and exotic examples of wireless communications and control include:

Global System for Mobile Communication (GSM) -- a digital mobile telephone system used in Europe and other parts of the world; the de facto wireless telephone standard in Europe

General Packet Radio Service (GPRS) -- a packet-based wireless communication service that provides continuous connection to the Internet for mobile phone and computer users

Enhanced Data GSM Environment (EDGE) -- a faster version of the Global System for Mobile (GSM) wireless service

Universal Mobile Telecommunications System (UMTS) -- a broadband, packet-based system offering a consistent set of services to mobile computer and phone users no matter where they are located in the world

Wireless Application Protocol (WAP) -- a set of communication protocols to standardize the way that wireless devices, such as cellular telephones and radio transceivers, can be used for Internet access

i-Mode -- the world's first "smart phone" for Web browsing, first introduced in Japan; provides color and video over telephone sets

Wireless can be divided into:
Fixed wireless -- the operation of wireless devices or systems in homes and offices, and in particular, equipment connected to the Internet via specialized modems

Mobile wireless -- the use of wireless devices or systems aboard motorized, moving vehicles; examples include the automotive cell phone and PCS (personal communications services)

Portable wireless -- the operation of autonomous, battery-powered wireless devices or systems outside the office, home, or vehicle; examples include handheld cell phones and PCS units

IR wireless -- the use of devices that convey data via IR (infrared) radiation; employed in certain limited-range communications and control systems

Cryptoperiod

A cryptoperiod (sometimes called a key lifetime or a validity period) is a specific time span during which a cryptographic key is authorized, or for which a key setting remains in effect. A key uses an algorithm to create ciphertext from plaintext (ordinary unencrypted text). The cryptoperiod is decided by weighing factors such as the sensitivity of the encrypted data, the risk of key compromise, and the cost of rekeying (encrypting the same material with a new key). Throughout the cryptoperiod, a key can be used to verify or decrypt data. The effective use of cryptoperiods is an important part of key management.
A cryptoperiod is usually expressed as a span of calendar or clock time, but may also be expressed as a maximum volume of data to be encrypted by an algorithm for a particular key. The span of some cryptoperiods can be a number of decades since keys may sometimes be archived for a very long time.

Blue Bomb

A "blue bomb" (also known as "WinNuke") is a technique for causing the Windows operating system of someone you're communicating with to crash or suddenly terminate. The "blue bomb" is actually an out-of-band network packet containing information that the operating system can't process. This condition causes the operating system to "crash" or terminate prematurely. The operating system can usually be restarted without any permanent damage other than possible loss of unsaved data when you crashed.
The blue bomb derives its name from the effect it sometimes causes on the display as the operating system is terminating - a white-on-blue error screen that is commonly known as blue screen of death. Blue bombs are sometimes sent by multi-player game participants who are about to lose or users of Internet Relay Chat (IRC) who are making a final comment. This is known as "nuking" someone. A commonly-used program for causing the

Secured Computing: A CISSP Study Guide, Copyright 2001

blue bomb is WinNuke. Many Internet service providers are filtering out the packets so they don't reach users.

Class C2

Class C2 is a security rating established by the U.S. National Computer Security Center (NCSC) and granted to products that pass Department of Defense (DoD) Trusted Computer System Evaluation Criteria (TCSEC) tests. A C2 rating ensures the minimum allowable levels of confidence demanded for government agencies and offices and other organizations that process classified or secure information. TCSEC standards were established in the 1985 DoD document, Department of Defense Trusted Computer System Evaluation Criteria, known unofficially as the "Orange Book" (evaluation criteria for networks, the Trusted Network Interpretation is known as the "Red Book"). NCSC's objectives in publishing the document were: to provide DoD users with a means of ensuring the security of sensitive information; to provide manufacturers with guidelines to be followed; and to provide those involved in acquisitions with criteria for specifications.

According to TCSEC, system security is evaluated at one of four broad levels, ranging from class D to class A1, each level building on the previous one, with added security measures at each level and partial level. Class D is defined as Minimum Security; systems evaluated at this level have failed to meet higher level criteria. Class C1 is defined as Discretionary Security Protection; systems evaluated at this level meet security requirements by controlling user access to data. Class C2, defined as Controlled Access Protection adds to C1 requirements additional user accountability features, such as login procedures. Class B1 is defined as Labeled Security Protection; systems evaluated at this level also have a stated policy model, and specifically labeled data. Class B2, defined as Structured Protection, adds to B1 requirements a more explicit and formal security policy. Class B3, defined as Security Domains, adds stringent engineering and monitoring requirements and is highly secure. Class A1 is defined as Verified Design; systems evaluated at this level are functionally equivalent to B3 systems, but include more formal analysis of function to assure security.

DMZ

In computer networks, a DMZ (demilitarized zone) is a computer host or small network inserted as a "neutral zone" between a company's private network and the outside public network. It prevents outside users from getting direct access to a server that has company data. (The term comes from the geographic buffer zone that was set up between North Korea and South Korea following the war in the early 1950s.) A DMZ is an optional and more secure approach to a firewall and effectively acts as a proxy server as well.

In a typical DMZ configuration for a small company, a separate computer (or host in network terms) receives requests from users within the private network for access to Web sites or other companies accessible on the public network. The DMZ host then initiates sessions for these requests on the public network. However, the DMZ host is not able to initiate a session back into the private network. It can only forward packets that have already been requested.

Users of the public network outside the company can access only the DMZ host. The DMZ may typically also have the company's Web pages so these could be served to the outside world. However, the DMZ provides access to no other company data. In the event that an outside user penetrated the DMZ host's security, the Web pages might be corrupted but no other company information would be exposed. Cisco, the leading maker of routers, is one company that sells products designed for setting up a DMZ.

Secured Computing: A CISSP Study Guide, Copyright 2001

Book References

Computer Security Handbook, Third edition, Arthur E, Hutt et al. 1995 John Wiley & Sons Inc.

Information Security Management Handbook, 4th edition, Harold F. Tipton, et al. 2000, Auerbach Publications.

Information Security Policies Made Easy, Version 6, Charles Cresson Wood, 1997

IPsec The new Security Standard for the Internet, intranets, and Virtual Private Networks, Naganand Doraswamy et al., 1999 Prentice Hall

Internet Besieged, Dorothy E. Denning et al., 1998, ACM Press

Security in Computing, Second edition, Charles P. Pfleeger, 1997 Prentice Hall

FIPS 113 May 1985, Computer Data Authentication

FIPS 140 Jan. 1994, Security Requirements for Cryptographic Modules

FIPS 180 April 1995, Secure Hash Standard

RFC 2828

RSA Laboratories' Frequently Asked Questions About Today's Cryptography, Version 4.1, Copyright © 1992-2000 RSA Security Inc.

RFC 2196 Site Security Handbook, RFC 2196, author B. Fraser, 1997, Investigating Computer related Crime, Peter Stephenson, CRC Press, 2000

CISSP Examination Textbooks Volume Ones, S. Rao Vallabhaneni, SRV Publications

Computer Security Basics, D. Russell, O'Reilly and Associates, 1991

ISC2 Code of Ethics, ISC2 Inc. 2001

Recommended Study Aids

RFCs are available online many places, try **www.faq.org**

<u>Kerberos</u> RFC 1510
<u>PKI</u> RFC 3039 and 3029
<u>NAT</u> RFC 3022
<u>ISP Security</u> RFC 3013
<u>SOCKS protocol</u> RFC1928
<u>Site Security Handbook</u>, RFC 2196
<u>Internet Standards and Processes</u> RFC 2026

<u>Study sites:</u> (These sites were all available at the time of publishing)

www.cissps.com - Online study website

http://www.cccure.org/

http://groups.yahoo.com/group/CISSPStudy - Online study forum

http://csrc.nist.gov/fips - Has all the NIST standards

http://www.infosyssec.net/ - Lists tons of security related sites on many topics

http://www.rsasecurity.com/rsalabs/faq/- Great source for cryptography information

<u>Test Questions</u>

www.boson.com has a CISSP practice test for purchase, Test #1 is recommended.

Glossary Terms*

Most definitions are taken directly from RFC 2828 and the TNI.

Access control
> The limiting of rights or capabilities of a subject to communicate with other subjects, or to use functions or services in a computer system or network. Restrictions controlling a subject's access to an object.

Access control list (ACL)
> A list of subjects authorized for specific access to an object. A list of entities, together with their access rights, which are authorized to have access to a resource.

Accountability
> Means of linking individuals to their interactions with an IT product, thereby supporting identification of and recovery from unexpected or unavoidable failures of the control objectives.

Accreditation
> The procedure for accepting an IT system to process sensitive information within a particular operational environment. The formal procedure for recognizing both the technical competence and the impartiality of an IT test laboratory (evaluation body) to carry out its associated tasks.

Address spoofing
> A type of attack in which the attacker steals a legitimate network (e.g. IP) address of a system and uses it to impersonate the system that owns the address

Administrative security
> Management procedures and constraints to prevent unauthorized access to a system. 'The management constraints, operational procedures, accountability procedures, and supplemental controls established to provide an acceptable level of protection for sensitive data.

Administrator
> A person in contact with the Target of Evaluation who is responsible for maintaining its operational capability.

Aggregation
> A circumstance in which a collection of information items is required to be classified at a higher security level than any of the individual items those comprise it.

Algorithm
> A computer can implement a finite set of step-by-step instructions for a problem-solving or computation procedure, especially one that.

Application gateway firewall
> A type of firewall system that runs an application, called a proxy, that acts like the server to the Internet client. The proxy takes all requests from the Internet client and, if allowed, forwards them to the Intranet server. Application gateways are used to make certain that the Internet client and the Intranet server are using the proper application protocol for communicating. Popular proxies include Telnet, ftp, and http. Building proxies requires knowledge of the application protocol.

Application program interface (API)
> System access point or library function that has a well-defined syntax and is accessible from application programs or user code to provide well-defined functionality.

Asymmetric algorithm
> An encryption algorithm that requires two different keys for encryption and decryption. These keys are commonly referred to as the public and private keys. Asymmetric algorithms are slower than symmetric algorithms. Furthermore, speed of encryption may be different than the speed of decryption. Generally asymmetric algorithms are either used to exchange symmetric session keys or to digitally sign a message. RSA, RPK, and ECC are examples of asymmetric algorithms.

Audit trail

A set of records that collectively provide documentary evidence of processing used to aid in tracing from original transactions forward to related records and reports, and/or backward from records and reports to their component source transactions

Authenticate

To verify the identity of a user, device, or other entity in a computer system, often as a prerequisite to allowing access to resources in a system. To verify the integrity of data that have been stored, transmitted, or otherwise exposed to possible unauthorized modification.

Authentication Header (AH)

An Internet IPsec protocol designed to provide connectionless data integrity service and data origin authentication service for IP datagrams, and (optionally) to provide protection against replay attacks. The receiver may select replay protection when a security association is established. AH authenticates upper-layer protocol data units and as much of the IP header as possible. However, some IP header fields may change in transit, and the value of these fields, when the packet arrives at the receiver, may not be predictable by the sender. Thus, the values of such fields cannot be protected end-to-end by AH; protection of the IP header by AH is only partial when such fields are present. AH may be used alone, or in combination with the IPsec ESP protocol, or in a nested fashion with tunneling. Security services can be provided between a pair of communicating hosts, between a pair of communicating security gateways, or between a host and a gateway. ESP can provide the same security services as AH, and ESP can also provide data confidentiality service. The main difference between authentication services provided by ESP and AH is the extent of the coverage; ESP does not protect IP header fields unless they are encapsulated by AH.

Availability

The ability to access a specific resource within a specific time frame as defined within the IT product specification. The ability to use or access objects and resources as required. The property relates to the concern that information objects and other system resources are accessible when needed and without undue delay.

Back door

A hardware or software mechanism that provides access to a system and its resources by other than the usual procedure, was deliberately left in place by the system's designers or maintainers, and usually is not publicly known

Baseline

A specification or product that has been formally reviewed and agreed upon, that thereafter serves as the basis for further development, and that can be changed only through formal change control procedures.

Bastion hosts

A strongly protected computer that is in a network protected by a firewall (or is part of a firewall) and is the only host (or one of only a few hosts) in the network that can be directly accessed from networks on the other side of the firewall. Filtering routers in a firewall typically restrict traffic from the outside network to reaching just one host, the bastion host, which usually is part of the firewall. Since only this one host can be directly attacked, only this one host needs to be very strongly protected, so security can be maintained more easily and less expensively. However, to allow legitimate internal and external users to access application resources through the firewall, higher layer protocols and services need to be relayed and forwarded by the bastion host.

Bell-LaPadula model

A formal, mathematical, state-transition model of security policy for multilevel-secure computer systems. The model separates computer system elements into a set of subjects and a set of objects. To determine whether or not a subject is authorized for a particular access mode on an object, the clearance of the subject is compared to the classification of the object. The model defines the notion of a 'secure state', in which the only permitted access modes of subjects to objects are in accordance with a specified security policy. It is proven that each state transition preserves security by moving

Secured Computing: A CISSP Study Guide, Copyright 2001

from secure state to secure state, thereby proving that the system is secure. In this model, a multilevel-secure system satisfies several rules, including the following:

- '*-property', pronounced 'star property: A subject has write access to an object only if classification of the object dominates the clearance of the subject.
- 'Simple security property': A subject has read access to an object only if the clearance of the subject dominates the classification of the object.

Benchmark

A standard against which measurements or comparisons can be made.

Bind

To inseparably associate by applying some mechanism, such as when a CA uses a digital signature to bind together a subject and public key in a public-key certificate.

Biometric authentication

A method of generating authentication information for a person by digitizing measurements of a physical characteristic, such as a fingerprint, a hand shape, a retina pattern, a speech pattern (voiceprint), or handwriting.

Block cipher

An encryption algorithm that breaks plaintext into fixed-size segments and uses the same key to transform each plaintext segment into a fixed-size segment of ciphertext.

Blowfish

A symmetric block cipher with variable-length key (32 to 448 bits) designed in 1993 by Bruce Schneier as an unpatented, license-free, royalty-free replacement for DES or IDEA.

Breach

The successful defeat of security controls that could result in a penetration of the system. A violation of controls of a particular information system such that information assets or system components are unduly exposed.

Brute force

A cryptanalysis technique or other kind of attack method involving an exhaustive procedure that tries all possibilities, one-by-one. For example, for ciphertext where the analyst already knows the decryption algorithm, a brute force technique to finding the original plaintext is to decrypt the message with every possible key.

Buffer overflow

This happens when more data is put into a buffer or holding area, then the buffer can handle. This is due to a mismatch in processing rates between the producing and consuming processes.

CA certificate

'A certificate for one CA issued by another CA.) That is, a digital certificate whose holder is able to issue digital certificates. A v3 X.509 public-key certificate may have a 'basic Constraints' extension containing a 'CA' value that specifically 'indicates whether or not the public key may be used to verify certificate signatures.'

Call back

An authentication technique for terminals that remotely access computer via telephone lines. The host system disconnects the caller and then calls back on a telephone number that was previously authorized for that terminal. A procedure for identifying a remote terminal. In a call back, the host system disconnects the caller and then dials the authorized telephone number of the remote terminal to reestablish the connection.

Cellular transmission
> Data transmission via interchangeable wireless (radio) communications in a network of numerous small geographic cells. Most current technology is analog - represented as electrical levels, not bits. However, the trend is toward digital cellular data transmission.

Centralized authorization
> A scheme in which a central, third party authorization agent is consulted for access control. All access control rules are defined in the database of the central authorization agent.

Certificate
> An electronic identifier from a certificate authority that includes the CA signature made with its private key. Other users who trust the CA's public key validate the authenticity of the signature. Certificates are data, which is used to verify digital signatures. A certificate is only as trustworthy as the agency, which issued it. A certificate is used to verify a particular signed item, such as an Email message or a web page. A mathematical program processes all the digital signature, the item and the certificate. It is possible to say, if the signature is valid, that 'According to the agency which issued the certificate, the signer was (some name)'.

Certificate revocation list (CRL)
> A data structure that enumerates digital certificates that have been invalidated by their issuer prior to when they were scheduled to expire. 'A signed list indicating a set of certificates that are no longer considered valid by the certificate issuer. After a certificate appears on a CRL, it is deleted from a subsequent CRL after the certificate's expiry. CRLs may be used to identify revoked public-key certificates or attribute certificates and may represent revocation of certificates issued to authorities or to users. The term CRL is also commonly used as a generic term applying to all the different types of revocation lists, including CRLs, ARLs, ACRLs, etc.'

Certification
> Comprehensive evaluation of the technical and no technical security features of an AIS and other safeguards, made in support of the approval/accreditation process, to establish the extent to which a particular design and implementation meet a set of specified security requirements. Note: There remain two other definitions in active common usage that differ according to circumstances. The issue of a formal statement confirming the results of an evaluation, and that the evaluation criteria used were correctly applied. Synonym for IT security certification

Certification authority (CA)
> An entity that issues digital certificates (especially X.509 certificates) and vouches for the binding between the data items in a certificate. 'An authority trusted by one or more users to create and assign certificates. Optionally, the certification authority may create the user's keys. Certificate users depend on the validity of information provided by a certificate. Thus, a CA should be someone that certificate users trust, and usually holds an official position created and granted power by a government, a corporation, or some other organization. A CA is responsible for managing the life cycle of certificates and, depending on the type of certificate and the CPS that applies, may be responsible for the life cycle of key pairs associated with the certificates.

Challenge/response
> An authentication process that verifies an identity by requiring correct authentication information to be provided in response to a challenge. In a computer system, the authentication information is usually a value that is required to be computed in response to an unpredictable challenge value.

Channel
> An information transfer path within a system. An information transfer path within a system. May also refer to the mechanism by which the path is effected.

Checksum
> A value that is computed by a function that is dependent on the contents of a data object and is stored or transmitted together with the object, for the purpose of detecting changes in the data To gain confidence that a data object has not been changed, an entity that later uses the data can compute a checksum and compare it with the checksum that was stored or transmitted with the object. Computer systems and networks employ checksums (and other mechanisms) to detect accidental changes in data.

Chernobyl packet

> A network packet that induces a broadcast storm and network meltdown. Typically an IP Ethernet datagram that passes through a gateway with both source and destination Ether and IP address set as the respective broadcast addresses for the subnetworks being gated between

Chosen-ciphertext attack

> A cryptanalysis technique in which the analyst tries to determine the key from knowledge of plaintext that corresponds to ciphertext selected (i.e., dictated) by the analyst.

Chosen-plaintext attack

> A cryptanalysis technique in which the analyst tries to determine the key from knowledge of ciphertext that corresponds to plaintext selected (i.e., dictated) by the analyst.

Cipher

> A cryptographic algorithm for encryption and decryption.

Cipher block chaining (CBC)

> An block cipher mode that enhances electronic codebook mode by chaining together blocks of ciphertext it produces. This mode operates by combining (exclusive OR-ing) the algorithm's ciphertext output block with the next plaintext block to form the next input block for the algorithm.

Cipher feedback (CFB)

> An block cipher mode that enhances electronic code book mode by chaining together the blocks of ciphertext it produces and operating on plaintext segments of variable length less than or equal to the block length. This mode operates by using the previously generated ciphertext segment as the algorithm's input (i.e., by 'feeding back' the ciphertext) to generate an output block, and then combining (exclusive OR-ing) that output block with the next plaintext segment (block length or less) to form the next ciphertext segment.

Ciphertext

> Data that has been transformed by encryption so that its semantic information content (i.e., its meaning) is no longer intelligible or directly available. Data produced through the use of encipherment. The semantic content of the resulting data is not available.

Ciphertext-only attack

> A cryptanalysis technique in which the analyst tries to determine the key solely from knowledge of intercepted ciphertext (although the analyst may also know other clues, such as the cryptographic algorithm, the language in which the plaintext was written, the subject matter of the plaintext, and some probable plaintext words.)

Classification level

> A grouping of classified information to which a hierarchical, restrictive security label is applied to increase protection of the data. The level of protection that is required to be applied to that information.

Clean system

> A computer system in which the operating system and application system software and files have just been freshly installed from trusted software distribution media. A clean system is not necessarily in a secure state.

Clearance level

> The security level of information to which a security clearance authorizes a person to have access.

Cleartext

> Data in which the semantic information content (i.e., the meaning) is intelligible or is directly available.

Client

A system entity that requests and uses a service provided by another system entity, called a 'server'. Usually, the requesting entity is a computer process, and it makes the request on behalf of a human user. In some cases, the server may itself be a client of some other server.

CLIPPER chip

The Mykotronx, Inc. MYK-82, an integrated microcircuit with a cryptographic processor that implements the SKIPJACK encryption algorithm and supports key escrow. The key escrow scheme for a chip involves a SKIPJACK key common to all chips that protects the unique serial number of the chip, and a second SKIPJACK key unique to the chip that protects all data encrypted by the chip. The second key is escrowed as split key components held by NIST and the U.S. Treasury Department.

Common Criteria

The Common Criteria is a standard for evaluating information technology products and systems, such as operating systems, computer networks, distributed systems, and applications. It states requirements for security functions and for assurance measures. Canada, France, Germany, the Netherlands, the United Kingdom, and the United States (NIST and NSA) began developing this standard in 1993, based on the European ITSEC, the Canadian Trusted Computer Product Evaluation Criteria (CTCPEC), and the U.S. 'Federal Criteria for Information Technology Security' (FC) and its precursor, the TCSEC. Work was done in cooperation with ISO/IEC Joint Technical Committee 1 (Information Technology), Subcommittee 27 (Security Techniques), Working Group 3 (Security Criteria). Version 2.1 of the Criteria is equivalent to ISO's International Standard 15408. The U.S. Government intends that this standard eventually will supersede both the TCSEC and FIPS PUB 140-1. The standard addresses data confidentiality, data integrity, and availability and may apply to other aspects of security. It focuses on threats to information arising from human activities, malicious or otherwise, but may apply to non-human threats. It applies to security measures implemented in hardware, firmware, or software. It does not apply to (a) administrative security not related directly to technical security, (b) technical physical aspects of security such as electromagnetic emanation control, evaluation methodology or administrative and legal framework under which the criteria may be applied, (d) procedures for use of evaluation results, or (e) assessment of inherent qualities of cryptographic algorithms.

Communication channel

The physical media and devices that provide the means for transmitting information from one component of a network to (one or more) other components

Communications security (COMSEC)

Measures that implement and assure security services in a communication system, particularly those that provide data confidentiality and data integrity and that authenticate communicating entities. Usually understood to include cryptographic algorithms and key management methods and processes, devices that implement them, and the life cycle management of keying material and devices.

Computer architecture

The set of layers and protocols (including formats and standards that different hardware and software must comply with to achieve stated objectives) which define a computer system. Computer architecture features can be available to application programs and system programmers in several modes, including a protected mode. e.g. the system-level features of computer architecture may include: (1) memory management, (2) protection, (3) multitasking, (4) input/output, (5) exceptions and multiprocessing, (6) initialization, (7) coprocessing and multiprocessing, (8) debugging, and (9) cache management.

Computer emergency response team (CERT)

An organization that studies computer and network INFOSEC in order to provide incident response services to victims of attacks, publish alerts concerning vulnerabilities and threats, and offer other information to help improve computer and network security. For example, the CERT Coordination Center at Carnegie-Mellon University (sometimes called 'the' CERT) and the Computer Incident Advisory Capability.

Confidentiality

The assurance that information is not disclosed to inappropriate entities or processes. The property that information is not made available or disclosed to unauthorized entities. The prevention of the

Secured Computing: A CISSP Study Guide, Copyright 2001

unauthorized disclosure of information. The concept of holding sensitive data in confidence, limited to an appropriate set of individuals or organizations.

Configuration

In configuration management, the functional and physical characteristics of hardware or software as set forth in technical documentation or achieved in a product

Configuration management

A discipline applying technical and administrative direction and surveillance to identify and document the functional and physical characteristics of a configuration item, control changes to those characteristics, record and report change processing and implementation status, and verify compliance with specified requirements.

Confinement

The prevention of the leaking of sensitive data from a program.

Context-dependent access control

Access control in which access is determined by the specific circumstances under which the data is being accessed.

Contingency plan

A plan for emergency response, backup operations, and post-disaster recovery in a system as part of a security program to ensure availability of critical system resources and facilitate continuity of operations in a crisis

Control zone

The space, expressed in feet of radius, surrounding equipment processing sensitive information, that is under sufficient physical and technical control to preclude an unauthorized entry or compromise.

Cookies

Cookies register information about a visit to a web site for future use by the server. A server may receive information of cookies of other sites as well which create concern in terms of breach of privacy.

Covert channel

A communication channel that allows a process to transfer information in a manner that violates the system's security policy. A covert channel typically communicates by exploiting a mechanism not intended to be used for communication.

Crack

A popular hacking tool used to crack passwords. System administrators also use Crack to assess weak passwords by novice users in order to better secure his/her system

Cross-certification

The act or process by which two CAs each certify a public key of the other, issuing a public-key certificate to that other CA.Cross-certification enables users to validate each other's certificate when the users are certified under different certification hierarchies.

Cryptanalysis

The mathematical science that deals with analysis of a cryptographic system in order to gain knowledge needed to break or circumvent the protection that the system is designed to provide. The analysis of a cryptographic system and/or its inputs and outputs to derive confidential variables and/or sensitive data including cleartext.

Cryptographic algorithm

An algorithm that employs the science of cryptography, including encryption algorithms, cryptographic hash algorithms, digital signature algorithms, and key agreement algorithms.

Cryptographic key

Usually shortened to just 'key'. An input parameter that varies the transformation performed by a cryptographic algorithm. 'A sequence of symbols that controls the operations of encipherment and decipherment. If a key value needs to be kept secret, the sequence of symbols (usually bits) that comprise it should be random, or at least pseudo-random, because that makes the key hard for an adversary to guess.

Cryptography

The principles, means, and methods for rendering information unintelligible, and for restoring encrypted information to intelligible form. The transformation of ordinary text, or 'plaintext,' into coded form by encryption and the transformation of coded text into plaintext by decryption. Cryptography can be used to support digital signature, key management or exchange, and communications privacy,

Cryptology

The science that includes both cryptography and cryptanalysis, and sometimes is said to include steganography.

Cut-and-paste attack

An active attack on the data integrity of ciphertext, effected by replacing sections of ciphertext with other ciphertext, such that the result appears to decrypt correctly but actually decrypts to plaintext that is forged to the satisfaction of the attacker.

Data diddling

An attack in which the attacker changes the data while en route from source to destination.

Data Encryption Algorithm (DEA)

A symmetric block cipher, defined as part of the U.S. Government's Data Encryption Standard. DEA uses a 64-bit key, of which 56 bits are independently chosen and 8 are parity bits, and maps a 64-bit block into another 64-bit block. This algorithm is usually referred to as 'DES'.

Data Encryption Standard (DES)

A cryptographic algorithm for the protection of unclassified data, published in U.S. Federal Information Processing Standard (FIPS) 46. The DES, which was approved by the U.S. National Institute of Standards and Technology (NIST), is intended for public and government use.

Data security

The protection of data from disclosure, alteration, destruction, or loss that either is accidental or is intentional but unauthorized. Both data confidentiality service and data integrity service are needed to achieve data security.

Database management system (DBMS)

A computer system whose main function is to facilitate the sharing of a common set of data among many different users. It may or may not maintain semantic relationships among the data items.

Datagram

A self-contained, independent entity of data carrying sufficient information to be routed from the source to the destination.

Decode

Convert encoded data back to its original form of representation.

Decrypt

Cryptographically restore ciphertext to the plaintext form it had before encryption.

Degauss

Apply a magnetic field to permanently remove, erase, or clear data from a magnetic storage medium, such as a tape or disk. Reduce magnetic flux density to zero by applying a reversing magnetic field.

Denial of service

The prevention of authorized access to system assets or services or the delaying of time-critical operations. Any action or series of actions that prevents any part of a system from functioning in

Secured Computing: A CISSP Study Guide, Copyright 2001

accordance with its intended purpose. This includes any action that causes unauthorized destruction, modification, or delay of service.

Dictionary attack

An attack that uses a brute-force technique of successively trying all the words in some large, exhaustive list. For example, an attack on an authentication service by trying all possible passwords; or an attack on encryption by encrypting some known plaintext phrase with all possible keys so that the key for any given encrypted message containing that phrase may be obtained by lookup.

Diffie-Hellman

A key agreement algorithm published in 1976 by Whitfield Diffie and Martin Hellman Diffie-Hellman does key establishment, not encryption. However, the key that it produces may be used for encryption, for further key management operations, or for any other cryptography. The difficulty of breaking Diffie-Hellman is considered to be equal to the difficulty of computing discrete logarithms modulo a large prime. The algorithm is described in and. In brief, Alice and Bob together pick large integers that satisfy certain mathematical conditions, and then use the integers to each separately compute a public-private key pair. They send each other their public key. Each person uses their own private key and the other person's public key to compute a key, k that, because of the mathematics of the algorithm, is the same for each of them. Passive wiretapping cannot learn the shared k, because k is not transmitted, and neither are the private keys needed to compute k. However, without additional mechanisms to authenticate each party to the other, a protocol based on the algorithm may be vulnerable to a man-in-the-middle attack.

Digital certificate

A certificate document in the form of a digital data object (a data object used by a computer) to which is appended a computed digital signature value that depends on the data object Although the recommended definition can be interpreted to include those items, the security community does not use the term with those meanings.

Digital envelope

A digital envelope for a recipient is a combination of encrypted content data (of any kind) and   the content encryption key in an encrypted form that has been prepared for the use of the recipient

Digital signature

 A method for verifying that a message originated from a principal and that it has not changed en route. Encrypting a digest of the message with the private key of the signing party typically performs digital signatures. A non-forgeable transformation of data that allows the proof of the source (with non-repudiation) and the verification of the integrity of that data.

Digital signature algorithm (DSA)

An asymmetric cryptographic algorithm that produces a digital signature in the form of a pair of large numbers. The signature is computed using rules and parameters such that the identity of the signer and the integrity of the signed data can be verified.

Digital Signature Standard (DSS)

The U.S. Government standard that specifies the Digital Signature Algorithm (DSA), which involves asymmetric cryptography. A U.S. Federal Information Processing Standard proposed by NIST (National Institute of Standards and Technology) to support digital signature.

Digitized signature

used mainly to refer to various forms of digitized images of handwritten signatures, the term should be avoided because it might be confused with 'digital signature'.

Disaster plan

A synonym for contingency plan.

Discretionary access control (DAC)

A means of restricting access to objects based on the identity of subjects and/or groups to which they belong. The controls are discretionary in the sense that a subject with a certain access permission is capable of passing that permission (perhaps indirectly) on to any other subject (unless restrained by mandatory access control).

Distributed computing environment (DCE)

      Open Group's integration of a set of technologies for application development and deployment in a distributed environment. Security features include a Kerberos-based authentication system, GSS API interface, ACL-based authorization environment, delegation, and audit

DNS spoofing

      Assuming the DNS name of another system either by corrupting the name service cache of a victim system or by compromising a domain name server for a valid domain.

Domain

      Security usage: An environment or context that is defined by a security policy, security model, or security architecture to include a set of system resources and the set of system entities that have the right to access the resources. Internet usage: That part of the Internet domain name space tree that is at or below the name the specifies the domain. A domain is a subdomain of another domain if it is contained within that domain.

Domain Name System (DNS)

      The main Internet operations database, which is distributed over a collection of servers and used by client software for purposes such as translating a domain name-style host name into an IP address (e.g., 'rosslyn.bbn.com' is '192.1.7.10') and locating host that accepts mail for some mailbox address.

El Gamal algorithm

      An algorithm for asymmetric cryptography, invented in 1985 by Taher El Gamal, that is based on the difficulty of calculating discrete logarithms and can be used for both encryption and digital signatures. electronic codebook (ECB) An block cipher mode in which a plaintext block is used directly as input to the encryption algorithm and the resultant output block is used directly as ciphertext.

Electromagnetic interference (EMI)

      Electromagnetic phenomena which either directly or indirectly can contribute to a degradation in the performance of an electronic system.

Electronic data interchange (EDI)

      Computer-to-computer exchange, between trading partners, of business data in standardized document formats EDI formats have been standardized primarily by ANSI X12 and by EDIFACT (EDI for Administration, Commerce, and Transportation), which is an international, UN-sponsored standard primarily used in Europe and Asia. X12 and EDIFACT are aligning to create a single, global EDI standard.

Elliptic curve cryptography

      A type of asymmetric cryptography based on mathematics of groups that are defined by the points on a curve. The most efficient implementation of ECC is claimed to be stronger per bit of key (against cryptanalysis that uses a brute force attack) than any other known form of asymmetric cryptography. ECC is based on mathematics different than the kinds originally used to define the Diffie-Hellman algorithm and the Digital Signature Algorithm. ECC is based on the mathematics of groups defined by the points on a curve, where the curve is defined by a quadratic equation in a finite field. ECC can be used to define both an algorithm for key agreement that is an analog of Diffie-Hellman and an algorithm for digital signature that is an analog of DSA.

Emanations

      An signal (electromagnetic, acoustic, or other medium) that is emitted by a system (through radiation or conductance) as a consequence (i.e., byproduct) of its operation, and that may contain information. Unintentional data-related or intelligence-bearing signals that, if intercepted and analyzed, disclose the information transmission received, handled, or otherwise processes by any information processing equipment.

Encapsulating Security Payload (ESP)

      An Internet IPsec protocol designed to provide a mix of security services--especially data confidentiality service--in the Internet Protocol. ESP may be used alone, or in combination with the IPsec AH protocol, or in a nested fashion with tunneling. Security services can be provided between a pair of communicating hosts, between a pair of communicating security gateways, or between a host and a gateway. The IP header encapsulates the ESP header, and the ESP header encapsulates either the upper layer protocol header (transport mode) or an IP header (tunnel mode). ESP can provide data confidentiality service, data origin authentication service, connectionless data integrity service, an anti-replay service, and limited traffic flow confidentiality. The set of services depends on the placement of the implementation and on options selected when the security association is established.

Encrypt

Cryptographically transform data to produce ciphertext.

Encryption

The process of making information indecipherable to protect it from unauthorized viewing or use, especially during transmission or storage. Encryption is based on an algorithm and at least one key. Even if the algorithm is known, the information cannot be decrypted without the key(s).

End-to-end encryption

Continuous protection of data that flows between two points in network, provided by encrypting data when it leaves its source, leaving it encrypted while it passes through any intermediate computers (such as routers), and decrypting only when the data arrives at the intended destination. When two points are separated by multiple communication links that are connected by one or more intermediate relays, end-to-end encryption enables the source and destination systems to protect their communications without depending on the intermediate systems to provide the protection.

Entrapment

The deliberate planting of apparent flaws in a system for the purpose of detecting attempted penetrations.

European Information Technology Security Evaluation Criteria (ITSEC)

Commission of the European Communities, European Information Technology Security Evaluation Criteria (ITSEC), Provisional Harmonized Criteria: Version 1.2, Office for Official Publications of the European Communities, Luxembourg, June 1991

Extranet

A computer network that an organization uses to carry application data traffic between the organization and its business partners. An extranet can be implemented securely, either on the Internet or using Internet technology, by constructing the extranet as a VPN.

Fail-safe

A mode of system termination that automatically leaves system processes and components in a secure state when a failure occurs or is detected in the system.

Fault tolerance

A method of ensuring continued operation through redundancy and diversity.

Federal Information Processing Standards (FIPS)

The Federal Information Processing Standards Publication (FIPS PUB) series issued by the U.S. National Institute of Standards and Technology as technical guidelines for U.S. Government procurements of information processing system equipment and services. Issued under the provisions of section 111 of the Federal Property and Administrative Services Act of 1949 as amended by the Computer Security Act of 1987, Public Law 100-235.

File Transfer Protocol (FTP)

A TCP-based, application-layer, Internet Standard protocol for moving data files from one computer to another.

Filtering router

An Internet work router that selectively prevents the passage of data packets according to a security policy. A filtering router may be used as a firewall or part of a firewall. A router usually receives a packet from a network and decides where to forward it on a second network. A filtering router does the same, but first decides whether the packet should be forwarded at all, according to some security policy. The policy is implemented by rules (packet filters) loaded into the router. The rules mostly involve values of data packet control fields (especially IP source and destination addresses and TCP port numbers).$ financial institution. An establishment responsible for facilitating customer-initiated transactions or transmission of funds for the extension of credit or the custody, loan, exchange, or issuance of money.

Firewall

An internetwork gateway that restricts data communication traffic to and from one of the connected networks (the one said to be 'inside' the firewall) and thus protects that network's system resources against threats from the other network (the one that is said to be 'outside' the firewall). A firewall typically protects a smaller, secure network (such as a corporate LAN, or even just one host) from a larger network (such as the Internet). The firewall is installed at the point where the networks connect, and the firewall applies security policy rules to control traffic that flows in and out of the protected network. A firewall is not always a single computer.

Firmware

Computer programs and data stored in hardware--typically in read-only memory (ROM) or programmable read-only memory (PROM)--such that the programs and data cannot be dynamically written or modified during execution of the programs.

Flooding

An attack that attempts to cause a failure in (especially, in the security of) a computer system or other data processing entity by providing more input than the entity can process properly.$ flow analysis An analysis performed on a nonprocedural formal system specification that locates potential flows of information between system variables. By assigning security levels to the variables, the analysis can find some types of covert channels.

Fortezza

A registered trademark of NSA, used for a family of interoperable security products that implement a NIST/NSA-approved suite of cryptographic algorithms for digital signature, hash, encryption, and key exchange. The products include a PC card that contains a CAPSTONE chip, serial port modems, server boards, smart cards, and software implementations.

Gateway

A relay mechanism that attaches to two (or more) computer networks that have similar functions but dissimilar implementations and that enables host computers on one network to communicate with hosts on the other; an intermediate system that is the interface between two computer networks. In theory, gateways are conceivable at any OSI layer. In practice, they operate at OSI layer 3 or layer 7. When the two networks differ in the protocol by which they offer service to hosts, the gateway may translate one protocol into another or otherwise facilitate interoperation of hosts.

Generic Security Service Application Program Interface (GSS-API)

An Internet Standard protocol that specifies calling conventions by which an application (typically another communication protocol) can obtain authentication, integrity, and confidentiality security services independently of the underlying security mechanisms and technologies, thus allowing the application source code to be ported to different environments. A GSS-API caller accepts tokens provided to it by its local GSS-API implementation and transfers the tokens to a peer on a remote system; that peer passes the received tokens to its local GSS-API implementation for processing.

Granularity

Relative fineness or coarseness to which an access controls mechanism or other IT product aspect can be adjusted.

Hash function

An algorithm that computes a value based on a data object (such as a message or file; usually variable-length; possibly very large), thereby mapping the data object to a smaller data object (the 'hash result') which is usually a fixed-size value. A (mathematical) function which maps values from a large (possibly very large) domain into a smaller range. A 'good' hash function is such that the results of applying the function to a (large) set of values in the domain will be evenly distributed (and apparently at random) over the range. The kind of hash function needed for security applications is called a 'cryptographic hash function', an algorithm for which it is computationally infeasible (because no attack is significantly more efficient than brute force) to find either a data object that maps to a pre-specified hash result (the 'one-way' property) or two data objects that map to the same hash result (the 'collision-free' property).

HMAC

A keyed hash that can be based on any iterated cryptographic hash (e.g., MD5 or SHA-1), so that the cryptographic strength of HMAC depends on the properties of the selected cryptographic hash. Assume that H is a generic cryptographic hash in which a function is iterated on data blocks of length B bytes. L is the length of the of hash result of H. K is a secret key of length L <= K <= B. The values IPAD and OPAD are fixed strings used as inner and outer padding and defined as follows: IPAD = the byte 0x36 repeated B times, OPAD = the byte 0x5C repeated B times. HMAC is computed by H(K XOR OPAD, H(K XOR IPAD, inputdata)). The goals of HMAC are as follows:

- To use available cryptographic hash functions without modification, particularly functions that perform well in software and for which software is freely and widely available.
- To preserve the original performance of the selected hash without significant degradation.
- To use and handle keys in a simple way.
- To have a well-understood cryptographic analysis of the strength of the mechanism based on reasonable assumptions about the underlying hash function.
- To enable easy replacement of the hash function in case a faster or stronger hash is found or required.

Honey pot

A system (e.g., a web server) or a system resource (e.g., a file on a server), that is designed to be attractive to potential crackers and intruders, like honey is attractive to bears.

HTTPS

When used in the first part of a URL (the part that precedes the colon and specifies an access scheme or protocol), this term specifies the use of HTTP enhanced by a security mechanism, which is usually SSL.

Hybrid encryption

An application of cryptography that combines two or more encryption algorithms, particularly a combination of symmetric and asymmetric encryption. Asymmetric algorithms require more computation than equivalently strong symmetric ones. Thus, asymmetric encryption is not normally used for data confidentiality except in distributing symmetric keys in applications where the key data is usually short (in terms of bits) compared to the data it protects.

Hypertext Markup Language (HTML)

A platform-independent system of syntax and semantics for adding characters to data files (particularly text files) to represent the data's structure and to point to related data, thus creating hypertext for use in the World Wide Web and other applications.

Hypertext Transfer Protocol (HTTP)

A TCP-based, application-layer, client-server, Internet protocol used to carry data requests and responses in the World Wide Web.

ICMP flood

A denial of service attack that sends a host more ICMP echo request ('ping') packets than the protocol implementation can handle.

Identification

Process that enables recognition of an entity by an IT product. Process that enables recognition of an entity by an IT product/system that may be by the use of unique machine-readable user names.

Incident

Event that has actual or potentially adverse effects on an information system. Any intrusion or attempted intrusion into a computer system. Incidents can include probes of multiple computer systems.

Information Technology Security Evaluation Criteria (TCSEC)

Standard developed for use in the European Union; accommodates wider range of security assurance and functionality combinations than the TCSEC. Superseded by the Common Criteria.

Information warfare

Actions taken to achieve information superiority by affecting adversary information, information based processes, and information systems, while defending our own information, information based processes, and information systems. Any action to deny, exploit, corrupt, or destroy the enemy's information and its functions, protect our selves against those actions; and exploiting our own military information functions.

INFOSEC

Abbreviation for 'information security', referring to security measures that implement and assure security services in computer systems (i.e., COMPUSEC) and communication systems (i.e., COMSEC).

Integrity

Correctness and appropriateness of the content and/or source of a piece of information. The prevention of the unauthorized modification of information.

International Data Encryption Algorithm (IDEA)

This is a symmetric encryption algorithm that is popular outside of the United States and Canada. However, DES is still the most popular symmetric algorithm anywhere.

Internet Architecture Board (IAB)

A technical advisory group of the ISOC, chartered by the ISOC Trustees to provide oversight of Internet architecture and protocols and, in the context of Internet Standards, a body to which decisions of the IESG may be appealed. Responsible for approving appointments to the IESG from among nominees submitted by the IETF nominating committee.

Internet Assigned Numbers Authority (IANA)

From the early days of the Internet, the IANA was chartered by the ISOC and the U.S. Government's Federal Network Council to be the central coordination, allocation, and registration body for parameters for Internet protocols. Superseded by ICANN.

Internet Control Message Protocol (ICMP)

An Internet Standard protocol that is used to report error conditions during IP datagram processing and to exchange other information concerning the state of the IP network.

Internet Engineering Task Force (IETF)

A self-organized group of people who make contributions to the development of Internet technology. The principal body engaged in developing Internet Standards, although not itself a part of the ISOC. Composed of Working Groups, which are arranged into Areas (such as the Security Area), each coordinated by one or more Area Directors. A committee selected at random from regular IETF meeting attendees who have volunteered makes nominations to the IAB and the IESG. Internet Message Access Protocol, version 4 (IMAP4) An Internet protocol by which a client workstation can dynamically access a mailbox on a server host to manipulate and retrieve mail messages that the server has received and is holding for the client.

Internet Protocol (IP)

A Internet Standard protocol (version 4 and version 6) that moves datagrams (discrete sets of bits) from one computer to another across an internetwork but does not provide reliable delivery, flow control, sequencing, or other end-to-end services that TCP provides. In the OSIRM, IP would be located at the top of layer 3.

Internet Protocol security (IPsec)

The name of the IETF working group that is specifying security architecture and protocols to provide security services for Internet Protocol traffic. A collective name for that architecture and set of protocols. (Implementation of IPsec protocols is optional for IP version 4, but mandatory for IP version 6.)

Interoperability

The ability of computers to act upon information received from one another.

Intranet

A computer network, especially one based on Internet technology, that an organization uses for its own internal, and usually private, purposes and that is closed to outsiders.

Intrusion detection

A security service that monitors and analyzes system events for the purpose of finding, and providing real-time or near real-time warning of, attempts to access system resources in an unauthorized manner. Pertaining to techniques that attempt to detect intrusion into a computer or network by observation of security logs or audit data. Detection of break-ins or attempts either manually or via software expert systems that operate on logs or other information available on the network

IP spoofing

An attack whereby a system attempts to illicitly impersonate another system by using IP network address.

IPsec Key Exchange (IKE)

An Internet, IPsec, key-establishment protocol (partly based on OAKLEY) that is intended for putting in place authenticated keying material for use with ISAKMP and for other security associations, such as in AH and ESP.

Isolation

The containment of subjects and objects in a system in such a way that they are separated from one another, as well as from the protection controls of the operating system.

IT security certification

The issue, by an independent body, of a formal statement or certificate confirming the results of an evaluation of a TOE, and the fact that the evaluation criteria used were correctly applied. Note: this term could also be called 'TOE certification' to make its application clearer.

Kerberos

A third-party trusted host authentication system devised at MIT within Project Athena. The Kerberos authentication server is a central system that knows about every principal and its passwords. It issues tickets to principals who successfully authenticate themselves. These tickets can be used to authenticate one principal (e.g. a user) to another (e.g. a server application). Moreover, Kerberos sets up a session key for the principals that can be used to protect the privacy and the integrity of the communication. For this reason, the Kerberos system is also called a Key Distribution Center (KDC).

Key

A long string of seemingly random bits used with cryptographic algorithms to create or verify digital signatures and encrypt or decrypt messages and conversations. The keys must be known or guessed to forge a digital signature or decrypt an encrypted message

Key distribution center (KDC)

A type of key center (used in symmetric cryptography) that implements a key distribution protocol to provide keys (usually, session keys) to two (or more) entities that wish to communicate securely A KDC distributes keys to Alice and Bob, who (a) wish to communicate with each other but do not currently share keys, (b) each share a KEK with the KDC, and may not be able to generate or acquire keys by themselves. Alice requests the keys from the KDC. The KDC generates or acquires the keys and makes two identical sets. The KDC encrypts one set in the KEK it shares with Alice, and sends that encrypted set to Alice. The KDC encrypts the second set in the KEK it shares with Bob, and either sends that encrypted set to Alice for her to forward to Bob, or sends it directly to Bob.

Key recovery

A process for learning the value of a cryptographic key that was previously used to perform some cryptographic operation. Techniques that provide an intentional, alternate (i.e., secondary) means to access the key used for data confidentiality service in an encrypted association. We assume that the encryption mechanism has a primary means of obtaining the key through a key establishment algorithm or protocol. For the secondary means, there are two classes of key recovery techniques-- key escrow and key encapsulation:

- 'Key escrow': A key recovery technique for storing knowledge of
- Cryptographic key or parts thereof in the custody of one or more third parties called 'escrow agents', so that the key can be recovered and used in specified circumstances. Key escrow is typically implemented with split knowledge techniques. For example, the Escrowed Encryption Standard entrusts two components of a device-unique split key to separate escrow agents. The agents provide the components only to someone legally authorized to conduct electronic surveillance of telecommunications encrypted by that specific device. The components are used to reconstruct the device-unique key, and it is used to obtain the session key needed to decrypt communications.
- 'Key encapsulation': A key recovery technique for storing knowledge of a cryptographic key by encrypting it with another key and ensuring that that only certain third parties called 'recovery agents' can perform the decryption operation to retrieve the stored key. Key encapsulation typically allows direct retrieval of the secret key used to provide data confidentiality.

A broad term that applies to many different techniques including key-escrow, commercial key recovery, cryptographic backup and recovery, and trusted third party. Implementations can include split knowledge using two or more trusted third parties and key encrypting keys

Key-escrow

Keys are used to encrypt and decrypt files. key-escrow is used to store keys for use by third parties to access the data in encrypted files.

Known-plaintext attack

A cryptanalysis technique in which the analyst tries to determine the key from knowledge of some plaintext-ciphertext pairs (although the analyst may also have other clues, such as the knowing the cryptographic algorithm

Lattice model

A security model for flow control in a system, based on the lattice that is formed by the finite security levels in a system and their partial ordering. The model describes the semantic structure formed by a finite set of security levels, such as those used in military organizations. A lattice is a finite set together with a partial ordering on its elements such that for every pair of elements there is a least upper bound and a greatest lower bound. For example, a lattice is formed by a finite set S of security levels -- i.e., a set S of all ordered pairs (x, c), where x is one of a finite set X of hierarchically ordered classification levels (X1, ..., Xm), and c is a (possibly empty) subset of a finite set C of non-hierarchical categories (C1, ..., Cn) -- together with the 'dominate' relation.

Layer 2 Tunneling Protocol (L2TP)

An Internet client-server protocol that combines aspects of PPTP and L2F and supports tunneling of PPP over an IP network or over frame relay or other switched network. PPP can in turn encapsulate any OSI layer 3 protocol. Thus, L2TP does not specify security services; it depends on protocols layered above and below it to provide any needed security

Leapfrog attack

Use of userid and password information obtained illicitly from one host to compromise another host. The act of TELNETing through one or more hosts in order to confuse a trace (a standard cracker procedure).

Least privilege

The principle that a security architecture should be designed so that each system entity is granted the minimum system resources and authorizations that the entity needs to do its work.

Lightweight Directory Access Protocol (LDAP)

A client-server protocol that supports basic use of the X.500 Directory (or other directory servers) without incurring the resource requirements of the full Directory Access Protocol (DAP). Designed for simple management and browser applications that provide simple read/write interactive directory service. Supports both simple authentication and strong authentication of the client to the directory server.

Link encryption

Stepwise protection of data that flows between two points in a network, provided by encrypting data separately on each network link, i.e., by encrypting data when it leaves a host or subnetwork relay and decrypting when it arrives at the next host or relay. Each link may use a different key or even a different algorithm.

Logic bomb

Malicious logic that activates when specified conditions are met. Usually intended to cause denial of service or otherwise damage system resources. A resident computer program that triggers the perpetration of an unauthorized act when particular states of the system are realized. A resident computer program which, when executed, checks for particular conditions or particular states of the system which, when satisfied, triggers the perpetration of an unauthorized act.

Magnetic remanence

A measure of the magnetic flux density remaining after removal of the applied magnetic force. Refers to any data remaining on magnetic storage media after removal of the power.

Mail bomb

The mail sent to surge others to send, massive amounts of email to a single system or person with the intent to crash the recipient's system. Mail bombing is widely regarded as a serious offense.

Maintenance hook

Special instructions in software to allow easy maintenance and additional feature development. These are not clearly defined during access for design specification. Hooks frequently allow entry into the code at unusual points or without the usual checks, so they are a serious security risk if they are not removed prior to live implementation. Maintenance hooks are special types of trap doors.

Malicious code

Hardware, software, or firmware that is intentionally included in a system for an unauthorized purpose; e.g. a Trojan horse.

Man-in-the-middle

A form of active wiretapping attack in which the attacker intercepts and selectively modifies communicated data in order to masquerade as one or more of the entities involved in a communication association. For example, suppose Alice and Bob try to establish a session key by using the Diffie-Hellman algorithm without data origin authentication service. A 'man in the middle' could (a) block direct communication between Alice and Bob and then (b) masquerade as Alice sending data to Bob, masquerade as Bob sending data to Alice, (d) establish separate session keys with each of them, and (e) function as a clandestine proxy server between them in order to capture or modify sensitive information that Alice and Bob think they are sending only to each other.

Mandatory access control (MAC)

An access control service that enforces a security policy based on comparing (a) security labels (which indicate how sensitive or critical system resources are) with (b) security clearances (which indicate system entities are eligible to access certain resources). This kind of access control is called 'mandatory' because an entity that has clearance to access a resource may not, just by its own volition, enable another entity to access that resource. A means of restricting access to objects based on the sensitivity (as represented by a label) of the information contained in the objects and the

Secured Computing: A CISSP Study Guide, Copyright 2001

formal authorization (i.e., clearance) of subjects to access information of such sensitivity.' A means of restricting access to objects based on the sensitivity (as represented by a label) of the information contained in the objects and the formal authorization (i.e. clearance) of subjects to access information of such sensitivity.

MD2

A cryptographic hash that produces a 128-bit hash result, was designed by Ron Rivest, and is similar to MD4 and MD5 but slower.

MD4

A cryptographic hash that produces a 128-bit hash result and was designed by Ron Rivest.

MD5

A cryptographic hash that produces a 128-bit hash result and was designed by Ron Rivest to be an improved version of MD4.

Metadata

Data referring to other data; data (such as data structures, indices, and pointers) that are used to instantiate an abstraction (such as 'process,' 'task,' 'segment,' 'file,' or 'pipe'). A special database also referred to as a data dictionary, containing descriptions of the elements (e.g. relations, domains, entities, or relationships) of a database.

MIME Object Security Services (MOSS)

An Internet protocol that applies end-to-end encryption and digital signature to MIME message content, using symmetric cryptography for encryption and asymmetric cryptography for key distribution and signature. MOSS is based on features and specifications of PEM.

Multipurpose internet mail extensions (MIME)

An Internet protocol that enhances the basic format of Internet electronic mail messages to be able to use character sets other than US-ASCII for textual headers and text content, and to carry non-textual and multi-part content.

National Institute of Standards and Technology (NIST)

A U.S. Department of Commerce agency that promotes U.S. economic growth by working with industry to develop and apply technology, measurements, and standards. Has primary Government responsibility for INFOSEC standards for unclassified but sensitive information.

Network reference monitor

An access-control concept that refers to an abstract machine that mediates all access to objects within the network by subjects within the network

Network security

The protection of networks and their services from unauthorized modification, destruction, or disclosure. Providing an assurance that the network performs its critical functions correctly and there are no harmful side-effects. Includes providing for information accuracy.

Network security architecture

A subset of network architecture specifically addressing security-relevant issues.

Non-discretionary access control

A means of restricting access to objects based largely on administrative actions.

Non-repudiation

The reasonable assurance that a principal cannot deny being the originator of a message after sending it. Non-repudiation is achieved by encrypting the message digest using a principal's private key. A trusted certification authority must certify the public key of the principal.

Nonce

A random or non-repeating value that is included in data exchanged by a protocol, usually for the purpose of guaranteeing aliveness and thus detecting and protecting against replay attacks.

Secured Computing: A CISSP Study Guide, Copyright 2001

OAKLEY

A key establishment protocol (proposed for IPsec but superseded by IKE) based on the Diffie-Hellman algorithm and designed to be a compatible component of ISAKMP. OAKLEY establishes a shared key with an assigned identifier and associated authenticated identities for parties. I.e., OAKLEY provides authentication service to ensure the entities of each other's identity, even if the Diffie-Hellman exchange is threatened by active wiretapping. Also, provides public-key forward secrecy for the shared key and supports key updates, incorporation of keys distributed by out-of-band mechanisms, and user-defined abstract group structures for use with Diffie-Hellman.

Object

A passive entity that contains or receives information. Access to an object potentially implies access to the information it contains. Examples of objects are records, blocks, pages, segments, files, directories, directory trees, and programs, as well as bits, bytes, words, fields, processors, video displays, keyboards, clocks, printers, network nodes, etc.

Object reuse

The reassignment and reuse of a storage medium (e.g., page frame, disk sector, magnetic tape) that once contained one or more objects. To be securely reused and assigned to a new subject, storage media must contain no residual data (magnetic remanence) from the object(s) previously contained in the media.' The reassignment and reuse of a storage medium (e.g. page frame, disk sector, magnetic tape) that once contained one or more objects. To be securely reused and assigned to a new subject, storage media must contain no residual data (magnetic remanence) from the object(s) previously contained in the media. The reassignment of a medium (e.g. page frame, disk sector, magnetic tape) that contained one or more objects to some subject. To be securely reassigned, such media must contain no residual data from the previously contained object(s). The reassignment to some subject of a medium (e.g. page frame, disk sector, magnetic tape) that contained one or more objects. To be securely reassigned, such media must contain no residual data from the previously contained object(s).

One-time pad

An encryption algorithm in which the key is a random sequence of symbols and each symbol is used for encryption only one time--to encrypt only one plaintext symbol to produce only one ciphertext symbol--and a copy of the key is used similarly for decryption. To ensure one-time use, the copy of the key used for encryption is destroyed after use, as is the copy used for decryption. This is the only encryption algorithm that is truly unbreakable, even given unlimited resources for cryptanalysis, but key management costs and synchronization problems make it impractical except in special situations

One-way encryption

Irreversible transformation of plaintext to ciphertext, such that the plaintext cannot be recovered from the ciphertext by other than exhaustive procedures even if the cryptographic key is known.

One-way function

A (mathematical) function, f, which is easy to compute, but which for a general value y in the range, it is computationally difficult to find a value x in the domain such that $f(x) = y$. There may be a few values of y for which finding x is not computationally difficult.

Out of band

Transfer of information using a channel that is outside (i.e., separate from) the channel that is normally used. Out-of-band mechanisms are often used to distribute shared secrets (e.g., a symmetric key) or other sensitive information items (e.g., a root key) that are needed to initialize or otherwise enable the operation of cryptography or other security mechanisms.$ output feedback (OFB) A block cipher mode that modifies electronic codebook mode to operate on plaintext segments of variable length less than or equal to the block length. This mode operates by directly using the algorithm's previously generated output block as the algorithm's next input block (i.e., by 'feeding back' the output block) and combining (exclusive OR-ing) the output block with the next plaintext segment (of block length or less) to form the next ciphertext segment.

Overt channel

A path within a computer system or network that is designed for the authorized transfer of data. Compare covert channel. An overt channel is a path within a network that is designed for the authorized transfer of data. Communications path within a computer system or network that is designed for the authorized transfer of data.

Packet filter

A type of firewall in which each IP packet is examined and either allowed to pass through or rejected. Normally packet filtering is a first line of defense and is typically combined with application proxies for more security.

Passive attack

Attack, which does not result in an unauthorized state change, such as an attack that only monitors and/or records data.

Pass phrase

A pass phrase is a long password. It is often composed of several words and symbols to make it harder to guess.

Password

A secret data value, usually a character string that is used as authentication information. A password is usually matched with a user identifier that is explicitly presented in the authentication process, but in some cases the identity may be implicit. Using a password as authentication information assumes that the password is known only by the system entity whose identity is being authenticated. Therefore, in a network environment where wiretapping is possible, simple authentication that relies on transmission of static (i.e., repetitively used) passwords as cleartext is inadequate

Password Authentication Protocol (PAP)

A simple authentication mechanism in PPP. In PAP, a user identifier and password are transmitted in cleartext.

Password sniffing

Passive wiretapping, usually on a local area network, to gain knowledge of passwords. Sniffers are programs that monitor all traffic on a network, collecting a certain number of bytes from the beginning of each session, usually the part where the password is typed unencrypted on certain common Internet services such as FTP and Telnet

Penetration

Successful, repeatable, unauthorized access to a protected system resource. The successful act of bypassing the security mechanisms of a system. The successful act of bypassing the security mechanisms; the unauthorized access to an automated system. The successful violation of a protected system.

Penetration test

A system test, often part of system certification, in which evaluators attempt to circumvent the security features of the system. Penetration testing may be performed under various constraints and conditions. However, for a TCSEC evaluation, testers are assumed to have all system design and implementation documentation, including source code, manuals, and circuit diagrams, and to work under no greater constraints than those applied to ordinary users.

Piggyback attack

A form of active wiretapping in which the attacker gains access to a system via intervals of inactivity in another user's legitimate communication connection. Sometimes called a 'between-the-lines' attack.

Ping of death

An attack that sends an improperly large ICMP echo request packet (a 'ping') with the intent of overflowing the input buffers of the destination machine and causing it to crash. The use of Ping with an address number higher than 65,507. This will cause a SYN flood, and cause a denial of service. RFC-791 says IP packets can be up to 65,535, with the IP header of 20 bytes, and ICMP header of 8 octets (65535-20-8 =65507). Sending a bigger packet greater than 65507 octets causes the originating system to fragment the packet.

Ping sweep

    An attack that sends ICMP echo requests ('pings') to a range of IP addresses, with the goal of finding hosts that can be probed for vulnerabilities.

Plaintext

    Data that is input to and transformed by an encryption process, or that is output by a decryption process. Usually, the plaintext input to an encryption operation is cleartext. But in some cases, the input is ciphertext that was output from another encryption operation.

Point-to-point protocol (PPP)

    An Internet Standard protocol for encapsulation and full-duplex transportation of network layer (mainly OSI layer 3) protocol data packets over a link between two peers, and for multiplexing different network layer protocols over the same link. Includes optional negotiation to select and use a peer entity authentication protocol to authenticate the peers to each other before they exchange network layer data. The point-to-point protocol, defined in RFC 1661, provides a method for transmitting packets over serial point-to-point links. There are many other RFCs, which define extensions to the basic protocol.

Point-to-point tunneling protocol (PPTP)

    An Internet client-server protocol (originally developed by Ascend and Microsoft) that enables a dial-up user to create a virtual extension of the dial-up link across a network by tunneling PPP over IP. PPP can encapsulate any Internet Protocol Suite network layer protocol (or OSI layer 3 protocol). Therefore, PPTP does not specify security services; it depends on protocols above and below it to provide any needed security. PPTP makes it possible to divorce the location of the initial dial-up server (i.e., the PPTP Access Concentrator, the client, which runs on a special-purpose host) from the location at which the dial-up protocol (PPP) connection is terminated and access to the network is provided (i.e., the PPTP Network Server, which runs on a general-purpose host). PPTP is combination of data and control packets. Data packets are PPP packets encapsulated using the Internet Generic Routing Encapsulation Protocol Version 2. Control packets perform PPTP service and maintenance functions.

POSIX

    Portable Operating System Interface for Computer Environments, standard [FP151, IS9945-1] (originally IEEE Standard P1003.1) that defines an operating system interface and environment to support application portability at the source code level. It is intended to be used by both application developers and system implementers. P1003.1 supports security functionality like those on most UNIX systems, including discretionary access control and privilege. IEEE Draft Standard P1003.6.1 specifies additional functionality not provided in the base standard, including (a) discretionary access control, (b) audit trail mechanisms, privilege mechanisms, (d) mandatory access control, and (e) information label mechanisms.

Post Office Protocol, version 3 (POP3)

    An Internet Standard protocol by which a client workstation can dynamically access a mailbox on a server host to retrieve mail messages that the server has received and is holding for the client. POP3 has mechanisms for optionally authenticating a client to server and providing other security services.

Pretty Good Privacy (PGP)

    Trademarks of Network Associates, Inc., referring to a computer program (and related protocols) that uses cryptography to provide data security for electronic mail and other applications on the Internet. PGP encrypts messages with IDEA in CFB mode, distributes the IDEA keys by encrypting them with RSA, and creates digital signatures on messages with MD5 and RSA. To establish ownership of public keys, PGP depends on the web of trust. A program, developed by Phil Zimmerman, which cryptographically protects files and electronic mail from being read by others. It may also be used to digitally sign a document or message, thus authenticating the creator.

Privacy Enhanced Mail (PEM)

    An Internet protocol to provide data confidentiality, data integrity, and data origin authentication for electronic mail. PEM encrypts messages with DES in CBC mode, provides key distribution of DES keys by encrypting them with RSA, and signs messages with RSA over either MD2 or MD5. To establish ownership of public keys, PEM uses a certification hierarchy, with X.509 public-key certificates and X.509 CRLs that are signed with RSA and MD2. PEM is designed to be compatible with a wide range of key management methods, but is limited to specifying security services only for

Secured Computing: A CISSP Study Guide, Copyright 2001

text messages and, like MOSS, has not been widely implemented in the Internet. Internet email, which provides confidentiality, authentication, and message integrity using various encryption methods.

Private key

The secret component of a pair of cryptographic keys used for asymmetric cryptography. '(In a public key cryptosystem) that key of a user's key pair which is known only by that user.' A cryptographic key used with a public key cryptographic algorithm, uniquely associated with an entity, and not made public. The undisclosed key in a matched key pair - private key and public key - that each party safeguards for public key cryptography.

Privilege

An authorization or set of authorizations to perform security-relevant functions, especially in the context of a computer operating system. Special authorization that is granted to particular users to perform security-relevant operations.

Protection ring

One of a hierarchy of privileged operation modes of a system that gives certain access rights to processes authorized to operate in that mode. One of a hierarchy of privileged modes of a system that gives certain access rights to user programs and processes authorized to operate in a given mode.

Protocol suite

A complementary collection of communication protocols used in computer network.

Protocols

A set of rules (i.e., formats and procedures) to implement and control some type of association (e.g., communication) between systems. (E.g., see: Internet Protocol.) In particular, a series of ordered steps involving computing and communication that are performed by two or more system entities to achieve a joint objective. A set of rules and formats, semantic, and syntactic, that permits entities to exchange information.

Proxy server

A computer process--often used as, or as part of, a firewall--that relays a protocol between client and server computer systems, by appearing to the client to be the server and appearing to the server to be the client. In a firewall, a proxy server usually runs on a bastion host, which may support proxies for several protocols (e.g., FTP, HTTP, and TELNET). Instead of a client in the protected enclave connecting directly to an external server, the internal client connects to the proxy server which in turn connects to the external server. The proxy server waits for a request from inside the firewall, forwards the request to the remote server outside the firewall, gets the response, then sends the response back to the client. The proxy may be transparent to the clients, or they may need to connect first to the proxy server, and then use that association to also initiate a connection to the real server. Proxies are generally preferred over SOCKS for their ability to perform caching, high-level logging, and access control. A proxy can provide security service beyond that which is normally part of the relayed protocol, such as access control based on peer entity authentication of clients, or peer entity authentication of servers when clients do not have that capability. A proxy at OSI layer 7 can also provide finer-grained security service than can a filtering router at OSI layer 3. For example, an FTP proxy could permit transfers out of, but not into, a protected network. A software agent that acts on behalf of something or someone else; decides whether or not the user has permission to use the proxy, perhaps does additional authentication, then connects to a remote destination on behalf of the user.

Pseudo-flaw

An apparent loophole deliberately implanted in an operating system program as a trap for intruders.

Public key

The publicly disclosable component of a pair of cryptographic keys used for asymmetric cryptography. (In a public key cryptosystem) that key of a user's key pair which is publicly known.' The key in a matched key pair - private key and public key - that may be published, e.g. posted in a directory, for public key cryptography

Public-key certificate

   A digital certificate that binds a system entity's identity to public key value, and possibly to additional data items; a digitally signed data structure that attests to the ownership of a public key. The digital signature on a public-key certificate is unforgeable. Thus, the certificate can be published, such as by posting it in a directory, without the directory having to protect the certificate's data integrity. The public key of a user, together with some other information, rendered unforgeable by encipherment with the private key of the certification authority which issued it.

Public-key cryptography

   The popular synonym for 'asymmetric cryptography'. Cryptography using two matched keys (or asymmetric cryptography) in which a single private key is not shared by a pair of users. Instead, users have their own key pairs. Each key pair consists of a matched private and public key. Public key cryptography can perform digital signature, secure transmission or exchange of secret keys, and/or encryption and decryption. Examples of public key cryptography are DSS (Digital Signature Standard) and RSA (Rivest, Shamir, and Adleman).

Public-key infrastructure (PKI)

   A system of CAs (and, optionally, RAs and other supporting servers and agents) that perform some set of certificate management, archive management, key management, and token management functions for a community of users in an application of asymmetric cryptography. PKIX usage: The set of hardware, software, people, policies, and procedures needed to create, manage, store, distribute, and revoke digital certificates based on asymmetric cryptography. The core PKI functions are (a) to register users and issue their public-key certificates, (b) to revoke certificates when required, and to archive data needed to validate certificates at a much later time. Key pairs for data confidentiality may be generated (and perhaps escrowed) by CAs or RAs, but requiring a PKI client to generate its own digital signature key pair helps maintain system integrity of the cryptographic system, because then only the client ever possesses the private key it uses. Also, an authority may be established to approve or coordinate CPSs, which are security policies under which components of a PKI operate. A number of other servers and agents may support the core PKI, and PKI clients may obtain services from them. The full range of such services is not yet fully understood and is evolving, but supporting roles may include archive agent, certified delivery agent, confirmation agent, digital notary, directory, key escrow agent, key generation agent, naming agent who ensures that issuers and subjects have unique identifiers within the PKI, repository, ticket-granting agent, and time stamp agent. Public and private keys, digital certificates, certification authorities, certificate revocation lists, and the standards that govern the use and validity of these elements make up an infrastructure where principals can engage in private and non-reputable transactions. This combination is called the Public Key Infrastructure.

Rainbow Series

   A set of more than 30 technical and policy documents with colored covers, issued by the NCSC, that discuss in detail the TCSEC and provide guidance for meeting and applying the criteria.

Read-only memory (ROM)

   A storage area in which the contents can be read but not altered during normal computer processing.

Real time

   The actual time in which something, such as the communication of information, takes place.

Reference monitor

   An access control concept that refers to an abstract machine that mediates all accesses to objects by subjects. A reference monitor should be complete (i.e., it mediates every access), isolated (i.e., it cannot be modified by other system entities), and verifiable (i.e., small enough to be subjected to analysis and tests to ensure that it is correct). Access mediation concept that refers to an abstract machine that mediates all accesses to objects by subjects

Remote access software

   This software allows a computer to use a modem to connect to another system. It also allows a computer to 'listen' for calls on a modem (this computer provides 'remote access service'.) Remote access software may provide access to a single computer or to a network.

Remote Authentication Dial-In User Service (RADIUS)

An Internet protocol for carrying dial-in users' authentication information and configuration information between a shared, centralized authentication server (the RADIUS server) and network access server (the RADIUS client) that needs to authenticate the users of its network access ports. A user of the RADIUS client presents authentication information to the client, and the client passes that information to the RADIUS server. The server authenticates the client using a shared secret value, then checks the user's authentication information, and finally returns to the client all authorization and configuration information needed by the client to deliver service to the user.

Residual risk

The risk that remains after countermeasures have been applied. The portion of risk that remains after security measures have been applied.

Residue

Data left in storage after processing operations are complete, but before degaussing or rewriting has taken place.

Risk

The expected loss due to, or impact of, anticipated threats in light of system vulnerabilities and strength or determination of relevant threat agents.

Risk analysis

The process of identifying security risks, determining their magnitude, and identifying areas needing safeguards. Risk analysis is a part of risk management.

A process that systematically identifies valuable system resources and threats to those resources, quantifies loss exposures (i.e., loss potential) based on estimated frequencies and costs of occurrence, and (optionally) recommends how to allocate resources to countermeasures so as to minimize total exposure. The analysis lists risks in order of cost and criticality, thereby determining where countermeasures should be applied first. It is usually financially and technically infeasible to counteract all aspects of risk, and so some residual risk will remain, even after all available countermeasures have been deployed.

Risk management

The process of identifying, controlling, and eliminating or minimizing uncertain events that may affect system resources. The total process of identifying, controlling, and eliminating or minimizing uncertain events that may affect system resources. It includes risk analysis, cost-benefit analysis, selection, implementation and test, security evaluation of safeguards, and overall security review. The total process to identify, control, and minimize the impact of uncertain events. The objective of the risk management program is to reduce risk and obtain and maintain DAA approval.

Role-based access control (RBAC)

A form of identity-based access control where the system entities that are identified and controlled are functional positions in an organization or process.

Root certificate

A certificate for which the subject is a root. Hierarchical PKI usage: The self-signed public-key certificate at the top of a certification hierarchy.

Router

A computer that is a gateway between two networks at OSI layer and that relays and directs data packets through that internetwork. The most common form of router operates on IP packets. Internet usage: In the context of the Internet protocol suite, networked computer that forwards Internet Protocol packets that are not addressed to the computer itself.

Salami technique

The process of secretly and repetitively slicing away tiny amounts of money in a way that is unlikely to be noticed.

Secured Computing: A CISSP Study Guide, Copyright 2001

Salt

A random value that is concatenated with a password before applying the one-way encryption function used to protect passwords that are stored in the database of an access control system. Salt protects a password-based access control system against a dictionary attack.

Sand boxed environment

The enforcement of access control by a native programming language such that an applet can only access limited resources. Java applets run in a sandboxed environment where an applet cannot read or write local files, cannot start or interact with local processes, and cannot load or link with dynamic libraries. While a sandboxed environment provides excellent protection against accidental or malicious destruction or abuse of local resources, it does not address the security issues related to authentication, authorization, privacy, integrity, and non-repudiation

Scavenging

Searching through object residue to acquire unauthorized data.

Screening router

A synonym for 'filtering router'. The condition of information being protected from being known by any system entities except those who are intended to know it.

Secret key

The key that two parties share and keep secret for secret key cryptography. Given secret key algorithms of equal strength, the approximate difficulty of decrypting encrypted messages by brute force search can be measured by the number of possible keys. e.g. a key length of 56 bits is over 65,000 times stronger or more resistant to attack than a key length of 40 bits.

Secret-key cryptography

A synonym for 'symmetric cryptography'. Cryptography based on a single key (or symmetric cryptography). It uses the same secret key for encryption and decryption. Messages are encrypted using a secret key and a secret key cryptographic algorithm, such as Skipjack, DES (Data Encryption Standard), RC2 (Rivest Cipher 2), or RC4 (Rivest Cipher 4

Secure Electronic Transaction (SET)

A protocol developed jointly by MasterCard International and Visa International and published as an open standard to provide confidentiality of transaction information, payment integrity, and authentication of transaction participants for payment card transactions over unsecured networks, such as the Internet.

Secure hash algorithm (SHA)

A message digest algorithm that digests a message of arbitrary size to 160 bits. SHA is a cryptographic checksum algorithm.

Secure Hash Standard (SHA-1)

The U.S. Government standard that specifies the Secure Hash Algorithm (SHA-1), a cryptographic hash function that produces a 160-bit output (hash result) for input data of any length < 2**64 bits.

Secure hypertext transfer protocol (S-HTTP)

A Internet protocol for providing client-server security services for HTTP communications. S-HTTP was originally specified by CommerceNet, a coalition of businesses interested in developing the Internet for commercial uses. Several message formats may be incorporated into S-HTTP clients and servers, particularly CMS and MOSS. S-HTTP supports choice of security policies, key management mechanisms, and cryptographic algorithms through option negotiation between parties for each transaction. S-HTTP supports both asymmetric and symmetric key operation modes. S-HTTP attempts to avoid presuming particular trust model, but it attempts to facilitate multiply rooted hierarchical trust and anticipates that principals may have many public key certificates. An extension to the HTTP protocol to protect the privacy and integrity of HTTP communications

Secure shell (SSH)

A protocol for secure remote login and other secure network services over an insecure network. Consists of three major components:

Secured Computing: A CISSP Study Guide, Copyright 2001

- Transport layer protocol: Provides server authentication, confidentiality, and integrity. It may optionally also provide compression. The transport layer will typically be run over a TCP/IP connection, but might also be used on top of any other reliable data stream.
- User authentication protocol: Authenticates the client-side user to the server. It runs over the transport layer protocol.
- Connection protocol: Multiplexes the encrypted tunnel into several logical channels. It runs over the user authentication protocol.

Secure single sign-on (SSSO)

Secure single sign-on, or SSSO satisfies three synergetic sets of requirements. From an end-user perspective, SSSO refers to the ability of using a single user ID and a single password to logon once and gain access to all resources that one is allowed to access. From an administrative perspective, SSSO allows management of all security-related aspects of one's enterprise from a central location. This includes adding, modifying, and removing users as well as granting and revoking access to resources. From an enterprise perspective, SSSO provides the ability to protect the privacy and the integrity of transactions as well as to engage in auditable and non-repudiable transactions.

Secure Sockets Layer (SSL)

An Internet protocol (originally developed by Netscape Communications, Inc.) that uses connection-oriented end-to-end encryption to provide data confidentiality service and data integrity service for traffic between a client (often a web browser) and a server, and that can optionally provide peer entity authentication between the client and the server. SSL is layered below HTTP and above a reliable transport protocol (TCP). SSL is independent of the application it encapsulates, and any higher-level protocol can layer on top of SSL transparently. However, IPsec might better serve many Internet applications. SSL has two layers: (a) SSL's lower layer, the SSL Record Protocol, is layered on top of the transport protocol and encapsulates higher level protocols. One such encapsulated protocol is SSL Handshake Protocol. (b) SSL's upper layer provides asymmetric cryptography for server authentication (verifying the server's identity to the client) and optional client authentication (verifying the client's identity to the server), and also enables them to negotiate a symmetric encryption algorithm and secret session key (to use for data confidentiality) before the application protocol transmits or receives data. A keyed hash provides data integrity service for encapsulated data.

Secure state

A system condition in which no subject can access any object in an unauthorized manner. A condition in which no subject can access any object in an unauthorized manner.

Security architecture

A plan and set of principles that describe the security services that a system is required to provide to meet the needs of its users, the system elements required to implement the services, and the performance levels required in the elements to deal with the threat environment. A security architecture is the result of applying the system engineering process. A complete system security architecture includes administrative security, communication security, computer security, emanations security, personnel security, and physical security (e.g., see:). A complete security architecture needs to deal with both intentional, intelligent threats and accidental kinds of threats. The subset of computer architecture dealing with the security of the computer or network system.

Security breach

A violation of controls of a particular information system such that information assets or system components are unduly exposed.

Security certificate

A chunk of information (often stored as a text file) that is used by the SSL protocol to establish a secure connection.

Security kernel

'The hardware, firmware, and software elements of a trusted computing base that implement the reference monitor concept. It must mediate all accesses, be protected from modification, and be verifiable as correct.' That is, a security kernel is an implementation of a reference monitor for a given hardware base. The hardware, firmware, and software elements of a TCB that implement the reference monitor concept. It must mediate all accesses, be protected from modification, and be

Secured Computing: A CISSP Study Guide, Copyright 2001

verifiable as correct. The hardware, firmware, and software elements of a Trusted Computing Base (or Network Trusted Computing Base partition) that implement the reference monitor concept. It must mediate all accesses, be protected from modification, and be verifiable as correct. The hardware, firmware, and software elements of a Trusted Computing Base that implement the reference monitor concept. It must mediate all accesses, be protected from modification, and be verifiable as correct.

Security label

A marking that is bound to a system resource and that names or designates the security-relevant attributes of that resource. The recommended definition is usefully broad, but usually the term is understood more narrowly as a marking that represents the security level of an information object, i.e., a marking that indicates how sensitive an information object is. System security mechanisms interpret security labels according to applicable security policy to determine how to control access to the associated information, otherwise constrain its handling, and affix appropriate security markings to visible (printed and displayed) images thereof. A piece of information that represents the security level of an object.

Security model

A schematic description of a set of entities and relationships by which a specified set of security services are provided by or within a system. An example is the Bell-LaPadula model.

Sensitivity label

A piece of information that represents the security level of an object and that describes the sensitivity (e.g. classification) of the data in the object. Sensitivity labels are used by the TCB/NTCB as the basis for mandatory access control decisions. A piece of information that represents the security level of an object. Sensitivity labels are used by the TCB/NTCB as the basis for mandatory access control decisions.

Separation of duties

The practice of dividing the steps in a system function among different individuals, so as to keep a single individual from subverting the process.

Session hijacking

Taking over an authorized user's terminal session, either physically when the user leaves his terminal unattended or electronically when the intruder carefully connects to a just-disconnected communications line.

Session key

In the context of symmetric encryption, a key that is temporary or is used for a relatively short period of time. Usually, a session key is used for a defined period of communication between two computers, such as for the duration of a single connection or transaction set, or the key is used in an application that protects relatively large amounts of data and, therefore, needs to be rekeyed frequently. A temporary symmetric key that is only valid for a short period. Session keys are typically random numbers that can be chosen by either party to a conversation, by both parties in cooperation with one another, or by a trusted third party.

Simple key management for IP (SKIP)

A protocol for protecting the privacy and integrity of IP packets.

Simple Mail Transfer Protocol (SMTP)

A TCP-based, application-layer, Internet Standard protocol for moving electronic mail messages from one computer to another.

Simple Network Management Protocol (SNMP)

A UDP-based, application-layer, Internet Standard protocol for conveying management information between managers and agents. SNMP version 1 uses cleartext passwords for authentication and access control. Version 2 adds cryptographic mechanisms based on DES and MD5. Version 3 provides enhanced, integrated support for security services, including data confidentiality, data integrity, data origin authentication, and message timeliness and limited replay protection.

Simple security condition

A Bell-LaPadula security model rule allowing a subject read access to an object only if the security level of the subject dominates the security level of the object.

Simple security property

A Bell-LaPadula security model rule allowing a subject read access to an object only if the security level of the subject dominates the security level of the object. An invariant state property allowing a subject read access to an object only if the security level of the subject dominates the security level of the object.

Single sign-on

A system that enables a user to access multiple computer platforms (usually a set of hosts on the same network) or application systems after being authenticated just one time. Typically, a user logs in just once, and then is transparently granted access to a variety of permitted resources with no further login being required until after the user logs out. Such a system has the advantages of being user friendly and enabling authentication to be managed consistently across an entire enterprise, and has the disadvantage of requiring all hosts and applications to trust the same authentication mechanism.

Skipjack

A Type II block cipher with a block size of 64 bits and key size of 80 bits, that was developed by NSA and formerly classified at the U.S. Department of Defense 'Secret' level. On 23 June 1998, NSA announced that SKIPJACK had been declassified. A classified 64-bit block encryption, or secret key encryption algorithm. The algorithm uses 80-bit keys (compared with 56 for DES) and has 32 computational rounds or iterations (compared with 16 for DES). Skipjack supports all DES modes of operation. Skipjack provides high-speed encryption when implemented in a key-escrow chip.

Smart card

A credit card sized device containing one or more integrated circuit chips, which perform the functions of a computer's central processor, memory, and input/output interface. Sometimes this term is used rather strictly to mean a card that closely conforms to the dimensions and appearance of the kind of plastic credit card issued by banks and merchants. At other times, the term is used loosely to include cards that are larger than credit cards, especially cards that are thicker, such as PC cards. A 'smart token' is a device that conforms to the definition of smart card except that rather than having standard credit card dimensions, the token is packaged in some other form, such as a dog tag or door key shape. A tamper-resistant hardware device where sensitive information can be stored. Typically a smart card stores the private key(s) of a principal. Smart cards can also be used to encrypt or decrypt data on the card directly. This has the desirable effect of not exposing the private keys, even to the owner of the key. Smart cards are password protected; in order for an application to use the keys and functions of a smart card the user must enter the correct password to open the card.

Smurf

Software that mounts a denial-of-service attack ('smurfing') by exploiting IP broadcast addressing and ICMP ping packets to cause flooding. A smurf program builds a network packet that appears to originate from another address, that of the 'victim', either a host or an IP router. The packet contains an ICMP ping message that is addressed to an IP broadcast address, i.e., to all IP addresses in a given network. The echo responses to the ping message return to the victim's address. The goal of smurfing may be either to deny service at a particular host or to flood all or part of an IP network.

Snarf

To grab a large document or file for the purpose of using it with or without the author's permission.

Sneaker

An individual hired to break into places in order to test their security; analogous to tiger team.

Sniffer

A program to capture data across a computer network. Used by hackers to capture user id names and passwords. Software tool that audits and identifies network traffic packets.

Social engineering

A euphemism for non-technical or low technology means--such as lies, impersonation, tricks, bribes, blackmail, and threats--used to attack information systems. An attack based on deceiving users or administrators at the target site. Telephoning users or operators and pretending to be an authorized user, to attempt to gain illicit access to the systems, typically carry out social engineering attacks.

SOCKS

An Internet protocol that provides a generalized proxy server that enables client-server applications-- such as TELNET, FTP, and HTTP; running over either TCP or UDP--to use the services of a firewall. SOCKS is layered under the application layer and above the transport layer. When a client inside a firewall wishes to establish a connection to an object that is reachable only through the firewall, it uses TCP to connect to the SOCKS server, negotiates with the server for the authentication method to be used, authenticates with the chosen method, and then sends a relay request. The SOCKS server evaluates the request, typically based on source and destination addresses, and either establishes the appropriate connection or denies it. networking middleware that creates a secure, proxy data channel between two computers; SOCKS v5 adds strong authentication and encryption.

Source integrity

The degree of confidence that can be placed in information based on the trustworthiness of its sources.

Spam

To indiscriminately send unsolicited, unwanted, irrelevant, or inappropriate messages, especially commercial advertising in mass quantities.

Split knowledge

Security techniques in which two or more entities separately hold data items that individually convey no knowledge of the information that results from combining the items. 'A condition under which two or more entities separately have key components which individually convey no knowledge of the plaintext key which will be produced when the key components are combined in the cryptographic module.' A condition under which two or more entities separately have key components, which individually convey no knowledge of the plaintext key which will be produced when the key components are combined in the cryptographic module.

Spoofing

An attempt to gain access to a system by posing as an authorized user.

Star Trek attack

An attack that penetrates your system where no attack has ever gone before.

Steganography

Methods of hiding the existence of a message or other data. This is different than cryptography, which hides the meaning of a message but does not hide the message itself. An example of a steganographic method is 'invisible' ink.

Stream cipher

An encryption algorithm that breaks plaintext into a stream of successive bits (or characters) and encrypts the n-th plaintext bit with the n-th element of a parallel key stream, thus converting the plaintext bit stream into a ciphertext bit stream.

Symmetric algorithm

An algorithm where the same key can be used for encryption and decryption.

Symmetric cryptography

A branch of cryptography involving algorithms that use the same key for two different steps of the algorithm (such as encryption and decryption, or signature creation and signature verification). Symmetric cryptography has been used for thousands of years. A modern example of a symmetric encryption algorithm is the U.S. Government's Data Encryption Algorithm. Symmetric cryptography is sometimes called 'secret-key cryptography' (versus public-key cryptography) because the entities that share the key, such as the originator and the recipient of a message, need to keep the key secret. For example, when Alice wants to ensure confidentiality for data she sends to Bob, she encrypts the data with a secret key, and Bob uses the same key to decrypt. Keeping the shared key secret entails both cost and risk when the key is distributed to both Alice and Bob. Thus, symmetric cryptography has a key management disadvantage compared to asymmetric cryptography.

Syn flood

A denial of service attack that sends a host more TCP SYN packets (request to synchronize sequence numbers, used when opening a connection) than the protocol implementation can handle. When the SYN queue is flooded, no new connections can be opened.

System integrity

The quality of a system fulfilling its operational purpose while preventing unauthorized users from making modifications to resources or using resources, and preventing authorized users from making improper modifications to resources or making improper use of resources. The quality that a system has when it performs its intended function in an unimpaired manner, free from deliberate or inadvertent unauthorized manipulation of the system. 'The quality that a system has when it can perform its intended function in a unimpaired manner, free from deliberate or inadvertent unauthorized manipulation.' The quality of a system fulfilling its operational purpose while: preventing unauthorized users from making modifications to resources or using resources preventing authorized users from making improper modifications to resources or making improper use of resources. The quality that a system has when it performs its intended function in an unimpaired manner, free from deliberate or inadvertent unauthorized manipulation of the system.

System-high security mode

A mode of operation of an information system, wherein all users having access to the system possess a security clearance or authorization, but not necessarily a need-to-know, for all data handled by the system. This mode is defined formally in U.S. Department of Defense policy regarding system accreditation, but the term is widely used outside the Defense Department and outside the Government. The mode of operation in which system hardware and software is only trusted to provide discretionary protection between users. In this mode, the entire system, to include all components electrically and/or physically connected, must operate with security measures commensurate with the highest classification and sensitivity of the information being processed and/or stored. All system users in this environment must possess clearances and authorization for all information contained in the system. All system output must be clearly marked with the highest classification and all system caveats until the information has been reviewed manually by an authorized individual to ensure appropriate classifications and that caveats have been affixed. Compare Dedicated Security Mode, Multi-Level Security Mode.

Target of Evaluation (TOE)

An IT product or system and its associated administrator and user guidance documentation that is the subject of an evaluation. An IT product, which is subjected to security evaluation under the Common Criteria. An IT system, product, or component that is identified/subjected as requiring security evaluation. An IT system, product, or component that is subjected to security evaluation.

TEMPEST

A nickname for specifications and standards for limiting the strength of electromagnetic emanations from electrical and electronic equipment and thus reducing vulnerability to eavesdropping. This term originated in the U.S. Department of Defense. The study and control of spurious electronic signals emitted by electrical equipment, such as computer equipment

Threat

An action or event that might prejudice security. Sequence of circumstances and events that allows a human or other agent to cause an information-related misfortune by exploiting vulnerability in an IT product.

Ticket

A synonym for 'capability'. A ticket is usually granted by a centralized access control server (ticket-granting agent) to authorize access to a system resource for a limited time. Tickets have been implemented with symmetric cryptography, but can also be implemented as attribute certificates using asymmetric cryptography. A credential used in a third-party trusted host model. A ticket is encrypted with the password of the principal to whom the ticket is presented. A ticket contains a session key as well as the identity of the principal to whom the ticket is issued. Tickets have an expiration time.

Secured Computing: A CISSP Study Guide, Copyright 2001

Tiger team
>   Government and industry-sponsored teams of computer experts who attempt to break down the
>   defenses of computer systems in an effort to uncover, and eventually patch, security holes.

Time bomb
>   A logic bomb that is triggered by reaching some preset time, either once or periodically. A variant of
>   the Trojan horse in which malicious code is inserted to be triggered later.

Token
>   General usage: An object that is used to control access and is passed between cooperating entities
>   in a protocol that synchronizes use of a shared resource. Usually, the entity that currently holds the
>   token has exclusive access to the resource. Authentication usage: A data object or a portable, user-
>   controlled, physical device used to verify an identity in an authentication process. Cryptographic
>   usage: See: cryptographic token.4. SET usage: 'A portable device [e.g., smart card or PCMCIA card]
>   specifically designed to store cryptographic information and possibly perform cryptographic functions
>   in a secure manner.' A hardware device that is used to augment password-based authentication by
>   challenging a principal to prove that possesses the token.

Traffic analysis
>   Inference of information from observable characteristics of data flow(s), even when the data is
>   encrypted or otherwise not directly available. Such characteristics include the identities and locations
>   of the source(s) and destination(s), and the presence, amount, frequency, and duration of
>   occurrence. 'The inference of information from observation of traffic flows (presence, absence,
>   amount, direction, and frequency).
>   'The generation of spurious instances of communication, spurious data units, and/or spurious data
>   within data units.'

Trap-door
>   Hidden software or hardware mechanism that can be triggered to permit protection mechanisms in an
>   Automated Information System to be circumvented. Note: A trap-door is usually activated in some
>   innocent-appearing manner (e.g. a special random key sequence at a terminal). Software developers
>   often write trap doors in their code that enable them to reenter the system to perform certain
>   functions.

Triple DES (3DES)
>   A block cipher, based on DES, that transforms each 64-bit plaintext block by applying the Data
>   Encryption Algorithm three successive times, using either two or three different keys, for an effective
>   key length of 112 or 168 bits. IPsec usage: The algorithm variation proposed for ESP uses a 168-bit
>   key, consisting of three independent 56-bit quantities used by the Data Encryption Algorithm, and a
>   64-bit initialization value. Each datagram contains an IV to ensure that each received datagram can
>   be decrypted even when other datagrams are dropped or sequence of datagrams is reordered in
>   transit. A triple-wrapped S/MIME usage: Data that has been signed with a digital signature, and then
>   encrypted, and then signed again.

Trojan horse
>   A computer program that appears to have a useful function, but also has a hidden and potentially
>   malicious function that evades security mechanisms, sometimes by exploiting legitimate
>   authorizations of a system entity that invokes the program. A computer program with an apparently or
>   actually useful function that contains additional (hidden) functions that surreptitiously exploit the
>   legitimate authorizations of the invoking process to the detriment of security or integrity. A computer
>   program with an apparently or actually useful function that contains additional (hidden) functions that
>   surreptitiously exploit the legitimate authorizations of the invoking process to the detriment of security;
>   e.g. making a 'blind copy' of a sensitive file for the creator of the Trojan horse. A program which
>   carries within itself a means to allow the creator of the program access to the system using it. An
>   apparently useful and innocent program containing additional hidden code which allows the
>   unauthorized collection, exploitation, falsification, or destruction of data. Computer program
>   containing an apparent or actual useful function that contains additional (hidden) functions that allow
>   unauthorized collection, falsification or destruction of data.

Trust

Information system usage: The extent to which someone who relies on a system can have confidence that the system meets its specifications, i.e., that the system does what it claims to do and does not perform unwanted functions. 'trusted vs. trustworthy': In discussing a system or system process or object, this Glossary (and industry usage) prefers the term 'trusted' to describe a system that operates as expected, according to design and policy. When the trust can also be guaranteed in some convincing way, such as through formal analysis or code review, the system is termed 'trustworthy'; this differs from the ABA Guidelines definition. PKI usage: A relationship between a certificate user and a CA in which the user acts according to the assumption that the CA creates only valid digital certificates. 'Generally, an entity can be said to 'trust' a second entity when it (the first entity) makes the assumption that the second entity will behave exactly as the first entity expects. This trust may apply only for some specific function. The key role of trust in [X.509] is to describe the relationship between an entity and a authority; an entity shall be certain that it can trust the certification authority to create only valid and reliable certificates.

Trusted certificate

A certificate upon which a certificate user relies as being valid without the need for validation testing; especially a public-key certificate that is used to provide the first public key in a certification path. A trusted public-key certificate might be the root certificate in a hierarchical PKI, the certificate of the CA that issued the user's own certificate in a mesh PKI, or any certificate accepted by the user in a trust-file PKI

Trusted computing base (TCB)

'The totality of protection mechanisms within a computer system, including hardware, firmware, and software, the combination of which is responsible for enforcing a security policy.' The totality of protection mechanisms within a computer system -including hardware, firmware, and software - the combination of that is responsible for enforcing a security policy. A TCB consists of one or more components that together enforce a unified security policy over a product or system. The ability of a Trusted Computing Base to correctly enforce a security policy depends solely on the mechanisms within the TCB and on the correct input by system administrative personnel of parameters (e.g. a user's clearance) related to the security policy. The totality of protection mechanisms within a computer system -including hardware, firmware, and software - the combination of that is responsible for enforcing a security policy. It creates a basic protection environment and provides additional user services required for a Trusted Computer System. The ability of a Trusted Computing Base to correctly enforce a security policy depends solely on the mechanisms within the TCB and on the correct input by system administrative personnel of parameters (e.g. a user's clearance) related to the security policy. The totality of protection mechanisms within a computer system, including hardware, firmware, and software, the combination of that is responsible for enforcing a security policy. A TCB consists of one or more components that together enforce a unified security policy over a product or system. The ability of a TCB to correctly enforce a security policy depends solely on the mechanisms within the TCB and on the correct input by system administrative personnel of parameters (e.g. a user's clearance) related to the security policy. The totality of protection mechanisms within a computer system, including hardware, firmware, and software, the combination of that is responsible for enforcing a security policy. A TCB consists of one or more components that together enforce a unified security policy over a product or system. The ability of a TCB to enforce correctly a unified security policy depends solely on the mechanisms within the TCB and on the correct input by system administrative personnel of parameters (e.g. a user's clearance level) related to the security policy. Totality of protection mechanisms within an IT product, including hardware, firmware, software, and data, the combination of that is responsible for enforcing a technical security policy. Note: The ability of an organization to achieve an organizational security policy depends jointly on the correctness of the mechanisms within the TCB, the protection of those mechanisms to ensure their correctness, and on adherence to associated usage security policies by authorized users.)

Tunnel

A communication channel created in a computer network by encapsulating (carrying, layering) a communication protocol's data packets in (on top of) a second protocol that normally would be carried above, or at the same layer as, the first one. Tunneling can involve almost any OSI or TCP/IP protocol layers; for example, a TCP connection between two hosts could conceivably be tunneled through email messages across the Internet. Most often, a tunnel is a logical point-to-point link -- i.e., an OSI layer 2 connection--created by encapsulating the layer 2 protocol in a transport protocol (such as TCP), in a network or internetwork layer protocol (such as IP), or in another link layer protocol. Often, encapsulation is accomplished with an extra, intermediate protocol, i.e., a tunneling protocol (such as L2TP) that is layered between the tunneled layer 2 protocol and the encapsulating protocol. Tunneling can move data between computers that use a protocol not supported by the network connecting them. Tunneling also can enable a computer network to use the services of a second network as though the second network were a set of point-to-point links between the first network's nodes. SET usage: The name of a SET private extension that indicates whether the CA or the payment gateway supports passing encrypted messages to the cardholder through the merchant.

Tunneled VPN

A bi-directional virtual private network that encapsulates data and transmits relatively securely across an untrusted network.

Uniform resource locator (URL)

A type of formatted identifier that describes the access method and location of an information resource object on the Internet. For example: www.etresearch.com is a URL.

User

Any person who interacts directly with a computer system or with a network system. This includes both those persons who are authorized to interact with the system and those people who interact without authorization (e.g. active or passive wiretappers).

User identifier (user ID)

A character string or symbol that is used in a system to uniquely name a specific user or group of users. Often verified by a password in an authentication process. Unique symbol or character string that is used by an IT system, product, or component to uniquely identify a specific user.

Validation

The process carried out by the NIAP Oversight Body leading to the issue of a validation certificate. The process of assessing the usefulness of a system in relation to its intended use or purpose. The process of evaluating software during or at the end of the development process to determine whether it satisfies specified requirements.

Value-added network (VAN)

A computer network or subnetwork (which is usually a commercial enterprise) that transmits, receives, and stores EDI transactions on behalf of its customers. A VAN may also provide additional services, ranging from EDI format translation, to EDI-to-FAX conversion, to integrated business systems.

Virtual private network (VPN)

A restricted-use, logical (i.e., artificial or simulated) computer network that is constructed from the system resources of relatively public, physical (i.e., real) network (such as the Internet), often by using encryption (located at hosts or gateways), and often by tunneling links of the virtual network across the real network. For example, if a corporation has LANs at several different sites, each connected to the Internet by a firewall, the corporation could create a VPN by using encrypted tunnels to connect from firewall to firewall across the Internet and not allowing any other traffic through the firewalls. A VPN is generally less expensive to build and operate than a dedicated real network, because the virtual network shares the cost of system resources with other users of the real network. A way of using a public network (typically the Internet) to link two sites of an organization. Protecting the privacy and integrity of the communication line using a secret session key typically sets up a VPN. The secret session key is usually negotiated using the public keys of the two principals.

Virus

Malicious software, a form of Trojan horse, which reproduces itself in other executable code. A self-propagating Trojan horse, composed of a mission component, a trigger component, and a self-propagating component.

Vulnerability assessment

An aspect of the assessment of the effectiveness of a Target of Evaluation, namely, whether known vulnerabilities in that Target of Evaluation could in practice compromise its security as specified in the security target. A measurement of vulnerability, which includes the susceptibility of a particular

288
Secured Computing: A CISSP Study Guide, Copyright 2001

system to a specific attack and the opportunities available to a threat agent to mount that attack. A measurement of vulnerability, which includes the susceptibility of a particular system to a specific attack and the opportunities available to a threat agent to mount that attack. An aspect of the assessment of the effectiveness of a Target of Evaluation, namely whether known vulnerabilities in that Target of Evaluation could in practice compromise its security as specified in the security target.

War dialer

A computer program that automatically dials a series of telephone numbers to find lines connected to computer systems, and catalogs those numbers so that a cracker can try to break into the systems. A cracking tool, a program that calls a given list or range of numbers and records those which answer with handshake tones.

Web of trust

PGP usage: A trust-file PKI technique used in PGP for building file of validated public keys by making personal judgments about being able to trust certain people to be holding properly certified keys of other people. A trust network among people who know and communicate with each other. Digital certificates are used to represent entities in the web of trust. Any pair of entities can determine the extent of trust between the two, based on their relationship in the web.

Work factor

General security usage: The estimated amount of effort or time that can be expected to be expended by a potential intruder to penetrate a system, or defeat a particular countermeasure, when using specified amounts of expertise and resources. Cryptography usage: The estimated amount of computing time and power needed to break a cryptographic system. An estimate of the effort or time needed by a potential penetrator with specified expertise and resources to overcome a protective measure.

Worm

A computer program that can run independently, can propagate a complete working version of itself onto other hosts on a network, and may consume computer resources destructively. A computer program, which replicates itself and is self-propagating. Worms, as opposed to viruses, are meant to spawn in network environments. Network worms were first defined by Shoch &Hupp of Xerox in ACM Communications (March 1982). The Internet worm of November 1988 is perhaps the most famous; it successfully propagated itself on over 6,000 systems across the Internet. A computer program which replicates itself and is self-propogating. Worms, as opposed to viruses, are meant to spawn in network environments. A program or executable code module which resides in distributed systems or networks. It will replicate itself, if necessary, in order to exercise as much of the systems's resources as possible for its own processing. Such resources may take the form of CPU time, I/O channels, or system memory. It will replicate itself from machine to machine across network connections, often clogging networks and computer systems as it spreads.

X.400

An ITU-T Recommendation that is one part of a joint ITU-T/ISO multi-part standard (X.400-X.421) that defines the Message Handling Systems. (The ISO equivalent is IS 10021, parts 1-7.)

X.500 Directory

An ITU-T Recommendation that is one part of a joint ITU-T/ISO multi-part standard (X.500-X.525) that defines the X.500 Directory, a conceptual collection of systems that provide distributed directory capabilities for OSI entities, processes, applications, and services. (The ISO equivalent is IS 9594-1 and related standards, IS 9594-x.) The X.500 Directory is structured as a tree (the Directory Information Tree), and information is stored in directory entries. Each entry is a collection of information about one object, and each object has a DN. A directory entry is composed of attributes, each with a type and one or more values. For example, if a PKI uses the Directory to distribute certificates, then the X.509 public-key certificate of an end user is normally stored as a value of an attribute of type 'userCertificate' in the Directory entry that has the DN that is the subject of the certificate.

X.509

An ITU-T Recommendation that defines a framework to provide and support data origin authentication and peer entity authentication services, including formats for X.509 public-key certificates, X.509 attribute certificates, and X.509 CRLs. (The ISO equivalent is IS 9498-4.) X.509

describes two levels of authentication: simple authentication based on a password, and strong authentication based on a public-key certificate.

X.509 certificate

Either an X.509 public-key certificate or an X.509 attribute certificate. This Glossary uses the term with the precise meaning recommended here. However, some who use the term may not be aware that X.509 specifies attribute certificates that do not contain a public key. Even among those who are aware, this term is commonly used as an abbreviation to mean 'X.509 public-key certificate.

Zeroization

A method of erasing electronically stored data by altering the contents of the data storage so as to prevent the recovery of the data.

Zeroize

Use erasure or other means to render stored data unusable and unrecoverable, particularly a key stored in a cryptographic module or other device. Erase electronically stored data by altering the contents of the data storage so as to prevent the recovery of the data.

CISSP Practice Exam

Allow yourself at least 2 hours to take this exam. It is designed to be of similar content and context as the real exam. It has 80 questions. Once completed, look up all wrong answers and take the exam again until you can answer at least 75 of the 80 correctly. Good luck!

1. Match the following:
    A. Orange Book   1. Password Management
    B. Dark Blue Book   2.TCSEC
    C. Light Green Book   3. Trusted Network Interpretation (TNI)
    D. Red Book   4. Magnetic Remanance guidelines

2. The planning horizon makes up what types of planning (Choose 3):
    A. Operation
    B. Tactical
    C. Financial
    D. Strategic

3. An undocumented access path is called a:
    A. Logic bomb
    B. Maintenance hook
    C. Trojan Horse
    D. Covert access path

4. Attempts to assign monetary or numeric vales to components of risk are called Qualitative analysis.
    A. True
    B. False

5. Which countermeasure selection principle states that safeguards must have shutdown capability and default lack of permission?
    A. Minimum human intervention
    B. Override & Failsafe defaults
    C. Compartmentalization
    D. Sustainability

6. Which represents the ALE calculation?
    A. Gross loss expectancy X Probability
    B. Single loss expectancy X biannual rate of occurrence
    C. Annual rate of occurrence X Single loss expectancy
    D. Single rate of occurrence X Gross loss expectancy

7. What major US Federal act was past for the need for attention on the need to fight computer crime?
    A. Medical computer crime Act 1984
    B. Privacy Act 1974
    C. Comprehensive Crime Control Act of 1986
    D. Comprehensive Crime Control Act of 1984

8.NFPA construction standards state that the flame spread rating for a sprinkler system should be?
    A.   <= 30
B. <= 25
C. <= 20
D. <= 15

9. No noise or voltage fluctuations defines which of the following:
    A. Quiet load
    B. Clean Power
    C. Whiteout
    D. Silent runner

10. What is the accepted standard for enrollment time in biometric devices?

A. 1 min
B. 2 min.
C. 5.min
D. 30 sec.

11. Which of the following is NOT an operation security attack?
A. Exhaustive attack
B. Known plain text attack
C. Incomplete parameter checking
D. Denial of use attack

12. What facilitates rapid recovery measures to lessen the impact to the business during a disaster?
A. BCP
B. DRP
C. DRiP
D. RPD

13. Recovery of a data center needs what type of recovery plan?
A. DRP
B. End-user contingency plan
C. Business resumption plan
D. BCP

14. The main difference between a BCP and a DRP is what?
A. DRP is the challenge to recover from disruptions and to continue support of critical business functions, A BCP is the challenge to recover from a disaster and restore critical functions to normal operation.
B. BCP is the challenge to recover from disruptions and to continue support of critical business functions, A DRP is the challenge to recover from a disaster and restore critical functions to normal operation.
C. DRP is the challenge to uncover from disruptions and to discontinue support of critical business functions, A BCP is the challenge to recover from a disaster and restore critical functions to abnormal operation.
D. BCP is the challenge to recover from bad business decisions and to continue support of critical business functions, A DRP is the challenge to recover from a disruption and restore basic functions to normal operation.

15. The composition technique for building new objects from 2 or more existing objects that support the new objects required interfaces describes what?
A. OOP channel
B. Inference
C. Aggregation
D. Object re-use

16. Writing to storage by one process and reading by another of a lower security level is _____ .
A. Covert storage channel
B. Strong * property
C. Covert timing
D. Lattice based access restriction

17. A small program residing on a host computer that is downloaded to a client computer to be executed is what?
A. Certificate
B. Applet
C. Cookie
D. OLE

18. Analyzing databases using tools that look for trends or anomalies without knowing what the data is about is referred to as?
A. Data scooping
B. Data mining
C. Garbage collection
D. Data analysis

Secured Computing: A CISSP Study Guide, Copyright 2001

19. _____ describes a suite of programs that managed large structured sets of persistent data with ad hoc query capabilities for users?
   A.   Query sets
   B.   SQL
   C.   DBMS
   D.   KBS

20. A network of very simple processors each with a small amount of memory and is able to learn from examples and ability to do generalizations is called what?
   A.   TNI
   B.   ANN
   C.   AIS
   D.   ANDF

21. Assignment of system privileges should be:
   A.   Tightly controlled and a single persons duty
   B.   Tightly controlled and a shared duty
   C.   Loosely controlled and a single persons duty
   D.   Tightly controlled only

22. Iteratively producing a more defined version of an object by replacing values and variables is called?
   A.   Polymorphism
   B.   Polyinstantiation
   C.   Polywannacracker
   D.   Polyinstantitoration

23. Different objects responding to the same command in different ways it called?
   A.   Inheritance
   B.   Inference
   C.   Polyinstantiation
   D.   Polymorphism

25. Creating a new class from more than one parent class is referred to:
   A.   Encapsulation
   B.   Inheritance
   C.   Multiple inheritance
   D.   Association Mechanisms

26. What is one advantage of content dependent protection of information?
   A.   It confine the usage of data
   B.   It provides granular control
   C.   It provides minor access control changes
   D.   It prevents data locking

27. Overwriting medium reused in the same system or environment is called:
   A.   Degaussing
   B.   Clearing
   C.   Purging
   D.   Overwriting

28. What is noise distributed over the spectrum so that the power-per-unit bandwidth is constant?
   A.   White Noise
   B.   Shielding signals
   C.   Constant rate flow
   D.   Spurious signals

29. What type of token device uses a polonius challenge response scheme and uses a one-time pad?
   A.   Asynchronous
   B.   Synchronous
   C.   Bi-synchronous
   D.   Integrated circuit chip

30. Which token implementation authenticates users, then passes it to the host for fixed password logon?
   A.   Front-end
   B.   Back-end
   C.   Host resident
   D.   Backend resident

31. _____ helps protect against fraud, provides cross training and provides trained back up.
   A.   Separation of duties
   B.   Least privilege
   C.   Rotation of duties
   D.   Max Factor

32. During the kerberos authentication process, when the user enters a password in to the client workstation it generates the users secret password that will _____
on the client workstation.
   A.   Not reside
   B.   Temporarily reside
   C.   Permanently reside
   D.   Dynamically reside

33. Match the following:
   A.   Tuple   1.Number of columns
   B.   Row   2.Number of rows
   C.   Foreign key   3.Columns making each new row unique
   D.   Primary key   4.columns
   E.   Degree   5.Row
   F.   Cardinality   6. Attribute of one relation that is the primary key of some
        other relation

34. What type of intrusion detection monitors behavior, then develops and maintains profiles for normal behavior and compares that to an audit file?
   A.   Rule Based
   B.   Anomaly based
   C.   Signature based
   D.   Statistical based

35. What are the three protection mechanisms used in security architecture?
   A.   Layering, Data hiding, embedding
   B.   Layering, Data hiding, abstraction
   C.   Layering, Data mining, abstraction
   D.   Data mining, Data layering, data obfuscation

36. The main storage used to hold instructions and data during computing is called?
   A.   Virtual space
   B.   Real space
   C.   Primary space
   D.   Open systems space

37. Interleaved execution of two or more programs by a processor is called?
   A.   Multi-tasking
   B.   Multiprocessing
   C.   Multiprogramming
   D.   Multi-task processing

38.Which CPU state executes only non-privileged instructions and is intended for application programs?
   A.   Supervisor state
   B.   Problem state
   C.   Safe mode
   D.   Basic state

39. What includes all protection mechanisms within a computer, is partially responsible for enforcing security policy and is in hardware, firmware and software?
   A.   TNI
   B.   TCB
   C.   TCBY
   D.   INI

40. Match the following:
   A.   Bell-LaPadula   1. Discretionary security model
   B.   Biba   2. *-property A subject cannot modify an object of
         a higher integrity level
   C.   Clark & Wilson   3. Invocation property

   D.   Goguen & Meseguer   4. Relies upon the well formed transaction
                                                5. Addresses all three integrity goals
                                                   ss-property A subject cannot read/access an
                     object of a higher classification (no read up)
                                                6. Capability System and Domain Systems

41. An abstract math model that state variables represent system state?
   A.   Non-interference model
   B.   State Matrix model
   C.   Access Matrix model
   D.   State Machine model

42. Match the following:
   A.   C1   1. Controlled access protection, Object reuse and audit
   B.   C2   2. Formal methods, Verified design
   C.   B1   3. Sensitivity and device labels
   D.   B2   4. More granularity, procedures for system starting securely
   E.   B3   5. Discretionary security protection
   F.   A1   6. Security Domains

43. _____ chooses a piece of cipher text and attempts to obtain the corresponding decrypted plaintext.
   A.   Chosen plaintext attack (CPA)
   B.   Chosen Cipher text attack (CCA)
   C.   Cipher text only attack (COA)
   D.   Known plaint text attack (KPA)

44. _____ is the weakest form of authentication and is a ANSI X9.9 standard.
   A.   DES
   B.   MAC
   C.   Digital signatures
   D.   MD5

45. _____ attacks rely on block ciphers exhibiting a high degree of mathematical structure.
   A.   Differential crypto
   B.   Algebraic Crypto
   C.   Linear Crypto
   D.   Differential linear crypto

46. Which topology has two rings and is very fault tolerant in nature
   A.   Token ring
   B.   FDDI
   C.   Ethernet
   D.   Gigabit Ethernet

47. _____ splits private keys into multiple parts, each separately registered with escrow agents. Combined these will generate the original key.
   A.   Key escrow encryption
   B.   Fair Public-Key Cryptosystems

Secured Computing: A CISSP Study Guide, Copyright 2001

    C.   Shared key Cryptosystems
    D.   Skipjack

48. What LAN transmission method from source to destination address?
    A.   Unicast
    B.   Multicast
    C.   Broadcast
    D.   Wincast

49. Match the following:
    A.   Packet filtering   1.Stateful inspection
    B.   Circuit level firewall   2.Deals with external servers on behalf of internal
    C.   Proxy firewall   3. Examines each packet, based on ACL's
    D.   Dynamic filter inspection   4. Does not require a special proxy for each service

50. _____ are caused by improper boundary checking in a program.
    A.   Rogue code
    B.   Malicious code
    C.   Buffer Overflows
    D.   Data contamination

51. What are the three main layers of access controls?
    A.   Administrative, Physical, logical
    B.   Administrative, Physical, abstract
    C.   Administrative, abstract, logical
    D.   Accountable, Physical, logical

52. File access, encryption and system access are what types of access control?
    A.   Physical
    B.   Logical
    C.   Abstract
    D.   Administrative

53. What types of controls are made to remedy changed original controls?
    A.   Detective
    B.   Corrective
    C.   Recovery
    D.   Compensating

54. Controls that cannot be made more permissive and are dictated by the system are?
    A.   Discretionary
    B.   Lattice based
    C.   Rule based
    D.   Mandatory

55. A _____ is a table that tells a computer OS which access rights a user has?
    A.   ACK
    B.   ACL
    C.   DCD
    D.   CRC

56. Tables that have protected identifiers that allow a subject specific rights based on the object being accessed are?
    A.   Constrained user interfaces
    B.   ACL
    C.   Capability table
    D.   Lattice controls

57. _____ refers to allowing employees only enough access to do their jobs?
    A.   Access controls
    B.   Least privilege
    C.   Segregation of duties

Secured Computing: A CISSP Study Guide, Copyright 2001

    D.   Lattice controls?

58. DAC stands for?
    A.   Discounted access control
    B.   Disuaded antonym content
    C.   Discretionary access controls

59. What access control model is an information flow model?
    A.   Biba
    B.   Bell-LaPadula
    C.   Crimson
    D.   Clark and Clark

60. Source, lifetime, storage and distribution are all?
    A.   Password filters
    B.   Password factors
    C.   IP headers
    D.   DLL control steps

61. _____ cards store but do not process information?
    A.   Access cards
    B.   Smart cards
    C.   Memory cards

62. What was designed to overcome both the extension limits on RADIUS and TACACS?
    A.   Smart Weavel
    B.   DIAMETER
    C.   CIRCUMFRUNCE
    D.   TACACS+

63. What type of intrusion detection system compares logs and then looks for what is seen as normal behavior?
    A.   Statistical
    B.   Bi-directional
    C.   Signature based
    D.   Rule based (TIM)

64. What is the final steps in doing a penetration test?
    A.   Tell the management
    B.   Report the results
    C.   Do the actual test
    D.   Create a test plan

65. TCP and UDP fall at what layer of the OSI model?
    A.   1
    B.   2
    C.   3
    D.   4
    E.   5

66. What does TTL stand for?
    A.   Time to live
    B.   Technical test level
    C.   Time to Leave
    D.   Triple Time levels

67. Ipv6 will have how many bits in its address?
    A.   16
    B.   32
    C.   128
    D.   254

68. IP is?
    A.   Connectionless

Secured Computing: A CISSP Study Guide, Copyright 2001

B.   Connection-orientated

69. _____ is a type of firewall that applies access controls when a connection is established.
    A.   Circuit level gateway
    B.   Proxy server
    C.   Stateful inspection
    D.   Packet filter

70. _____ is a high level statement of beliefs or goals.
    A.   Policy
    B.   Standard
    C.   Guideline
    D.   Baseline

71. _____ is an access control concept that refers to and abstract machine that will mediate all access.
    A.   Referral monitor
    B.   Reference monitor
    C.   DBMS
    D.   Client side scripting

72. Data about data is called_____?
    A.   Redundancy
    B.   Meta data
    C.   Meta drift data
    D.   Data mining

73. A storage device that loses its contents when turned off is called _____?
    A.   Virtual storage
    B.   Volatile Storage
    C.   Random storage
    D.   Real storage

74. _____ is software that tries to emulate the way people and resolve problems?
    A.   AI
    B.   Fuzzy nueronetworks
    C.   Aggregation
    D.   Buffer Overflow

75. What is it called when you put more data into a buffer than it could handle?
    A.   Override
    B.   Failsafe override
    C.   Buffer overflow
    D.   Buffer influx

76. Which comes first:
    A.   Certification
    B.   Accreditation

77. _____ are used to condense an arbitrary length message to a fixed size?
    A.   EAR
    B.   Basis
    C.   HASH
    D.   EES

78. When the cipher text remains the same but the order of the characters is shuffled is an example of?
    A.   Substitution cipher
    B.   Polyalphabetic cipher
    C.   Transposition cipher
    D.   Concealment cipher

79. A method of erasing electronic data by altering the contents is called?
    A.   Deference

Secured Computing: A CISSP Study Guide, Copyright 2001

B.   Degaussing
C.   Zeroization

80. _____ uses a certification hierarchy, with X.509 public key certificates?
    A.   S/MIME
    B.   SET
    C.   PEM
    D.   GSSAPI

1. AB4, C1, D3
2. A,B,D
3. D
4. B
5. B
6. C
7. D
8. B
9. B
10. B
11. B
12. A
13. A
14. B
15. C
16. A
17. B
18. B
19. C
20. B
21. B
22. B
23. D
24. –
25. C
26. B
27. B
28. A
29. A
30. A
31. C
32. B
33. A5, A,C6, D3,E1,F2
34. D
35. B

36. B
37. C
38. B
39. B
40. A1,B2,B3,C4,C5A6,D7
41. D
42. A5, B1, C3, D4, E6 F2
43. A
44. B
45. B
46. B
47. B
48. A
49. A3, B4, C2, D1
50. C
51. A
52. B
53. B
54. D
55. B
56. C
57. B
58. C
59. B
60. B
61. B
62. B
63. A
64. B
65. D
66. A
67. C
68. A
69. A
70. A
71. B
72. B
73. B
74. A
75. C
76. A

77. C
78. C
79. C
80. C

**Was this book helpful? Do you have questions?
Corrections? Errors?**

Please Contact Us at:

ETRESEARCH@HOTMAIL.COM

ISBN 155212889-X

9 781552 128893